W9-AQW-740

# Theater in America

# THEATER

# n America

## APPRAISAL AND CHALLENGE

### For the National Theatre Conference



Robert E. Gard  Marston Balch  Pauline B. Temkin



DEMBAR EDUCATIONAL RESEARCH SERVICES, INC.
Madison, Wisconsin
and THEATRE ARTS BOOKS, NEW YORK

# Theater in America



Printed in the United States of America
First Edition

Library of Congress Catalog Card Number: 68-25166

Published by
DEMBAR EDUCATIONAL RESEARCH SERVICES, INC.
Post Office Box 1148
Madison, Wisconsin 53701
and
THEATRE ARTS BOOKS
333 Sixth Avenue
New York 10014

*For David H. Stevens, great former Director of Humanities, The Rockefeller Foundation*

# PREFACE

IN NOVEMBER 1961, at the annual meeting of the National Theatre Conference (NTC) in New York, the Board of Trustees established a major project for a National Appraisal of the American Theater. The purpose of the project was to prepare an accurate, up-to-date, critical report of the "total, many-faceted image of theater in the United States in the third quarter of the twentieth century"—a picture, as it were, of the whole state of the theater, where it is and where it is going. Nothing comparable to this undertaking had been produced since Norris Houghton's *Advance from Broadway* (1941) and, before that, Kenneth Macgowan's *Footlights Across America* (1929)—both books by NTC members and both dealing primarily with decentralized, non-commercial theater activities as observed by their authors in the course of extensive, subsidized tours of inspection. In view of the innumerable changes and marked developments in the theater of this country since World War II, it was held that a new study, comprising all sectors of the theater, was needed and that NTC, despite too limited financial resources to permit extended travel, should undertake it. The membership confirmed the Trustee's decision.

Robert E. Gard, director of the Wisconsin Idea Theatre, The University of Wisconsin, was named chairman of the project. Marston Balch, director of the University Theater and head of the Department of Drama and Speech, Tufts University, and executive secretary of NTC, was named co-chairman.

Immediately thereafter, Gard, with a professional research assistant, Pauline Temkin, began gathering material for the Appraisal, initially by means of various questionnaires. The research fell naturally into two categories: one, a frank, individual assessment of the theater in its professional sectors and as a whole, as seen by the members of NTC and by others (directors, producers, playwrights, critics, scholars, teachers, and similar specialists); the second, a statistical survey of the theater in its various manifestations in the major centers of activity and in all the geographical regions of the United States.

By the November 1962 meeting, material sufficient both in substance and quality was in hand to warrant a search for funds that would permit a study in greater depth than was at first contemplated. Also, in view of Gard's commitment to serve as visiting professor at the University of Helsinki, Finland, during a term's leave of absence the following spring, and Balch's simultaneous availability for eight months' continuous research, it was decided that Balch should take over direction of the project—as he did, starting in March 1963. And the first of several donations and grants enabled the research to go forward on a more intensive scale.

In the course of the next three years, Balch and his research assistants—Jeannette Y. Rose, until September 1963, and thereafter for longer periods Lorelei F. Guidry—assembled and analyzed a vast quantity of pertinent data and opinions. The material came from many different sources—from further questionnaires, from correspondence, from surveys, books, articles, brochures, lectures, symposia, official documents, and from personal interviews with people in theater, government, and education—reflecting virtually every aspect of the theater situation in the United States.

In addition, several statistical and critical analyses, commissioned by NTC, were made of the impact of American drama and theater abroad: by Charles Landstone of London, for Great Britain and Ireland; by Serge Zanetti of Paris, for France; and by Dr. Günter Meyer of Darmstadt, for West Germany. These special studies, plus material obtained from other foreign countries, while enlarging the perspective of the present Appraisal, will find their major use in a second NTC report now in progress on the state of playwriting in America.

In November 1966, in order to expedite publication, it was decided that the chairman and co-chairman of the Appraisal should divide the project into two parts: Gard, with the assistance of Mrs. Temkin, to assume charge of drafting the general report; Balch; having gathered, in his research, the most complete body of current information yet assembled on the conditions and problems of the American playwright, to proceed with writing the special Appraisal report on that subject, due in 1969. Meanwhile, Balch also collaborated in the final revision of *Theater in America.*

The present book, consequently, represents the combined labors of its authors over a period of almost six years, drawing upon information, ideas, and expert opinions furnished by countless individuals and organizations, plus their own experience and insights. Clearly, the mountain of material could not be totally digested in a single brief summary. This report, far from being a statistical survey—although employing the findings from NTC's and other surveys—is intended as a condensed critical overview, at once diagnostic and prescriptive, of our nation's theater in the 1960's. Its panorama takes in current developments and trends in the theater's main sectors of commercial, community, educational, children's, and regional professional repertory. What is offered here in the name of the National Theatre Conference is an appraisal of that panorama from the standpoint of a genuine and continuing concern for the theater's future growth as a major factor of American culture.

This project was supported by grants and gifts from The Rockefeller Foundation, The John Golden Fund, Tufts University's Graduate Faculty Research Fund, Samuel French, Inc., Dramatists Play Service, Inc., and John F. Wharton, Esq., of New York City. NTC is deeply grateful to the generosity of these institutions and individuals for making this report possible.

The authors wish to record their indebtedness to the late John Gassner, scholar, teacher, and colleague in NTC, for his personal encouragement and advice, as well as for his timely help in securing funds for this project.

Special thanks are due NTC's historian, Dr. Tino Balio, of The University of Wisconsin, for his Introduction to this volume.

Acknowledgment and thanks are also extended to the following organizations for assistance in the collection of materials: Actors' Equity Association, the American Community Theatre Association, the American Educational Theatre Association, the American National Theatre and Academy, the Children's Theatre Conference, the Dramatists Guild, the Institute of Outdoor Drama, the International Theatre Institute, the League of New York Theatres, the League of Off-Broadway Theatres, the National Recreation and Park Association, the New Dramatists Committee, the New England Theatre Conference, The Rockefeller Brothers Fund, the U.S. Institute for Theatre Technology, and the Writers Guild of America, West.

The number of directors, producers, playwrights, actors, educators, scholars, and other spokesmen of the American theater who responded to NTC queries through questionnaires, letters, and interviews is so great that we can only humbly express the utmost gratitude for the generosity of their replies. The membership of NTC alone contributed wholeheartedly. We hope we have drawn from their collective knowledge, experience, and insight a representative picture of the American theater today—on the way to tomorrow.

Robert E. Gard
Marston Balch
Pauline B. Temkin
For the Trustees and Members of the
National Theatre Conference

March 1968

# ACKNOWLEDGMENTS

THE AUTHORS wish to express their gratitude to the following persons and publishers for their permission to reprint excerpts from their work in this book:

Ira Bilowit, *How to Organize an Off-Broadway Theatre, ANTA Booklet*—1964 (from Introduction).

Marston Balch, "The Right Play in the Right Place: An Idea for Community Theatres," *Theatre Arts,* XL, 8 (August 1956), pp. 64–68.

Alexander Cohen, "What's Right with Broadway?", *New York Herald Tribune,* (July 7, 1963).

Judith Crist on Joseph Papp's Shakespeare Festival, *New York Herald Tribune* (excerpt).

Hume Cronyn, *Best Plays of 1965–66,* pp. 58–62. Otis L. Guernsey, Jr., *Best Plays of 1965–66,* p. 41. Reprinted by permission of Dodd, Mead & Company, Inc. from *The Best Plays of 1965–66,* edited by Otis L. Guernsey, Jr. Copyright © 1966 by Dodd, Mead & Company, Inc.

Ogden Dwight on Community Theater from an article in *Des Moines Register & Tribune.*

Joseph Golden, *The Death of Tinker Bell,* Syracuse University Press, 1966, pp. 164–68 and 160–63.

Theodore Hoffman on Educational Theater from the *New York Times,* (September 1, 1963) (excerpts).

Theodore Hoffman on NYU Theater Program, *Tulane Drama Review,* (Winter 1965) (excerpt).

Burnet M. Hobgood, *Directory of American College Theater,* First edition, 1960.

Burnet M. Hobgood, "American Educational Theatre in the Present," paper prepared for delivery at the annual convention of AETA in New York, August 21, 1967.

Ted M. Kraus on Resident Theaters, *Critical Digest,* (March 20, 1967) (excerpt).

Samuel Selden lecture "Future Directions of Educational Theatre," *FUTURES IN AMERICAN THEATRE* (Lecture series), Department of Drama, University of Texas, Austin, 1963 (excerpt).

Sandra Schmidt from a series of articles on Regional Theatre, *Christian Science Monitor,* (July and August 1964).

Michael Smith, article on "Off off-Broadway," *TULANE DRAMA REVIEW* Vol. X, No. 4 (T 32) (Summer 1966), pp. 159–60 (excerpt).

Alvin Toffler, *The Culture Consumers: A Study of Art and Affluence in America,* New York, 1964, pp. 164–65.

*Tulane Drama Review,* (Summer 1966), report of TDR Conference on November 21, 1965, excerpts on Regional Theatre from remarks by: Theodore Hoffman, John O'Neal, Gordon Rogoff, André Gregory, Paul Gray, Edwin Sherin, Paul Sills.

*Variety,* (March 9, 1966), "Hinterland Legits Top B'way" (excerpt).

John Wharton on Broadway Ticket Situation (address to NTC in November, 1966) printed in Dramatists Guild Quarterly, (Winter 1967).

# CONTENTS

# INTRODUCTION

IN INITIATING in 1961 its project for a National Appraisal of the American Theater, the National Theatre Conference hoped "to help the theater learn about itself and help the American people and the people of other lands to understand the practical problems and real potentiality of a great cultural asset too long neglected."

That NTC would pursue such an ambitious goal is neither surprising nor inappropriate. NTC was the first permanent organization of the theater profession in the United States. Since its founding in 1925, at the height of the Little Theater movement, it has sought to mediate the exchange of ideas and to provide collective service between leading community and educational theaters, and between these and the professional theater.

With modest grants from the Carnegie Foundation (1932–35) and under the leadership of George Pierce Baker and Edith J. R. Isaacs, NTC set out to raise artistic standards. It published a series of theater handbooks which included Rosamond Gilder's *A Theatre Library* (1932), Stanley McCandless's *A Method of Lighting the Stage* (1932), Richard Boleslavsky's *Acting, the First Six Lessons* (1933), and Edith J. R. Isaacs' *Architecture for the New Theatre* (1935). During its early years, NTC also inaugurated such projects as the Play Release Project to encourage the writing and production of plays by untried playwrights, and Mrs. Isaacs' Survey of 400 Stock Towns, which proved to the Dramatists League that since certain areas no longer had stock companies there was no reason to delay the release of plays to amateur theaters in these areas. The latter project was of considerable financial benefit to most theaters outside New York.

In 1937 the Rockefeller Foundation chose NTC as the vehicle through which it would subsidize projects intended to insure the artistic growth of the noncommercial theater. To administer these funds efficiently, NTC underwent a reorganization. The open-membership policy was abandoned in favor of a trusteeship consisting of 25 leaders from community and educational theater. (The number was eventually raised to 100.) A new series of projects was initiated beginning with the Royalty Project, which helped amateur groups to secure quality plays at prices consonant with low incomes and limited budgets. This project eventually taught thousands of groups the value of collective bargaining and encouraged them to deal directly with play publishers and agents.

Among its other undertakings inaugurated before the war, NTC began publishing in 1939 a quarterly *Bulletin* which ran until the end of 1950; created a Free Placement Service; and administered a Fellowship Project with the twofold aim of enabling selected young men and women to prepare themselves for work in the noncommercial theater as actors, designers, and directors, and of providing nonprofessional theaters with competent staff assistants.

With the outbreak of World War II, NTC implemented national defense efforts by introducing the theater into the Army's morale program. Its Training Camp Entertainment Project demonstrated the need for entertainment by and for the soldiers and the need for expert supervision of the activity by men trained in university and community theaters. As a result, the Army to this day commissions men to act as theater advisers in training camps. NTC's other wartime activities included staging premières to raise initial money for war bond drives, sponsoring playwriting contests for plays dealing with army life, supplying military posts and camps with college and community theater performances, furnishing scholarships to theatrically talented servicemen, and, in the demobilization period, operating a Veterans Counseling Service on opportunities for theater training, apprenticeships, and jobs. During this latter period it also initiated, under Lee Norvelle, a New Play Project to supply new works of quality directly to nonprofessional theaters, and in 1946, under Hallie Flanagan Davis, launched a very successful New Playwrights Project whereby 33 young dramatic authors received grants to enable them to master their craft.

The philosophy guiding NTC's efforts after the war was formulated by Frederic McConnell, then director of the Cleveland Play House. In a speech at the 1945 annual meeting he said:

> Recognizing the need for a decentralized national theater, and believing that such a theater can best be achieved through establishment of non-profit professional theaters throughout the country, and that the nucleus for such theaters is already to be found in many existing competent and experienced amateur theaters, the National Theatre Conference, therefore, encourages and will endorse any effort on the part of such amateur theaters as will lead to achievement of professional status through the development and maintenance of a full-rounded professional ensemble of directors, actors, designers, technicians, and administrative personnel, and that, further, it will favor for membership those theaters and individuals who express the intention to operate on such a professional level and take constructive measures to achieve it.

Accordingly, NTC awarded generous fellowships to students for graduate work, to professors for research, and to directors for advanced study. It also helped establish university repertory companies, find employment for young actors, and provide intensive training for apprentice actors through its touring company at Indiana University.

The Rockefeller subsidy ended in 1950 because the Foundation regarded "its contribution over the past fifteen years to this phase of work in drama . . . as having been made." In summarizing NTC's contributions, Harry E. Davis, director of the theater at the University of North Carolina, also described the organization itself in saying that the National Theatre Conference:

> . . . provided a professional association in which the leading spirits of the educational and community theater movements could cooperate effectively in an exchange of ideas and experiences, in which these people could work together to establish standards of high order for the nonprofessional theater, and in which leaders in these nonprofessional theater movements could be afforded the prestige and status they deserved. Through its annual meetings, its projects, and its publications, NTC spoke authoritatively for the varied and discrete leadership in the theater outside of the commercial New York area, and generated a necessary and healthy comparison of standards, objectives, and achievements of these two principal areas of theater activity.

The cessation of the Rockefeller subsidy forced NTC to redefine its objectives. The curtailment of its projects and the end of its publication of the *Bulletin* were inevitable and much regretted. But in the years since, these losses have been partly offset by the enlargement of the Conference's representative membership of leaders not only in the university and community theater but, more recently, in the nonprofit professional theater throughout the country. Moreover, through its affiliations with the American Educational Theatre Association (AETA) and constituent groups in Community Theater, Secondary School Theater, and Children's Theater, as well as with the American National Theatre and Academy (ANTA) and the National Council of the Arts in Education (NCAIE), NTC has continued to exert a strong, high-level influence upon the noncommercial theater of America. While its primary concern has always been with this decentralized theater and the professionalizing of its standards, NTC, being a national body, has never ceased to regard Theater in America as a single entity and the health or sickness of any of its parts as vitally affecting the whole.

Marston Balch, the current Executive Secretary of NTC, speaking for a majority of the members said NTC still has "a significant role to play as an impartial leader in the movement to revitalize the American theater, to restore American drama and the whole institution of the theater to a stature commensurate with the other arts and with our national position in the world." By "impartial" Balch meant leadership not biased by one or another organizational affiliation, "standing in a sufficiently elevated place to take the entire panorama into its purview." With the National Appraisal of the American Theater, NTC is meeting the obligations of its new role.

Tino T. Balio
Wisconsin Center for Theater Research
The University of Wisconsin

# I. IN NEW YORK

# In New York

THE PROBLEMS and promise of theater in America are reflected vividly on the New York stage. There, both on and off Broadway, the dilemmas, complexities, and constant attempts to achieve a theatrical success are continuously being played out.

Theatrical success is measured differently by the various groups operating in New York. For the commercial theater, operated primarily as a profit venture, the monetary risks today are greater than ever, making sweeter than ever the lure of success in the form of a hit. The commercial theater has been and continues to be in the grip of the hit-or-flop psychology.

There are also in New York some theatrical groups which have attempted to break away from the tyranny of the dollar and are primarily interested in producing fine drama. For these nonprofit organizations, theatrical success is measured primarily in terms of critical acclaim and audience support, with the hope of being financially self-supporting. Paradoxically, however, the stronger the achievement artistically, the weaker the likelihood of financial independence, so that subsidy from government or philanthropic sources has become a necessity of existence.

In estimating the condition of the New York theater we must report the two categories separately: (1) the commercial theater known as Broadway and off-Broadway, and (2) the nonprofit organizations such as the APA–Phoenix, the Lincoln Center Repertory Company, the New York Shakespeare Festival, and others.

Information has been derived from all manner of publications; from surveys made by the present authors; from questionnaires addressed to producers, directors, and playwrights; from a voluminous correspondence with a variety of theatrical personalities; and from direct personal interviews. We do not intend what follows to be an exhaustive or intensive study, but rather a critical overview of the New York scene reflecting a variety of current, informed viewpoints.

## Commercial Theater - Broadway

What's wrong with Broadway today? This question was asked of many people, and we quote as representative the reply of Joseph Anthony, a well-known Broadway director:

> What's wrong with Broadway today? Well, of course, the one we've all been shouting about: costs, first. When even a modest production costs $100,000 everyone involved cannot help but in some measure distort the intent of theater, being harnessed with the responsibility of securing a return on that investment. The successful or "hit" play and the search for it, to the exclusion of all other concerns, interests, and passions, is, of course, destructive and aimless. There is no future in it, certainly none that would make the "great American theater" a rational goal. Audiences, too, if the price of a ticket is as high as it is today, even for off-Broadway, will seek out the security of the unanimously declared hit, and gone is the possibility of discovery and the exercise of individual judgment which make for constant and vigorous support.
>
> How can a change be brought about? I am pessimistic about its accomplishment on Broadway. The producers and managers about 30 years ago began creating this monster, and we artists and performers gave over our rights and original intent for the happy dollar and easy chair. The guilds and craft unions all fell into the trap of treating the theater as an industry and business, and our best efforts are really only coping with the monster.

### *Production Costs*

The fantastic rise in cost of a Broadway production is an undis puted fact and apparently still spiraling upward. In 1963 Jean Dal rymple, of the New York City Center, reported that a show once cost ing $8,000 to produce would cost $125,000. In 1967 Norris Houghton co-founder of the Phoenix Theatre in New York, stated that productio costs of the average straight play on Broadway would run between $100,000 and $150,000 and the cost of the average musical between $400,000 and $500,000.

Increased labor costs and the general inflationary rise of our economy account for a great part of the enormous rise in costs. Peculiar to the theatrical industry of Broadway, however, are other factors.[1]

## *Real Estate*

Real estate costs are a unique Broadway problem. The number of legitimate theaters on Broadway has been steadily declining: in 1966–67 there were only 37 operating in New York.

A neutral opinion regarding the real estate situation in New York was expressed by Margaret Jane Fischer, patron, commentator, and lecturer on the American theater:

> New York City building laws forbid the construction of a theater building except for the exclusive use as a theater. This has been a deterrent to new building. Further, since theater-owning is not always a paying proposition, theater owners include a stop-clause in all their contracts.
>
> As you know, a realtor can set the figure he expects a production to gross weekly if it is to occupy his theater, and if it falls below that, he can force the play out so that he can book a more promising attraction. Needless to say, the theater owner is not necessarily a person interested in the Theater as a cultural venture! This clause can be particularly hard on a straight play which may require time to find its audience. I do not know how many times it may have been invoked to the detriment of a worthy production, but its very existence places power in the wrong hands!
>
> I do think new commercial theaters should be built, and that some restriction of present laws should make it possible to combine a building that would house a theater and be used as well for other commercial purposes. The theater shortage in New York City, and elsewhere, is desperate, cutting down to a dangerous low the number of plays and musicals that can be seen in a given season, and this situation inevitably increases the greed of the theater owner. He makes the most of it by charging exorbitant rent, by invoking the stop clause at will, and often by deciding what can or cannot be booked.
>
> Theater owners, of course, would reply that they need the long-playing hits to meet their rising costs and make their investment pay off.

## *Unions*

A questionnaire sent to Broadway producers asked what they considered to be the point of greatest economic pressure and whether in their opinion unions' demands, featherbedding, or any other abuses constituted a serious menace to the commercial theater.

The replies do not furnish any authoritative answers to the question of whether union demands are excessive but do reflect the variety of opinions on this highly controversial subject.

Featherbedding, the requirement of some unions that members be paid for a minimum number of hours regardless of whether the services are needed or used, was cited by one-third of those replying as the greatest point of pressure. A few felt that Equity, the actors' union, was at fault; a few that the stagehands' union was excessive in its demands. Some producers expressed the view that there were no pressure points with regard to unions and that time was the great enemy. One producer temperately said that the unions were all doing the best for their members, a view with which union officials would certainly agree.

One-third of those replying did believe that union demands and featherbedding abuses constitute a serious menace to the commercial theater. Almost one-third disagreed and the remaining third expressed in-between views such as "they do increase pressure to do more popular plays," "no more than others," and "not in a successful play."

A greater variety of opinions came in reply to the question as to what might be done to limit union demands and control abuses. Some producers did not agree with the premise or did not know. Those who felt strongly about the issue recommended many different approaches, including: "stand together unanimously," "strengthen League of New York Theatres," "public pressure," "government pressure," "unions will respond to a mass conference for the good of the theater," "start all over," and "revolution!"[2]

The fact is that the New York theater is not only very highly unionized, but its employees are organized into many independent craft unions. Theater managements have to deal with as many different sets of union negotiators as there are job functions whenever the terms of a contract come into question. Moreover, so rigid are the lines defining the various kinds of work that in actual stage practice a simple function like moving a prop, which in the nonprofessional theater might be performed by anyone, may only be done by a stagehand. And if any kind of music is used in a play, even a tape recording, a stipulated number of union musicians must be added to the payroll. Even more burdensome to managements are the requirements of some of the noncraft trade unions that service the theater.

## *Theater Ticket System*

One of the effects of rising costs has been the increase in the price of tickets. If purchased at the box office, orchestra seats to a Broadway musical may cost $9.90, and to a straight play $6.60 or more. A licensed ticket broker will add a charge of $1.50 to the box office price. A speculator will charge whatever the traffic will bear, and prices may range from $25 to $125.

John F. Wharton, then consultant-director of the Legitimate Theatre Industry Exploratory Commission, in an address delivered in November 1966 to the National Theatre Conference, called the theater ticket system "Elizabethan, antediluvian, mythological, nay, prehistoric." He pointed out that the selling pattern of everything except theater tickets has changed radically in the last 350 years.

Each physical theater has its own box office to which the would-be purchaser must trudge or mail his order. In every other area of merchandising a buyer can telephone, charge his purchase, or use a credit card. In the theater, however, it is still cash-and-carry, Wharton told NTC:

> After about 300 years—in the first decades of this century—a segment of the public began to rebel against the cash-and-carry system and demand something more convenient. Since we live in a free enterprise society, some enterprising people decided to fill this demand. They came to be known as brokers, although, except for the name and the fact that for some unknown reason they have to be licensed, their activities bear no similarity to any brokerage business. They were (and are) retailers who bought tickets from the theater owner and retailed them at convenient spots, mostly hotels. They tried to keep on hand a supply of tickets for all plays. They took orders by telephone. They permitted charge accounts. They delivered the tickets. For these services they charged a modest amount over the price printed on the ticket.
>
> In their blissful ignorance of economics, most Americans in the early 1900's believed that the whole great American distribution system should be given to them free. If it cost $10 to make something at a factory, they felt they should be able to buy it for $10 at the nearest store; they believed that any increase in that price was due to wicked middlemen, and that these immoral creatures were parasitical speculators who should be legislated out of existence. In most cases, however, the producer of goods set, and advertised, a retail price; this of course included a markup for the retailer over the factory price, but since the buyer did not know about it, he felt that the seller paid it and raised no questions. But the theater people stuck to the pattern of a box office (or factory) price, with an increase over that price when sold conveniently by their retailers. And they brought down on themselves the wrath of the public, press and politicians which exists to this day.
>
> A spate of laws and regulations was enacted which has brought about the current ridiculous, insane situation. A so-called broker must first get a license, then buy the tickets from the theater, and resell them at no more than $1.50 increase. (Please note that he can mark up the price of a $3 ticket by 50 percent, but a $10 ticket only 15 percent; the least affluent buyer pays the heaviest toll.)

What's more, he must sell them at a place where nothing but tickets are sold. Moreover, the theater owners cannot legally pay brokers a commission, nor pay bonuses to big sales, nor give tie-in bargains. They cannot do what every other industry does as a matter of course.

The whole matter was further complicated by the appearance of buyers who not only wanted service, but also the privilege of buying choice seats at their convenience, right up to the last minute. Those buyers were ready, able and willing to pay far more than a $1.50 over the printed price. Again, in a free enterprise society, this produced a group of speculators who took the risk of supplying this last-minute demand. This drove the moral reformers into a frenzy of anger. Although the American people speculate in homes, corn, wheat and other necessities of life, the reformers declared ticket speculation to be dastardly, immoral and un-American. And further laws and regulations were enacted to legislate morality into the theater industry.

Laws such as these produce one sure result: a crop of people who violate them. Prohibition produced the bootlegger and the hijacker; in the theater we have an under-the-counter market. Over the years, millions of dollars have gone into the pockets of the men who run this market instead of going to playwrights, stars, honest producers and theater owners and their investors, or being used to lower the price of the other seats.

There is a myth that the elimination of ice would eliminate the under-the-counter market in hit tickets, or at least reduce the price asked in that market. Let us be clear here on the difference between so-called "ice" and a speculator's profit. If the printed price of a ticket is $9 and a speculator feels sure he can resell it for $25, he is often quite willing to pay to the box office man or the theater owners or producer (whoever controls the sale) a premium in order to get the ticket. Let us assume that the premium is $6. That $6 is ice. The speculator has then paid $9 plus $6 ice, or $15 for the ticket; then, when he sells it for $25, he has made $10. The $10 is speculator's profit. Now, if he did not have to pay the $6 of ice, he could resell at $19 and still make $10. But if you believe that this is the way of a speculator's life, you are more naïve than I think. He will charge the market price of $25, and the elimination of ice would only increase his speculative profit from $10 to $16. You never hear, and never will hear, a speculator telling a buyer that he is reducing the price because he got the tickets without having to pay ice.

Wharton concluded his speech, which appeared in the *Dramatists Guild Quarterly*, Winter 1967 by saying:

There has been entirely too much mystery about the sale of theater tickets, and the whole system ought to be brought out in the open. We should be able to set up a modern system which would enable the industry to get the money now going to ice-takers and speculators, to set up one scale of retail prices, and to have tickets

> sold at convenient locations. When this happens . . . you will see a scale of prices that goes down to the reach of the least affluent, and furthermore, one that regularly offers bargains.
>
> There are many different ways in which tickets could be sold, and, in a free economy, we should be free to choose the best ones. The theater has a choice—lots of choices. We don't have to retain the Terebratula Ticket System.

Wharton, as consultant-director of the Legitimate Theatre Industry Exploratory Commission which was set up by the League of New York Theatres,[3] evolved a ticket distribution plan that will discourage speculators and ice. Under his proposal legitimate ticket brokers would be allowed to sell the seats at prices the market can bear, particularly for hit shows. The revenue now going into the black market would end up with the producers, creators, performers and investors who do the work in the theater. The broker would be able to buy tickets at the theater box office and sell them to the public at the same price. This agreed-to price would be stamped on the ticket and the producer would then pay the broker a commission.

The new "open ticket" proposal has not yet been put into practice, but there is considerable optimism that the new scheme will help solve one of Broadway's most pesky problems.

### *Benefit Parties*

A benefit theater party is the merchandising device whereby a producer sells the house to the agents of a charitable organization who in turn add on a substantial levy for their particular cause and sell the tickets by subscription.

For the producer, this practice assures a certain amount of initial income for his show before it opens, and consequently before the critics have a chance to pan or praise it. If the show's advance publicity attracts a considerable number of theater-party sellouts, the income thus assured may tide an otherwise shaky production over the first rough weeks—seldom longer. For the subscriber, the heavy surcharge for his tickets is tax-exempt, since it goes to charity, and his participation in the party gives him the double gratification of serving a worthy cause while attending a new show that may become a hit. For the two or three leading agents who handle the large benefit parties in New York, the financial rewards are generally believed to be very substantial. Whether this practice has been entirely beneficial to Broadway, to say nothing of the theater or of drama at large, is debatable. On this question the National Theatre Conference sought out and received a number of different opinions.

In the view of most of the persons consulted, the party audience attends chiefly for social reasons, not because of any real interest in theater. Such an audience wants to be amused and diverted, not stimulated to self-analysis or provoked into a contemplation of serious problems. This accounts for the preponderant number of theater parties arranged for musicals, light comedies, and shows with popular stars. It is, furthermore, understandable that the person paying $25 to $100 for a ticket—even though most of the sum goes to charity—wants to be sure he is seeing a hit.

We shall have more to say later on the composition of the Broadway audience, but it may be appropriate to ask here: Who is victim and who is perpetrator of this hit-or-flop psychology?

Costs, prices, audiences are among the main factors that have created the uniquely Broadway situation which some defend and others criticize. The guts of this Pandora's box can perhaps best be illustrated by quoting at some length from one of the knowledgeable people that wrote to NTC on the subject.

The view of Margaret Jane Fischer follows:

> The problems that afflict the New York theater are so inextricably bound that it is difficult to separate them or even, in some instances, to distinguish between cause and effect!
>
> One of my own great fears is that we are rapidly becoming a musical theater to the extent that we are failing to encourage and develop playwrights and are, as well, losing an audience for the straight play.
>
> Granted that the musical is our particular forte and a form so peculiarly American that it is our contribution to World Theater, and granted that a *The King and I* or a *West Side Story* is a genuine work of art! But the very success of the really fine musical has inevitably led to imitation. We have reached a point where even a poor musical can have a run at least long enough for motion picture sales and record albums to absorb possible Broadway box office losses.
>
> Because of the possible financial reward, producers find it easier to raise money for a musical than for a straight play, despite the fact that the former requires twice the capitalization, increasing upwards now to half a million dollars.
>
> The musical has brought into being a totally new audience, unfortunately not in addition to the previously existing one, but, for the most part, instead of it! The person most likely to afford the high price of musical tickets is the expense-account executive or the out-of-town buyer. He cares little for the merit of what he sees, but prefers, always, to see a musical, feeling that he gets more for his money when there is music, dancing and elaborate scenery.
>
> The musical is also easier to sell for charitable benefits as, again, patrons more willingly pay the very high benefit prices (ranging

from $25 to $100 per ticket) with a feeling that more is offered for the money spent. There is also the promise of light and undemanding entertainment for what is essentially not an evening dedicated to theater but a social occasion. (Who can blame actors for loathing to play to benefit audiences?)

I am among those who feel that the ever-increasing theater benefit is an unfortunate development in the theater. Granted that it guarantees a producer enough sold-out houses to get his musical safely launched, no matter what the critics may say on opening night, but it has also made possible the fairly long runs of some most unworthy productions. Producers, in fairness, are not altogether to blame. Theirs is not an easy task, for they must work from scripts submitted months before the production is actually under way. The final production is often as disappointing to them as it is to the buyer, for not infrequently the very quality of the script that has prompted their choice of it has been altered beyond recognition during rehearsals, or the star or director or choreographer whose reputation has been a strong selling point has withdrawn from the production for which the brokers have already sold thousands of tickets.

### *Economic Summary*

Broadway has barely been able to be self-supporting according to the recent study by William J. Baumol and William G. Bowen, *Performing Arts: The Economic Dilemma.* From their scholarly and factual work, prepared and published in 1966 under the auspices of the Twentieth Century Fund, it is clear that the dilemma of all the performing arts is the constantly increasing gap between costs and earnings. With the exception of Broadway, the professional, live performing arts need a subsidy of over $20,000,000 annually in order to survive. Inasmuch as ticket prices cannot be raised high enough nor production methods streamlined low enough in an era of rising costs, the annual income gap is destined to grow.

While there is not as yet a large income gap in the overall operation of the Broadway commercial theater, the authors point out some distressing signs such as the drop in the number of productions (especially of new dramatic works) and the leveling off of attendance (at about 7,000,000) in an era of rising population and affluence.

*Variety,* the weekly journal which keeps its fingers on all the pulses of the manifold entertainment industry, credited Broadway with an unusually profitable season in 1965–66. In spite of 33 staggering failures (at the box office) out of a total of 68 productions, the fact that one in three paid off made it a successful season as Broadway dollars are measured. In the same terms, it noted a quantitative "rise" both on Broadway and on the "road" in the season of 1966–67, while attributing the marked increase of the total gross receipts to the rise of ticket prices, and admitting that "from the standpoint of quality, however, it was one of the most disappointing seasons in memory." It attributed the "large increase" in the number of shows in the "miscellaneous" classification in 1966–67 primarily to the repertory presentations of the APA-Phoenix, but also to the Broadway appearance of the National Repertory Theatre and the straight-play revival season at the City Center.

Nonetheless, Broadway's economic decline is real in the eyes of the majority of producers who replied to the NTC questionnaire. Chronic as the problem has been for several decades, there is, in their view today, genuine cause for alarm. Some feel that the chance of investors making the sort of profit to justify the risk is not good enough; others see little evidence of success in recent efforts to broaden the base of theatrical investments by increasing the number of small investors. As noted by Norris Houghton, of the APA-Phoenix Theatre, the total amount of money invested in Broadway has not declined much, but it is being invested in fewer shows, with the largest sums going into musicals. And it could be added that of late years even the musicals show more box office failures and have conspicuously fallen off in quality.

### *Critical Successes*

Success in the New York theater is measured in terms of financial success and critical success. A show can be a hit with the critics and a flop at the box office. Rarely, however, can a show be panned by the critics and a hit at the box office. For this reason New York critics wield an enormous power over the theater.

Some people are understandably bitter about "good" shows that never had a chance because the critics disapproved. Since an evening at the theater is so expensive (add dinner, transportation, and sitter to the price of the ticket), the average theatergoer feels he cannot afford to attend any show that is not a hit. He therefore waits to read what the critics say before he decides what to see.

Since the number of New York's daily newspapers has been drastically reduced, the few remaining critics have become even more powerful than a decade ago when there were "nine cold men" rendering verdicts on the shows. And it is now said that if producers cannot carry Walter Kerr's approval, they cannot make a go of it. It is doubtful that Walter Kerr or any other critic wants such undisputed power, but they undoubtedly have it.[4]

Paradoxically, the same two seasons (1965–66 and 1966–67) that *Variety* considered financially successful were far from being critically acclaimed. The consensus of drama critics was that, with few exceptions and most of those foreign imports, these seasons were, on the whole, shabby and dull. In the critics' opinion, what Broadway needs is more challenging fare. While old-fashioned, rousing musicals are fine for fun, there is a stupendous dearth of the vital, questioning drama that brings distinction to a nation's theatrical capital.

## *Producers, Plays and Playwrights*

What do producers look for in plays and what do they avoid? These and similar questions were asked in the NTC questionnaire sent to the producing group. While the number of replies is too small to be considered authoritative, the replies themselves seem sufficiently typical to report.

Most producers indicated that they are producing fewer plays per season than they used to. With notable exceptions, such as David Merrick, Alexander H. Cohen, and Arthur Fried (who reported that he managed to average three or four plays per season), the majority were averaging only one play per season.

There is apparently no one type of play that producers seek out. To quote from their replies, they are looking for "good, serious plays," "commercial plays with something to say," "serious comedies," "good comedy or drama with a low production budget," "musicals," "something unusual or potentially successful," "quality and distinction," "exciting theater," "anything that will move or entertain or stimulate." Clearly, producers have no set formula in mind.

Many producers do have a sense of humor which is revealed in some of the replies to the question: "What types of plays do you tend to avoid?" The gamut included musicals, light comedies, comedies set in brownstone houses, period or costume musicals, abstract and tasteless plays, dirty plays, absurd, ordinary, formula, far out, racial or minority problems, expensive, plays with devils, classical plays, and bad ones!

A frequent criticism of the Broadway producer is that he does not take enough chances with the new or little-known playwright. Our producers' replies on this subject indicated that this is not a wholly valid accusation. Over 60 percent protested it, some of them in strong terms. They listed the names of more than 40 playwrights they introduced when they were unknown, and claimed that many of these authors, such as Miller, Laurents, Wilder, Williams, and Inge, were first professionally produced on Broadway. It must be noted, however, that several of those mentioned, including Williams and Inge, had previously been discovered and given professional productions in regional playhouses, such as the late Margo Jones's Dallas Theatre-in-the-Round; others had seen their plays done in summer stock or off-Broadway.

Another criticism—this one voiced by established playwrights as well as new ones—concerns the functionaries who stand between the author and the producer and between the author's script and its production. In the entertainment industry, it seems, everyone must employ an agent, even agents themselves. Playwrights, and new ones in particular, are seldom in a position to market their own scripts; instead, they must depend upon a dramatic agent to whom they pay 10 percent of any royalties or other profits the script, in whatever form, may eventually earn. Good and reliable agents, they tell us, are few. The Broadway producer, in turn, employs one or more playreaders to sift the scripts that come in and select for his attention any that seem to have commercial quality. Since it takes unusual experience, patience, insight, and imagination for anyone to discover the potentialities of a given script, and since such qualifications are rare and hard to come by, the playwright's trouble often lies there. Unless his script happens to fit one of the accepted commercial formulae or happens to find the right reader, it is likely to be turned down before reaching the Master's desk. And if he is lucky enough to have a script accepted, says the playwright, he may still have to contend with the producer and director over the casting and over the interpretation of roles, scenes, or the play itself—as often as not, in vain.

Broadway producers all declare that they are interested in and looking for the "good" playwright. Most of them believe that, along with professional theatrical producers, the major television networks, motion picture corporations, and recording firms—all of which profit directly from the work of playwrights—have a clear responsibility to assist young dramatists at the source of their careers, for example through scholarships, residentships, grants-in-aid, and the like. Indeed, some beginnings in this direction have already been made, as in the fellowships offered through certain universities by the Shubert Foundation and those provided for television writers at the Yale School of Drama by the Columbia Broadcasting System. But the entertainment industry as a whole has been far too slow to recognize and assume its responsibility toward fostering the playwrights it will have to depend on in the future. Broadway producers, however, feel that they cannot take any more chances than they do with the new, the unknown, the untried author or play—and in the present state of their business they are probably right—but must leave the task of experiment to educational, regional, and community theaters. We shall consider, further on in the text, how they handle it.

If it is true that every producer would dearly love to see a great script cross his desk, why is not more significant drama being performed today? This is one of the imponderables that seems locked into a vicious cycle.

Most producers agree with the view that today's typical Broadway audience is not terribly interested in theater and is, in fact, more and more a coterie audience—hence the trend to musicals, to the lighter bill of fare and the "safe package." To this there are of course exceptions. *Who's Afraid of Virginia Woolf?* was produced successfully in 1962–63 without theater parties or advance sale. *The Subject Was Roses,* after a long struggle, finally caught on in 1964–65. And although Edward Albee's *Tiny Alice* failed in that season, his no less serious play, *A Delicate Balance,* proved a success in 1966–67. (Note: Albee is one of his own producers.) Yet, in spite of the exceptions, there is a definite reluctance to gamble on "drama." The fact is attested to by all recent surveys, including NTC's, that of the few commercial managements producing serious drama in the 1960's, virtually all are doing so at a deficit.

Even so, it would seem probable that some Broadway producer would be willing to stage a major American play—if only to foster, or keep alive the illusion of, native talent. Why, then, have our established playwrights been so scarce of late years on the commercial stage, and, when they have appeared, why have they been so brief and unlucky? Except for his rewrites of *The Milk Train,* Tennessee Williams's only recent Broadway plays have been his pair of one-acters, *Slapstick Tragedy,* which closed after seven performances in February 1966. William Inge's comedy *Where's Daddy?* ran but 22 performances in the following month. Arthur Miller has brought out no new plays in the past two seasons, and none on Broadway for many more. With the possible exception of Edward Albee's *A Delicate Balance,* there simply have been no major American plays to stage. But why?[5]

According to Lee Strasberg, the reason is that Broadway success is based on strictly commercial values—values which are intangible and unpredictable. The major American playwrights are stymied because they cannot write what they want to and they do not want to write what is commercially salable.

As an example of Broadway's unpredictability, Strasberg cited to NTC the 1967–68 hit comedy of Robert Anderson, *You Know I Can't Hear You When the Water's Running.* (Robert Anderson, incidentally, was one of the young ex-servicemen who were helped to playwriting careers by NTC fellowships.) Anderson, said Strasberg, wrote for the community theater, and not for Broadway, what are essentially four one-act plays with a common theme. In Strasberg's opinion, no seasoned Broadway producer would have taken a chance with this script, but two young, adventurous producers did, and it became one of the few

American hits of the 1966–67 season. This is the kind of unpredictable success story that keeps the lure of Broadway ever shiny, but also frustrates the serious playwright.[6]

## *Audiences and Taste*

Howard Lindsay, one of America's great actors and directors, expressed his views on this particular subject in an interview with an NTC representative.[7]

> I have to conclude that the theater has not changed the audiences. The audience has changed the theater. This is a different world we are living in. For example, one of the elements that kept good taste in the theater of a generation ago was the consciousness of the individual in the audience that he was sitting next to a stranger and he had a feeling that this stranger would appraise him by his reactions to the play. If he laughed at vulgarity, the stranger would put him down as a vulgar fellow. And he cared what his neighbor was thinking of him. Today, it seems to me that the individual in the audience just does not give a damn about what the people around him think of him.
>
> Many people believe the playwright has been responsible for this because of his abuse of shock. Now, to my mind, shock used to be one of the most valuable tools of the playwright, but it has been used for its own sake to such an extent that it has become dulled.
>
> It is probably true that the playwright has inured the audience to vulgarity and a lowering of taste, but it seems to me that the audience would not have accepted this use of four-letter words and obscenities if it had not been trained by social custom to be ready to accept it.

## *Production Standards*

There may be a decline on Broadway in creative and economic terms, but there has been no decline in standards of production.

Criticism is continually directed against Broadway that too many shows open under-rehearsed; that the script is not quite satisfactory to author or director; that the cast is still imperfectly acquainted with the play, their roles, and each other; that elements of the sets, lighting, costumes, music, or choreography are not yet in final shape.

In the majority view of producers, these charges are not true unless the show is done by inexperienced people. There may sometimes be errors of judgment—in the selection of the wrong director for the cast or the wrong cast for the play—but these do not reflect a decline in standards. In the opinion of most people interviewed by NTC, Broadway standards of production are still the highest in the world. Most producers reported that they rehearse their shows according to the Equity standard of four weeks for a straight play and five weeks for a musical, and follow this by extended tryouts in a series of theaters out of town. (It should be added, however, that these Equity rehearsal periods are considerably below the norms generally practiced by European professional theaters. Most of the latter, in addition, rotate their plays in repertory and so provide continuing rehearsal throughout a season, whereas many long-run shows in the United States betray a marked falling-off in quality of performance after the first six or seven weeks.)

Relatively new are preview runs on Broadway. The trend of paid previews at reduced prices was greatly encouraged by ANTA and seems to be working fairly well for comedy and serious drama. Producers, however, do not foresee a gradual elimination of out-of-town tryouts for straight plays, and they favor such tryouts for musicals because they are less expensive.

Before we leave the subject of Broadway's expertise, it may not be inappropriate to quote the remark of a Nigerian delegate to the 1967 Congress of the International Theatre Institute held in New York. According to the *New York Times* (June 12, 1967), this gentleman, in answer to a question as to what he thought of the Broadway shows he had just seen, said: "All technique. The husk, but not the kernel."

### Commentary

Producers and other Broadway professionals were asked by NTC to make any comments they cared to on the American theater generally, and we report a sampling of their remarks:

"The economic and artistic difficulty for both writers and producers causes too much turning to other fields, mainly motion pictures and other forms of writing. Motion pictures are improving from their contributions, but theater has too few creative, serious talents who will stick to it."

"The sooner New York loses its position as the fountain from which all good things flow, the better off the American theater will be."

"The theater is, or should be, a vital part of our life—of everyone's life. It is, and will, I suppose, continue to be of changing character. At present it has little meaning beyond temporary titillation and expertise. Thus it is in a decline. The intimate connection with television, insofar as writing talent is concerned, will prevent, for a time, any significant expansion (culturally) of the theater. But, as TV becomes surfeited with talent and prices for writers decline (as I am sure they will), writers will slowly drift back to the theater and seek their rewards, ultimately greater, there."

"It is healthier, when you look at the number of plays produced, than ever before. It is healthier when you look at the money an author can make even on short runs. The producer is the one who suffers most and risks all. He needs help more than authors, actors, or directors."

"Personally, I feel bleak about the theater as my own activity dwindles. I used to produce and/or direct one or two plays every season. Yet I know that the moment an exciting script reaches my desk all will be well. . . ."

"The fabulous invalid will always be fabulous and always be invalid."

Robert Whitehead, an outstanding New York producer, confirmed in an NTC interview that the New York theater's main problem is economic: diminishing business in an expanding economy. Where formerly Broadway would mount 250 new productions a season, now it does only 45 to 50. It is hard to make a profit with 1,200-seat houses, yet houses much larger are unsuited to straight plays. Broadway tries to keep alive on venture capital and this is ever harder to find. The hit-or-flop psychology: people don't just go to see a play any more, only a hit; with prices so high, if it is not a smash, they stay away.

In Whitehead's view, the commercial theater has a major selling job to do with the Federal Government. Not for subsidy, which he says no Broadway producer really wants, but for a complete revision: personal income tax spread over a wider span of years; corporate taxes eased for the performing arts. Whitehead also believes there should be important changes in New York's municipal tax structure, particularly with a reduction of real estate taxes on theater property.

He does not think, however, that Broadway will fold up. In fact Whitehead himself is returning to commercial production in 1967–68 after an absence of several seasons, during which he helped to plan the ANTA-Washington Square Playhouse and launch there the first Lincoln Center Repertory Company. Producers and their investors lose millions, it is true; but they also make millions—on balance, more than they lose. Very often the losses are due directly to poor management. New York has too many one-shot producers who raise capital for a single show and then cease. The established professional producers, averaging losses with gains, are not doing so badly, even today. In Whitehead's opinion, if they were, they would not stay in business.

Norris Houghton, NTC trustee and adviser on this New York theater section, agrees with Whitehead that Broadway is not yet done for. As he sees it, the kind of theatrical fare that is chiefly entertainment will continue to thrive there, but the more serious theater is bypassing the Great White Way and finding its place in the regional resident groups.

Alexander H. Cohen, prominent Broadway producer, in response to a letter from NTC soliciting his opinions, sent us a copy of an article he had written for the *New York Herald Tribune* in 1963 entitled, "What's Right With Broadway?" The article is presented here because it expresses an unusually optimistic view of the New York theater:

I would like to answer those amateur critics who think that the fashionable thing to do is aim broadsides at the theatrical industry.

First of all, let us acknowledge the recent "discovery" that flop shows lose money. Indeed they do—millions of dollars—and deservedly so. But that does not seem reason enough to overlook the many more millions earned by the hits. The commercial theater, when it gives the consumer what he wants, is commercially sound. Otherwise, might I suggest that all of us who produce for Broadway would have long since sought employment elsewhere. I am one of many producers who can go to work any time he pleases in commercial or toll television, producing shows or working for Hollywood. Why don't I? Because, happily, I do well on Broadway and, when I do, so do my employees, my associates and my investors.

Rousing himself from the gloom generated by the thought of Broadway's bankruptcy, our armchair critics' next complaint is that "the public can't buy tickets. The theater parties have them all!" Aside from the consideration of the hundreds of millions of dollars that theater parties have raised for deserving charities, one wonders if perhaps it is not time to start thinking of these audiences, who patronize the theater at advanced prices, as members, individually, of the public.

"Okay," our critic concedes, "so you can get tickets! But, at $6.90, who can afford to buy them?" Armies of bleary-eyed customers are staggering out of four-hour cinematic treats, having paid a dollar an hour for their labor. Others of their kind are riding back uptown from off-Broadway's vanity shops (those basements which have been financed by the entrepreneur's mother-in-law, whose donation of $7,000 has enabled her daughter's husband to mount and run *The Tulip Bulb* for a weekend), pleased with themselves for having spent only $5 a ticket, a reasonable price made possible by the generous consideration of the craft unions. While all this financial frivolity is going on, a lot of the legitimate theater's cheap seats are going begging.

Then there is the critic who says, "You call that a business! C'mon now—it's fun and all, but a business?" Yes, my friend, and a very efficiently run one. For instance, a musical spectacle involving the varied talents of 150 people—principals, singers, dancers, musicians and technicians of varying types—is completely mounted in a six-week period, having first been designed by qualified experts in each department. We are seldom, if ever, taxed by overtime. Our scenery is constructed and our costumes manufactured according to exact specifications on a rigid schedule and, together with properties and tons of sound and lighting equipment, is delivered to a theater on a particular day, and assembled in a matter of hours at a firm contracted price. Moreover, our grosses are totaled daily, our accounts are presented weekly, and our profits are distributed monthly.

"But," says our critical economist, "your production costs have more than doubled in two decades." True, but only in direct proportion to the nation's economy. Labor costs, material costs and creative costs have all risen—just as they have in every other industry. One inevitable result is that failure is more expensive than it ever was—witness either the Edsel or *Lorenzo*. Inevitably, too, there is less room for mediocrity. It is worth noting that this year three of the craft unions have received cost-of-living wage increases, all unions are sharing in pension plans, the city has added a 2.5 percent occupancy tax, and advertising lineage rates have gone up. In spite of all this, the price of admission to the public has remained the same.

Our self-appointed faultfinders then complain that "too much of what Broadway offers is imported." So are some of our best wines, books, paintings, cars and cheeses.

"Broadway never does anything new" is a strange complaint to encounter in an era in which every department of the theater has made major breakthroughs. The steps from Odets to Miller to Albee have been consistent and progressive.

Technically, the full use of contemporary electronics in lighting and sound has completely changed the mechanics of the theater. Production design has moved drastically from Belasco's realism to Alswang's abstractions.

"Theaters are physically uncomfortable," says the patron, and this complaint has been justified. Following the example of City Playhouses in New York and Jujamcyn Theatres on the road, Lawrence Shubert Lawrence, Jr., the managing director of the Shubert empire, has alloted a fortune for the refurbishing of the Shubert chain. Every theater in New York has been undergoing a face lifting and extensive renovation.

Turning from amateur to professional critics, New York State's Attorney General has a complaint—one which must be considered seriously, but which should not be exaggerated. The Attorney General alleges that some of the financial arrangements made by certain promoters are open to question and that legislation may be necessary to correct certain malpractices.

He is, I believe, correct in his concern. Every season some newcomers, wooed by hopes of vast profits, engage in the business of producing a play and because of their inexperience are unfamiliar with established practices. Mostly they fail, fold their tents and quietly return to some other pursuit. To the best of my knowledge, all professional producers, who are members of the League of New York Theatres, conduct their business in a meticulous way according to accepted professional and ethical procedures. The formation of limited partnerships is subject to the scrutiny of the Securities and Exchange Commission and standard theatrical certified public accounting procedures are strictly adhered to.

Producers are not transients—the day of the fly-by-night who stranded a company in Kansas City went out with gaslight. Producers are creative businessmen who have the courage to invest their energy and resources in the commercial theater.

The last criticism we always have is what a bad season it has been.

The total output of any living art form fluctuates from year to year. Some books are good, some don't make it; some movies are sellouts, some fold quickly; a new painter enjoys a vogue, while others continue to paint with less critical acclaim. So, too, with the theater, and surely, it is the continuity of production, season after season, that is irrefutable proof of the basic health of the industry.

## *Off-Broadway*

Before World War II, Broadway's theaters were practically the only professional ones in New York City. Except for Eva LeGallienne's Civic Repertory Theatre (1926–31), various units of the Federal Theatre (1935–39), some of the productions presented at the Provincetown and Cherry Lane playhouses in the 1920's and 30's, and others by workers', Yiddish, and miscellaneous groups, nearly all productions were of a semiprofessional or nonprofessional nature.[8]

About five or six years after the War ended, off-Broadway, as we know it today, began to take on a professional character. In an area of Manhattan roughly from Vandam Street to 103rd and from Ninth Avenue to Second, lofts, stores, old churches and warehouses were converted into theater facilities, and off-Broadway was born. Since 1950 it has grown until it has more playhouses than Broadway and many more productions.

The purpose of this movement was to allow people to work without the pressures imposed by the hit-or-flop syndrome. By working with drastically reduced costs, these young producers, managers, actors, and directors hoped to present more experimental drama, more new and classical works from abroad, more new American playwrights than Broadway was doing—and make a return on their investment.

The off-Broadway theater, as a rule, has an audience capacity of less than 300 seats, in order to satisfy the union and city licensing requirements. Of the 28 off-Broadway theaters operating in 1966–67, the average size is under 199.

At the beginning, actors, authors, directors, and even the craft unions were lured by the promise of off-Broadway and worked for minimal salaries to help the new movement grow. In recent years, however, the financial picture has changed radically with the spiraling index of costs and stronger union demands. Whereas the average cost of an off-Broadway production in 1963 was $15,000, the figure has risen in 1967 to $20,000. Largely responsible for the increase has been the unionization of off-Broadway theaters.

According to Paul Libin, president of the League of Off-Broadway Theatres and Producers and the operator of the Martinique Theatre, the average salary to actors is the Equity minimum, $65 weekly, which may rise again before 1968. For directors, $500 is the minimum payment and $750 the average. Required box office, press agent, and backstage personnel are also unionized. Royalty payments to authors range from 4 to 6 percent, as compared to a range of from 5 to 10 percent of the gross on Broadway. Ticket prices at off-Broadway performances have not changed much in recent years, ranging from $2 to $5 and averaging about $3.50—barely enough to meet expenses.

Libin sees the off-Broadway theater as revolving in peculiar circles and convolutions. While costs have risen and the union situation is complicated, the mood of producers is not one of despair. If the seasons of 1964–65 and 1965–66 were disappointing, he reports that in his sector of the business 1966–67 was an "up" year.[9]

Another experienced producer, Norris Houghton, admits that off-Broadway theater does not make much money, but notes certain phenomenal exceptions such as *The Threepenny Opera* and *The Fantastiks,* which broke records for long runs.

Before the days of off-Broadway unionization, according to Libin, there were a number of people with a yen for theater and a little money who tried their hand at producing. This gave rise to the term "vanity shops." Today, he says, the vanity shops have largely disappeared and off-Broadway belongs chiefly to the professionals.

Margaret Jane Fischer, on the other hand, expresses some reservations about these developments:

> The off-Broadway theater has all but lost the rich promise it had at the beginning when it was dedicated chiefly to the tryouts of promising new scripts or the revivals of classics. It has done fewer of each as time has passed. It has leaned heavily upon revivals of musicals, topical revues, and trivial comedies. Except for the work of Edward Albee, it has brought forth no new playwright of stature. Far too many productions have been done to satisfy the ego of some untalented person, and the quality of production itself has often been very low.

An even stronger view was expressed in an interview to NTC by John F. Wharton in 1964:

> Off-Broadway has lasted longer than I expected. There are apparently still plenty of groups willing to risk $25,000 or so, although I am told that the odds against them grow steadily worse.
>
> I do not have much sympathy with commercial off-Broadway. It exists by paying as little as possible to workers in the theater; the shrinkage of Broadway has created a buyer's market for actors.

This seems an unhealthy condition, and one that cannot last. The stagehands' union is threatening to kill it right now, and a substantial increase in acting opportunities would either destroy it or reduce its quality below any point of public acceptance.

Is the off-Broadway theater, in vying for the playgoer's dollar, a competitive threat to Broadway? We put this question to commercial producers and to Irving W. Cheskin, executive director of the League of New York Theatres, representing all the established Broadway producers and theater-owners. Their virtually unanimous reply was: no— or at least, no longer.

There have, of course, been times when an off-Broadway director like José Quintero, with *The Iceman Cometh* at the Circle in the Square, could "knock the spots off" the original Theatre Guild production of a major drama by O'Neill. Times, too, when critics and the public agreed that the revival of a modern foreign classic like Brecht's *Mother Courage* would have fared far better off-Broadway than on. There have been off-Broadway seasons more brilliant, varied, and exciting than anything then showing on the Great White Way. There have been summers, especially, when the play-loving visitor to New York has had to look to the smaller peripheral playhouses to find anything new or interesting. And when the city's first-string critics started covering off-Broadway premières, uptown producers and theater owners were impelled to take notice. At the very least, they had to recognize that off-Broadway was particularly good for revivals of musicals and ancient and modern classics, for the presentation of new foreign and American playwrights, and for the discovery and initial development of young producers, directors, designers, and actors.

In a "preliminary checklist" of plays presented off-Broadway during the 12 seasons from 1950–51 to 1961–62, Julia S. Price enumerates the titles and authors of no fewer than 322 new plays by American authors and 639 revivals of all kinds.[10] On a purely quantitative scale, off-Broadway theaters have surpassed Broadway repeatedly in number of productions, their biggest seasons being 1954–55 (106), 1955–56 (132), 1958–59 (112), and 1959–60 (102). Although its rate of production has diminished since 1962 (66 shows in 1965–66 as compared with 75 the year before), off-Broadway is still the place to look for most of the work by new American playwrights (William Alfred, Ronald Ribman, Jean–Claude van Itallie, for instance) and by avant-garde writers from England and the Continent. In the European tours of the Living Theatre, off-Broadway reciprocated by showing the work of recent American authors, such as Jack Gelber, to international audiences. Moreover, some of off-Broadway's best producers, such as Theodore

Mann (Circle in the Square) and the team formed by Richard Barr with Clinton Wilder and Edward Albee (Cherry Lane Theatre), having enjoyed hits on Broadway (e.g. *Who's Afraid of Virginia Woolf?*), turned a portion of their profits to the benefit of new playwrights by giving them the opportunity to see their work professionally performed in experimental productions in Greenwich Village (Theater '61, '62, etc.—the group is named by the performance year). Many other producers, like Judith R. Marechal and Paul Libin, have taken great financial risks and frequent losses in order to bring out significant fresh work (e.g. *In White America, Chicago*) on current subjects.

Finally, it must be noted, the example of off-Broadway theaters has stimulated the establishment of similar groups in many of the larger cities of the United States and Canada—enterprises now more commonly known as professional resident or regional theaters.

On balance, then, most Broadway producers regard off-Broadway as a useful testing ground and a necessary complement to their own work—they could hardly do less—on the principle that "the more theater, the better."

Ira J. Bilowit, who compiled and edited for ANTA a booklet called *How To Organize an Off-Broadway Theatre* (1964), wrote in his Introduction:

> Off-Broadway has become a higher-priced work medium. Although budgets are bigger, shows are not necessarily better. Off-Broadway remains an area of extremes of both quality and taste.
>
> Creative artists hope to make their mark and novice producers hope to make their fortune off-Broadway. Both are possible. As much public and trade attention is focused on a good off-Broadway production as on the biggest Broadway show.
>
> Off-Broadway, while laboring under the burden of increased costs, remains a vital force in the American theater.

## *Off Off-Broadway*

Burgeoning in the 1960's have been small groups of dedicated writers, actors, and directors creating highly experimental works, often of a most unconventional character, in the relaxed atmosphere of coffeehouses, vacated workshops, church lofts and the like, mainly in the east to west area south of Twelfth Street and centering in Greenwich Village. Impermanence being virtually their rule of life, many of these groups, such as the Open Theatre (begun in 1963 by Joseph Chaikin, then acting in the Living Theatre), have no fixed home but play wherever suitable space can be found, and members of one group often share in the work of others. This practice of mounting fairly simple, inexpensive, non-Equity productions began with poetry readings, then staged readings, then performances of original one act plays as early as 1959 at the Caffe Cino on Cornelia Street, where eventually more than 100 new playwrights saw their works produced. Another place, opened in 1960 by Ellen Stewart, was the Café La Mama, where performances were given from Wednesday through Sunday, with two each on Friday and Saturday nights, and much new creative talent was revealed. Other locales are the choir loft of the Judson Memorial Church on Washington Square South, where the Judson Poets' Theatre gives weekend programs of one-act plays (about one-half dozen productions per season) most of them directed by Lawrence Kornfeld; a church and a workshop on St. Mark's Place; the Village East; the Chelsea Theater Center on Ninth Avenue, and so on. There are now probably two dozen such theatrical groups, but as they tend to appear and disappear, and their aims and activities vary greatly, it has proved difficult, even for one involved in them, to supply any clear definitions of what has come to be known as "Off off-Broadway."[11]

One of its leading figures, Michael Smith, explains it as follows:

> Off off-Broadway is not a place or an idea or a movement or a method or even a group of people. It has no program, no rules, no image to maintain. It is as varied as its participants and they are constantly changing. At its best, it implies a particular point of view: that the procedures of the professional theater are inadequate; that integrity and the freedom to explore, experiment, and grow count more than respectable or impressive surroundings; that, above all, it is necessary to do the work.
>
> Freedom has been won, but not without sacrifice. No one makes a living in the Off off-Broadway theater. Accomplished professionals work side by side with rank beginners, and standards are unpredictable and uncontrolled. And, largely because of municipal licensing regulations, there are no theaters. These apparent limitations have often been turned to advantage. The very unprofessionality of Off off-Broadway, in fact, may finally be its contribution to the American theater.[12]

Some of these groups, to the extent that they are organized, operate as "experimental theater clubs," each participant and spectator paying dues of one dollar a week and adding contributions as they see fit; others are simply voluntary. One of them, the Open Theatre on Spring Street, has conducted as many as six weekly workshops, each with its particular function and director. Their theaters are necessarily of small capacity (75 seats or under), their technical facilities meager, their productions generally limited to fewer than ten performances with occasional repeats. New full-length playscripts by Off off-Broadway groups in the past two or three years have totaled around 30 to 35, with a much larger number of one-act plays and a smaller number of musical revues, miscellaneous revivals, and "happenings."

Important among the militant claims of their exponents is that they alone are laboring to find and develop new forms, hence the varied labels applied to their work: Film-theater, Chance Drama, Action Theater, Events, Inscapes, Total Theater, New Theater, Environments, and the like. Their work, too, has received extensive and often favorable critical attention in local journals such as *The Village Voice* and in at least one serious quarterly, the *Tulane Drama Review*—which, now that it is to be edited and published as *The Drama Review* at the neighboring New York University, can be expected to keep Americans abreast of Off off-Broadway's evolution.

Like the off-Broadway theater in the 1950's, however, these theater clubs have of late run into problems of unionization, notably from Actors' Equity. Several of them, including the oldest ones, have already folded. Those that survive, unless they are content to remain strictly amateur in their operations, must expect to face continual pressure from unions and licensing boards, and continued criticism for slapdash though earnest work. The new Off-off-Broadway Association may save them.

Perhaps the most that can now be said for Off off-Broadway is that it has begun to show us the potentialities of new kinds of theatrical work which, in due time, may make a significant contribution to the American theater.

## Nonprofit Organizations

Turning now from the experimental theater clubs—and even omitting from the present study numerous other agencies at work in New York in behalf of new plays and the apprenticeship of dramatic artists—NTC sought the advice of specialists on the problems of getting good theater to the people at large. It consulted, among others, one of America's foremost actresses, who is also an outstanding director and pioneer in repertory theater, Miss Eva LeGallienne. Here is her emphatic response:

> There is no question in my mind that the inaccessibility of live theater to the general public is the chief reason why it is said that only 15 to 20 percent of Americans see no more than one live play a year. Our people have lost the *habit* of attending the theater. How can they demand something with which they are almost totally unfamiliar?
>
> For this reason I believe there is more than ever a need for people's repertory theaters in all the great centers throughout the country: theaters which combine the highest standards of produc-

tion (acting, directing, and staging) with truly popular prices. At least for the first few years—until people get accustomed to using them—such theaters would probably need endowment, otherwise the standard of work will suffer, even if the prices are kept low. It is no use trying to lure the public back to live theater, in these days of moving pictures and television, unless they are offered the BEST.

These theaters would of course in no way conflict with, or try to supplant, show business. Our commercial theater is probably the best in the world—but what we lack, what we have always lacked here, are theaters comparable to the state-endowed organizations that exist as a matter of course in all the great cities of Europe: people's repertory theaters, which form a necessary and integral part of the life of the community.

In pursuit of goals akin to those Miss LeGallienne expresses, there have arisen in New York since the end of World War II a number of professional groups. As differentiated from the commercial theater, they are incorporated as nonprofit organizations. The first of such groups was the Living Theatre, founded in 1947 by Judith Malina and Julian Beck. (In recent seasons, following a variety of financial difficulties, it has been abroad, but is expected to return.) Next came the Circle in the Square, which won four off-Broadway awards in 1950. It was followed three years later by the Phoenix Theatre. The story of the Phoenix, as told to NTC by Norris Houghton, illustrates the problems and promise such groups face.

### *APA—Phoenix*

The Phoenix Theatre was started as a profit organization with limited partnership on December 1, 1953, by Norris Houghton and T. Edward Hambleton in a 1,200-seat house on lower Second Avenue. They remained there for seven seasons, making many structural changes. The public was wooed with a subscription series, and originally the Phoenix did five plays consecutively for approximately six weeks each. Their bill of fare included some new plays, some classics, some musicals. Sometimes they did one-night stands or single-week performances. However, each play was treated as a separate unit with its own cast and director.

In 1960, the Phoenix established a resident company with a full-time director. Stuart Vaughan, as artistic director, assembled an acting company which lasted for two years. When Vaughan left on a Ford Foundation fellowship, the company disintegrated and the Phoenix went back to its original program.

In September 1961, the organization moved to a more suitable theater on East 74th Street and gave a full season consisting of a series of alternating plays. They used the same plan for the 1962–63 season; but the third play, *Oh Dad, Poor Dad!* etc., turned out to be a hit. For obvious economic reasons, they kept the show running for 15 months, thereby disrupting their repertory program and policy.

In 1964, the Phoenix, which was by then re-organized as a nonprofit theater, invited the Association of Producing Artists (APA) to come and mount a dramatization of Tolstoy's *War and Peace*. The APA, with Ellis Rabb as director, was a troupe of actors who had been performing wherever they could find a home. After playing for several years at Princeton University's McCarter Theatre, they had just completed three successful seasons in the Professional Theatre Program at the University of Michigan. The APA had a repertory of plays: the Phoenix had the management, the subscription audience, the money, and the theater building (one they had just purchased), the Lyceum, on West 45th Street near Times Square. The two groups merged.

This fairly recent merger of the Phoenix and the APA has turned out to be an ideal combination, with Ellis Rabb as artistic director and T. Edward Hambleton as managing director.

Artistically speaking, the APA–Phoenix, as it is now known, has achieved success. According to Norris Houghton, it has won critical acclaim for five out of six productions at the Lyceum. "In the good old days," he said, "we averaged three out of five critical successes." Praise for the productions of the 1966–67 season was universal.

Financially speaking, while the APA–Phoenix has been drawing good audiences (70 percent of capacity in a 900-seat house), it is not self-supporting. Houghton estimates their 1967–68 season's loss, with only four plays in repertory, as "probably in excess of one-half million dollars." He said the Phoenix never had a season without a deficit. The income gap (difference between box office income and costs) for the first ten years of their existence was $100,000 a year, and "due to the rising costs, that income gap for the last four years has totaled about one million dollars."

The only way they can manage to keep going is through subsidy. In 1967–68 they received $250,000 from the National Endowment for the Arts and raised the balance from a variety of other sources. Repertory is far more expensive to produce than limited engagements. In Houghton's opinion, there are no theaters doing serious plays that are not having a deficit.

## *Lincoln Center Repertory Company*

The most ambitious and most publicized new repertory theater in the United States is the Lincoln Center Repertory Company in New York. Under the direction of Robert Whitehead and Elia Kazan, this group opened its first season in January 1964 at the "temporary" ANTA–Washington Square Theatre with a new play by Arthur Miller, *After the Fall.* Whitehead and Kazan, during their season-and-one-half in charge of the company, did six plays. Three were successful, although they had to weather caustic criticism. The public was unfamiliar with the practice and hazards of the repertory system; critics were impatient.

The Vivian Beaumont Theater in Lincoln Center, where the company now operates, was designed expressly to house a major metropolitan repertory company. It was completed in 1965 and opened that October, the first new theater constructed in New York since 1927. Designed by Jo Mielziner, it has, in addition to its main, open-stage auditorium, a small and intimate Forum theater downstairs where experimental work can be done.

Before the move to Lincoln Center, the company's direction was changed. Herbert Blau and Jules Irving, long-time directors of the Actor's Workshop in San Francisco, were called to take charge, and they brought their best actors with them for their opening season (1965–66). Blau and Irving have done ten plays in their first two seasons with one success, Brecht's *Galileo,* as the tenth production. In the spring of 1967 it was announced that Herbert Blau had resigned from his post at Lincoln Center to resume university teaching. Jules Irving continues as the director of the company.

Critics attribute many reasons for the lack of success to date. Some of these include: "poor acoustics" (and there was trouble in adjusting certain productions to the broad open stage), "lack of finish—less than APA's," "haphazard choice of actors," "run by self-conscious amateurs," "not a true repertory anyhow," "a building is not as important as an idea."

The criticism about repertory is of course correct: the Lincoln Center company does not rotate its bills of plays, but runs each play for five, six, or more weeks, then changes it for another production. It is estimated that the Vivian Beaumont Theater is currently losing about $750,000 a year. According to Jules Irving, it would still lose money even if every seat were sold at every performance. Were the management to adopt repertory practice and keep the scenery, costumes, and properties of four or five productions always in rotation throughout a season, the building could not contain them and the trucking and storage costs would be colossal. Fortunately, like the Metropolitan Opera and the Philharmonic Symphony nearby, the Lincoln Center Repertory Company benefits from very generous donors and foundation aid.

## *Problems of Repertory*

The histories of the APA-Phoenix and the Lincoln Center Repertory indicate two major problems that repertory faces: (1) the inability to exist without subsidy and (2) the difficulties of creating a cohesive and polished acting company.

In a recent interview with an NTC representative, Howard Lindsay expressed yet another problem of repertory, namely, selling the repertory idea to the American public:

> I'm glad to see repertory grow because it may train some audiences, but repertory is not a natural form of entertainment in America. Repertory demands that you are willing to see a play you have seen before. Few Americans are willing to do that. Repertory assumes that the primary interest of the audience is in interpretation. This is true in London, where the audience has been trained by seeing different actors in the same role. The English audience enjoys seeing the classics more and seeing the same actor in different parts.
>
> The best repertory theater in America is the Metropolitan Opera Company, where the audience has seen the same opera again and again. Their first interest is not in the story but in interpretation. An audience has to be trained for that.
>
> Repertory is great for actors. They love it because they sense that interest in interpretation is a more intelligent interest. Our audiences have been seduced by the new story. We had, during the first half of this century, so many good playwrights that the audience always had a new story. This created a lazier audience. The spectator only had to bring to the theater the price of admission.

In assessing the repertory groups in New York, Lindsay felt that the APA-Phoenix was the best. He was not sure of the practicality of the Vivian Beaumont Theater, where the pitch is so great that the actors are dwarfed. He said that the thrust stage is not easy to use. It makes a terrific demand on the director and he loses the curtain, which is one of the greatest forms of emphasis. Lindsay was not sure that intimacy in the theater is a "plus" since it makes both actors and audience self-conscious. He personally prefers the proscenium stage and commented that most plays have not been written for the thrust stage. "Exits and entrances are so important and the blackout cannot replace the curtain for emphasis."

Lindsay did see an enormous growth and improvement in lighting and scenery in the American theater.

In spite of his feeling that the audience has become inured to vulgarity, he felt that the vulgar play and the play about the sick personality have hurt the theater enormously. He recognized, however, that the audiences of today want to relax and, afraid of serious plays, they go to comedies and musicals. The producer, therefore, shies away from serious plays unless they have some sensational value. "Tragedy," Lindsay said, "should be elevating," but then he concluded wryly, "Perhaps it is the times that prevent the writing of great tragedy."

Howard Lindsay's remarks about repertory practice and the new theaters reflect, in part, an elder statesman's view of his profession and an old hand's habits of work. Young performers and directors today are taking the thrust and the open stage in their stride, indeed with alacrity. Jules Irving told NTC recently that by now he thinks they "have these problems licked." Meanwhile, most new theaters across the land today have some form other than, or in addition to, the proscenium stage with its curtain. As for repertory, examples are accumulating each year among the festival and regional theaters to indicate that, under a variety of conditions of work, a season's plays can safely and successfully be rotated.

### *Free Theater*

The New York Shakespeare Festival is a nonprofit theater organization that can boast of great success in terms of artistic achievement and public acclaim. Chartered by the New York State Board of Regents, it is supported by city and state as well as by private contributions.

Joseph Papp, a dynamic director with a vision, believes that every citizen needs and is entitled to a theater. He believes that the arts are indispensable to the full life and that a theater can and should be run for beauty and wisdom rather than for money. He has made, and continues to make, that dream come true. Although he started with a modest budget of $500 some 13 years ago, his program has expanded to a budget of well over $3,500,000.

Top-quality productions of Shakespeare are presented free of charge at the open-air Delacorte Theatre in Central Park. This auditorium, given to the City of New York, is a 2,300-seat amphitheater, where every summer tens of thousands wait in line for hours to gain admission.

Judith Crist wrote in the *New York Herald Tribune:*

> The essence of Papp's productions has been a restoration of Shakespeare to popularity, in its literal sense. . . . It is a matter of approaching Shakespeare as a playwright of the people, not by bastardizing the implications, de-poetizing the language or adding irrelevant décor for its own sake, but by an enthusiastic and vigorous approach, a clear understanding and even clearer speech. It is a matter of imagination—but imagination attuned to the playwright's; a matter of perceiving "how it was" and reproducing the essential values.[13]

An extension of the Festival in the Park is the Mobile Theatre, a caravan of six trucks containing a stage, lighting equipment and generator, dressing room, and seats for 1,600. In less than four hours a fully-equipped and handsomely lit Elizabethan theater is set up in the center of Harlem. This theater on wheels reaches out to all the boroughs of New York, and even presents one Spanish-speaking production. In its nine summers in New York City parks and schools the Festival has presented 33 plays to audiences totaling over 3,000,000.

The latest development in this successful venture is the renovation of the old Astor Library as a permanent winter home for the New York Shakespeare Festival. Two theaters are included in this new program, one of which will produce new scripts exclusively.

### *Actor's Studio and Actor's Studio Theatre*

There are additional theater groups in New York City which do not fall into the categories discussed above. One such group is the Actor's Studio, Inc., with its Actor's Studio Theatre.

Both organizations are chartered as nonprofit educational corporations, with Lee Strasberg as artistic director. The Actor's Studio was originally founded by Elia Kazan, Robert Lewis and Cheryl Crawford in 1947, and has become renowned for the Method approach to acting.

The Studio is not a school in the usual sense, since there are no courses, grades, or diplomas. Its primary function is to provide a workshop in which professional actors, directors, and playwrights can experiment and practice their craft before a small audience of other professionals.

Members are accepted as a result of auditions. Although an average of 100 auditions are held yearly, the present membership is about 350. Membership in the Actor's Studio is for life and is free. The Studio is supported entirely by contributions and benefits.

The Actor's Studio Theatre, a natural outgrowth of the goals of the Workshop, considers itself primarily a playwright's rather than an actor's theater. In the words of Lee Strasberg:

> The first responsibility of our theater is therefore to the playwright—the living playwright. While our work has dealt with the actor, our fight has been for the author. The actor can find his material not only in the present but in the drama of the past. But the living playwright must depend on the living actor. It is therefore our responsibility and our intention and our hope to create a place for the playwright, where the highest demands will be made upon him, where he will be encouraged to seek the fullest embodiment of his vision, where nothing but our own flaws and the natural

lapses of our talent will stop us from lending the fullest measure of our understanding and our devotion to bring his play to life. In the union of actor and playwright lies the magic of the theater.

A grant of $447,000 in subsidy for this relatively new theater and workshop came from the Ford Foundation. These funds allowed the theater to operate for two seasons, but the program was inoperative in 1967. Strasberg has a dream, he says, of two touring units of the Actor's Studio Theatre: one on the East coast, one on the West. They would have a midcontinent base where they would meet, and the two units would do five to ten plays. Their plan, as of early 1968, remained a dream unrealized, the ~~Actor's Studio~~ itself having folded, at least temporarily. Actor's Studio Theatre

## A Philosophical View

Mordecai Gorelik, American stage designer, critic, and more recently a playwright, who is in residence at Southern Illinois University, wrote to one of the present authors at some length about a chief evil plaguing the professional theater. Gorelik, an honorary member of NTC, stated:

> I shall confine myself to some observations on the effect of conformism on the American drama today. I consider this one of the basic problems of the theater, and one that is seldom discussed. Adult drama is not possible without genuine freedom of thought and conscience. Under present-day conditions it is easy to lose both, almost before one becomes aware of the loss.
>
> A theater that can no longer speak out without fear or favor loses its reason for being, and must deteriorate. On the other hand, no rise in production costs, no competition from films or T.V. can undermine a theater whose value to its audience remains unimpaired.
>
> At this moment the American people stand before a vast horizon. Great possibilities as well as frightful dangers loom before us: the threat of a nuclear war that could devastate this planet; the conquest of outer space; the population explosion; world poverty and malnutrition; racial, social and political antagonisms; a mounting crime rate; automation; the pollution of our air, water and food; and a host of related issues. But to suggest that these questions call for dramatic illumination in our playhouses is to risk a pitying smile from the "knowledgeable" critics who know enough to look down on crude soap opera, but who continue to call for a type of American drama and comedy which is now completely bankrupt.
>
> Broadway playscripts have no use for the great problems that confront the American people except perhaps as local color for a story of boy meets girl. Domestic squabbles and sexual abnormalities have become the staples of the New York theater, with little or no curiosity about the moral, social or political conditions out of which these conflicts arise. The critics find it much easier to go on

lamenting the decay of drama than to accept a new and possibly disquieting approach. Plays that concern themselves with human nature, that have true-to-life speech and emotion-packed excitement are relatively comforting in this shook-up world, especially when they are steeped in the theatrical deep fat known as *schmaltz,* and are seasoned with a hot mixture of violence and wisecracks. While our playscripts may be endowed with all these virtues, they are in full flight from the challenge of an atomic age. . . .

The *schmaltz* tradition seems to me to be incapable of reform. It will simply have to be replaced by a new, rational, scientific-minded procedure, one toward which Bertolt Brecht and Erwin Piscator have already blazed a path. Nor does this mean that a rational theater must be "cerebral," "unemotional," "statistical," "a dull lecture," or any of the other epithets that have been applied to Epic theater by those who know nothing about it. What it does mean is that our contemporary theater has been decapitated; we need a theater with a head on its shoulders.

Such a theater is not likely to come very soon. The "fabulous invalid" may have entered upon its terminal illness, but it will rally many times before its last gasp, and until then it will have its accepted modes of production, its apologists, and its (dwindling) audience. The coming of a new and healthy theater requires independent thought—and independence of thought is in very short supply these days. Even before the Cold War the regimentation of thought had become a global phenomenon. Sloganeering, official news handouts, a syndicated press, radio, film and television, official and private censorship, all combined to exert their pressure on nonconformists. The Cold War has intensified this state of affairs, creating a suffocating ideology.

Theater is one of the mass media of communication, and the world's politicians, whatever their political color, expect it to serve as a handmaid of any clique or administration that happens to be in power. This status is explicit in the authoritarian countries. In the democratic ones—the few that remain—the stultification of thought on stage is mainly self-imposed by the stage people themselves, though not without some rude nudging by official or self-appointed censors.

It may be too much to expect that a theater of real scope and objectivity can grow up in a mental climate of this sort. A mature drama, one that asserts the dignity of the human spirit, must be able to face life in all its complexity and contradictions, in its full dimensions of height, depth and width. For this the times have to be propitious—as they were in the spacious days of the Elizabethan dramatists, when Engand had freed itself of the tyranny of the feudal Church; or in Russia at the turn of the present century, when its men of genius were able to protest against the inhumanity of the Tsar. The era of mechanized communication has brought about a *Gleichshaltung*[14] whose rigor is unprecedented in history. In the United States the menace of McCarthyism has abated somewhat, but the same kind of simplistic pressure continues, and may return with even greater vehemence if America goes on having setbacks in the Cold War.

What can stage people do under these circumstances? They can begin to understand how far independent thinking has been eroded. Independence of thought and conscience is a guarantee of a nation's sanity, its protection against the mass hysteria that brought on Hitlerism in Germany, Stalinism in the Soviet Union and McCarthyism in the United States. And how can independent thought be protected in the theater? Not, I think, by expecting theater people to turn themselves into martyrs in its defense. The men and women of the theater, like people anywhere else, are not ready to be heroic except under official auspices. Indeed, they are not even aware that theater has any objective other than to please an audience. The American theater's first task, I believe, is to become aware of a standard different from that of a more sophisticated soap opera or jejune absurdism. With that accomplished, some progress can be made even under present-day restrictions—such as when an issue enlists a public response wide enough to support the theater's traditional defense of human values, as in the case of civil rights.

If Broadway and off-Broadway must both be written off, what of the academic and community theaters? These are reporting a tremendous advance in resources and professionalism. This is a heartening development, one that I have long spoken for. But the so-called tributary theater has yet to prove its independence of the Broadway pattern. For the past 40 years, at least, most of its repertory has consisted of warmed-over Broadway hits, and its young people still look to Broadway as the goal of their ambitions.

In some areas of the country, censorship by minor officialdom or by hard-shell university trustees has set local theaters back even more than the silent pressure exerted on the New York producers; and in a great many other areas the college or community box office operates on the Broadway model. Still, its audiences are not as "sophisticated," in a bad sense, as those of New York, and its theater people, if less expert, are also more receptive to ideas that serve the health of theater. I allow myself no overzealous forecasts; I can only guess that if a very different American theater will one day replace the moribund *schmaltz* theater of the present, it is among the national playhouses that it can be expected to take root. In any case it will not grow up automatically. It will have to be envisioned, worked toward and fought for, step by step. And its indispensible basis will be the theater's right to a clear conscience and an open mind.

Whether or not one agrees with each of Gorelik's trenchant strictures on the commercial theater that has dominated the American scene for so many years, one can turn with fresh anticipation to the "national playhouses," by which he means the decentralized, noncommercial theaters—community, educational, and especially resident professional—that will concern us throughout much of the remainder of this book.

II. IN COMMUNITIES - THE VOLUNTEER

## 1 Communities - The Volunteer

THERE ARE TWO main kinds of Community Theater in the United States today. The oldest d much the more prolific of these is the direct product of the amateur-lunteer movement which evolved out of the European art theater and e theater developments of the late 19th century and came to first namic fruition in this country around 1915. This American movement, ich was at first highly creative and experimental, was originally called t Theater, Little Theater or Civic Theater, but of late years has been nerally known as Community Theater. Like other national organiza-ns in the field, NTC accepts Community Theater as the proper term.

The second kind is the much younger regional professional resident eater. Since a whole section of this NTC appraisal is devoted to the ofessional Resident Theaters, nothing more will be said of them here cept to make the point that although they are a separate and distinct velopment, they share many characteristics and problems common to e Community Theater.

# Community Theater

The amateur-volunteer movemer is extremely widespread and profuse in the United States. Its audience run into many millions, and its producing groups are legion. If we wer to count all the local clubs, churches, camps, social and civic group and other organizations that put on dramatic presentations, the numbe might well run between 30,000 and 80,000. Since there exists no offici central counting agency, and since there is a certain mortality and flu among community theaters, to say nothing of generic and qualitati definitions, an exact count is impossible.

However, of established groups organized solely for the present tion of a regular seasonal bill of dramatic productions, the Stanfo Research Institute estimated 18,000 to be operating in 1962. NTC est mates that approximately 3,000 of these groups are doing drama produ tion at acceptable standards, and that perhaps 200 groups are producir drama at more or less professional standards, occasionally work of ve high quality.

Community Theater occupies a peculiarly important position in th American theater picture. It is the largest, by far, of the theater's n merous segments, and has the best chance of reaching the averag citizen and family. In the bigger cities its clientele is the neighborhoo in smaller ones, a fair cross section of the stable, educated populatio and to countless localities not served by the professional or the educ tional theater it offers the only opportunity to see live drama. Con munity Theater, consequently, is the ultimate retailer of the large quantity of dramatic material in America—plays and musicals of a varieties. It engages more people in theatrical activity, albeit part-tim than all the rest of the American theater put together, including schoo and colleges. And, as its best and strongest organizations become increa ingly professionalized, both in quality of workmanship and in paid staf it may well come to offer a substantial share of job opportunities f trained theater artists, managers, and technicians.

Community Theater is our most direct attempt in America today create a true popular or people's theater. Its groups are organiz mostly with frank dependence upon the localities in which they exi They reflect the community's image; they project the citizens' devoti to community service; and, in organization, they rely chiefly up volunteer workers.

It is well to recognize here the definition the authors of this bo had in mind when referring to amateur and professional theater worke Usually amateurs are volunteer workers who are interested and talent ut whose commitment to the theater is primarily avocational. Profes-ionals, on the other hand, are trained people with their vocational ommitment to the theater.

The rationale of Community Theater was succinctly formulated nany years ago by a distinguished member of NTC, the late Kenneth Aacgowan, in his book *Footlights Across America* (1929). Noting that The local theater is the product of local necessity," Macgowan reduced ll the arguments to a single issue with three "riders." In terms slightly pdated, it follows:

There is, in the public, a deep craving for live drama:

1. If a town wants live drama it will have to provide it for itself.
2. Any group can make a drama live on the stage if it will apply itself with intelligence, skill, and assiduity.
3. A Community Theater organization is the only financial set-up that can present live drama in the small towns and still pay the bills.[1]

Community Theater has a great burden of responsibility placed pon it, simply because it is the kind of theater most readily available. ertainly not a large portion of the American public is attending the rofessional theater. According to Baumol and Bowen's recent survey f the performing arts, only 4 percent of all residents of this country 8 years of age or older attend a professional live performance of any ind—theater, music, or dance—in any year.[2] But a fair proportion of he public does attend noncommercial, and particularly community heater productions. The Stanford Research Institute estimated in 1962 hat there were 50,000,000 spectators of amateur theater—more than one uarter of the nation's total population! NTC wishes this were so!

## *Iometown Drama*

Despite the social revolution caused by "automobility," with its pro-ound changes in everyday living, America is still very much under the nfluence of the "hometown" concept of entertainment. Research con-ucted in Wisconsin shows that only a relatively few citizens in com-nunities of under 10,000 travel far afield in search of cultural entertain-nent. When it comes to drama, even network television reaches far ewer people in such localities than the big-city resident imagines. Most f them accept what dramatic fare they have, or can get, on their own ome scene. Thus, the high school, the club, the church, and the com-nunity theater play take on a greater importance than they could other-vise claim.

Sadly enough, the quality of hometown drama has been generall deplorable. Its presentation of theater as an art has made a negative im pression generally upon the American public as a mass. Innumerable ar the instances in which persons undertake activities related to the crea tion of works of art, but never, or poorly, achieve such objectives. NT is not discussing here the basic objectives of recreation, or even of soci service, but those of an art demanding personal devotion to aestheti ideals.

This raises the question of whether any kind of theater is bette than none, and whether the mere activity of a drama group, on wha ever level or standard, does not help to create a climate for better ar NTC's answer is simple: Plays badly done are not worthwhile. Negativ values in theater production are neither helpful nor desirable.

NTC makes a further point: that, taking the nation as a whole, ther seems to be no dominant pattern of excellence, and that this is the singl greatest weakness of the American theater today.

For this lack of a dominant pattern of excellence Communit Theater may be chiefly to blame, although Educational Theater an Professional Theater also often contribute—and they, too, are produc of our society. The American public, for the most part, is still apt t evoke the tired frontier attitude that the theater is a frill in society an in education; a take-it-or-leave-it activity, harmless enough for thos who want to spend their time, money, and energy on it, but not ge erally excellent enough or compelling enough to make it a necessit Townspeople are often blamed for failing to recognize and support th efforts of a dramatic group. Usually, however, the fault lies in the indi ferent work of the group itself.

The great task of Community Theater must be to make live dram important to the public; and many local theater organizations throug out the country are striving mightily to do this. The old closed corp ration spirit or "tight little group" structure that characterized man adult drama clubs in past decades—as reported, for example, by NT members in earlier published surveys of the decentralized theater in th country[3]—is rapidly vanishing from the scene. Instead, NTC finds toda that nearly all community theater organizations sincerely invite the local public to full partnership in their enterprise and its activities.

## *The Volunteer*

Community Theater commands the chief asset for bringing abo a wide acceptance of live theater in America. This asset is without que tion the volunteer worker. Without the volunteer, there would be vi tually no live drama available to the one-third of America's populatio living in communities of under 10,000. With approximately 50 permane professional resident theaters, the U.S.A. is far behind the U.S.S.R., which has about 500—all State supported, of course. Yet our country has the greatest corps of volunteer theater workers in the world. Not only do community theaters but all our noncommercial theaters rely heavily upon volunteers for organization, operation, and public acceptance.

NTC asked the successful directors of two fine community theaters to comment on the volunteer as a force in the theater today. Ted Kehoe, who directs the influential Des Moines (Iowa) Playhouse, replied:

> The finest results will always belong to the professional, . . . but it is to the volunteer that most of America must look for most of its theater. He is central in the producing picture . . . dismissed cynically as "hobby theater." Berated by certain pat souls who feel he displaces the professional, belittled by many who notice the edge rather than the heart, the volunteer makes possible a theater that bubbles up all across the land. . . . It is to the volunteer that I look as the source and the result.

Art Cole, energetic and talented director of the flourishing Midland (Texas) Community Theatre, writes to NTC:

> Man will always make theater, and there will always be more volunteers working at it than professionals. Quite honestly, I gave up being concerned about the professional's plight years ago. Once I realized the enormous influence of the volunteer on all theater, my concern has been for him. The volunteer started theater a very long time ago, didn't he?
>
> No one can assess a value on the volunteer, but every one is worth cold cash. The community theater operating on a $100,000 annual budget is probably receiving an additional subsidy of $200,000 in volunteer services. This is a very conservative estimate.
>
> A Rochester, Minnesota, surgeon or a Midland Oil Company executive or an Omaha manufacturer does not work cheap; but Community Theater is the beneficiary of these talents for hundreds of hours each year for free.
>
> It would be economically impossible for any community theater to exist without the volunteer.
>
> The talents encompassed by this volunteer corps of theater workers are often remarkable. They range through expert seamstresses, cabinet makers, electronics experts, skilled artists, top management personnel to excellent actors and actresses.
>
> There is a new breed of volunteer abroad since the war, and particularly since the mid-1950's. He is to be found operating in many areas of civic interest. He is the young, successful businessman. By the mid-1950's, the young men of World War II were settled into careers, and being well educated, with more leisure than their fathers and grandfathers, they turned their attention to social and cultural agencies. Their impact has been great. Community Theater has particularly benefited from this new breed; for historically it was the province of the ladies and the artsy types.

> These young men have brought a new and robust vitality to Community Theater, whether it be the amateur or the professional resident companies. Motivated by a new social consciousness, a desire for better educational environments, a new awareness of the importance of our culture, these young men have brought great energy and sharp business acumen into areas long the province of aging philanthropists, dowagers, and dilettantes. Coming right behind them in the 1960's is an even broader base of new young manpower. Business, industry, and the professions recognize the impact of this volunteer force and now encourage it.

Unfortunately, all too few community theaters have directors of th caliber of the men we have just quoted, or the opportunities to provid the enthusiastic volunteer with the kind of training and direction he s desperately needs.

The necessity for training the volunteer in technical skills and bringing out his latent dramatic talents has long been recognized by community theater leaders. In 1957 a National Community Theatre Trainin Center was proposed, but the great philanthropic foundations refuse to support the plan and it never attained its potential. In the view c some leaders, this decision may have set the American theater back 2 years in national development. Hundreds of key volunteers, trained an ready to help raise artistic standards and create favorable communit attitudes for live drama, might have prepared the soil much sooner an much better for a proliferation of decentralized professional theater.

As it is, there has been no centering of training, no general recognition of the peculiar demands and opportunities of community theate operation, and no concerted attempt to give community theaters throughout the nation a deep sense of their national responsibility. Instead, ther has been a much too ready willingness to turn Community Theater o as a mere adjunct to "real theater" (whatever is meant by that) and t discount the contribution that Community Theater has already made an that, if properly stimulated, it could make.

NTC does not in the least regret the millions that the foundation have poured into the sparsely scattered regional professional operations but it does deplore the one-sided viewpoint demonstrated by foundation grants. Is it possible, one sometimes wonders, that foundation directors, like so many other Americans, still picture Community Theater i terms of a hometown production of *Aaron Slick of Punkin Crick?*

## *The American Community Theatre Association*

The fact is, on a national scale Community Theater has too lon lacked a working association with a central headquarters. Partly, thi is a result of the independent nature and spirit of each individual group

It is also a product of the same shortsightedness that we have just attributed to the foundations; namely, the failure to see Community Theater in national terms as a creative movement of limitless potentiality.

In the early years of this century, a degree of cohesion among the most ambitious Little Theater groups was obtained through the Drama League of America. Its constituent members could communicate their aims, ideas, and achievements through a regularly published bulletin, and could receive advice and information from the central office. With the growth and development of Educational Theater since the 1920's and the proliferation of independent local adult theater groups, the problems of coordination and intercommunication—to say nothing of standards—called for a new and broader organization. To cope with such problems as these at a high level, the National Theatre Conference was formed, and for more than two decades it was the chief spokesman, agency, and communication center for the joint interests of community and college theaters. With its members in key positions in the nonprofit theaters, it continues to address itself to these concerns. Meanwhile, NTC was instrumental in establishing the American Educational Theatre Association (AETA) and in promoting the American National Theatre and Academy (ANTA)—both organizations with unlimited membership, with regional units, and with various modalities for giving practical assistance to individual theaters and theater people. One of the divisions of the AETA is the American Community Theatre Association (ACTA), having as its specific province the area we are discussing. Through its separate governing board, its regional council, and its *Newsletter,* ACTA is striving to organize the community theaters of America and service them with information.

It is no disparagement of the work of ACTA to say that it has hardly scratched the surface of the field it seeks to cultivate. Its membership scarcely begins to cover Community Theater as a whole; its corporate representation at the annual AETA conventions has been disappointingly small, though growing slightly; and the vast majority of community theaters remain isolated from one another, seemingly unaware of or indifferent to the total movement. ACTA's peak achievement so far appears to have been its first Floating Conference, held in August 1966 at St. Paul, Minnesota, when 56 community theater directors gathered and discussed their mutual problems, including professionalization and the ways and means of lifting the sights of local theater groups to encompass the wider horizons of national and international Community Theater.

This kind of conference, like the Training Center mentioned earlier, is greatly needed. But no less useful to the health of the community theater movement would be the establishment of an organism similar to the Theatre Communications Group which the Ford Foundation created for the permanent professional resident theaters: a central agency for keeping each theater continually in touch with all the others, not only by conferences and newsletters, but by exchange visits of directors and managers and by mutual assistance and advice. Given adequate financial support from private or government foundations, ACTA might well form the nucleus of such an agency. NTC hopes it will be enabled to do so.

### *Objectives*

Unlike the Little Theaters of 50 years ago, which were imbued with a revolutionary sense of mission, the Community Theater of today presents too often the picture of a theater in search of a goal. We have called it a "movement," but how is it moving, and where is it moving to? What motives inspire and activate its leading members?

Since Community Theater is composed so largely of volunteers—that is, of amateurs, in the literal sense of people working for the love of it—NTC tried to discover whether its primary purpose is social or artistic and to what extent. Accordingly, NTC questionnaires asked: "Would you say that absolute theater or social service ranks highest in your organization's objectives?" In the replies, 52.8 percent said "absolute theater"; 26.4 percent checked "social service"; 13.9 percent said "both"; 1.4 percent indicated "neither"; 1.9 percent replied "'other"; and 3.6 percent ducked the question.

The large preponderance of "absolutes" is striking; but it may not be too trustworthy since many found the question confusing, and others were perhaps ashamed to admit that social service—still less, sociability—is more important to their members. And even though more than half of the total number of the theaters canvassed regard their primary objective as cultural rather than social, NTC is far from encouraged or satisfied by the response.

In response to the question: "What would you say is the major purpose of your organization?" typical replies included: "to produce good theater," "advancement of the art," "to present exciting theater," "entertainment for our members," "trying to keep 'live' theater ALIVE!", "to encourage new playwrights," and "to contribute to the social and cultural life of the community and give people opportunity to express themselves on stage and backstage." Even among these candid replies, a certain duality of purpose is evident.

In describing the historical transition from Little Theater to Community Theater, Dr. Joseph Golden, of Syracuse, New York, sets forth the dilemma in cogent terms:

> Having lost its sense of mission, its aura of combat for the great good cause, the Community Theater, in the late 1920's and early 1930's, found itself in a perilous vacuum. What banner shall be raised now? An obvious banner; one that had been waving sporadically and weakly over the American theater for 200 years: the quest for Culture. It was a pretentious banner, to be sure, but hardly unjustified. Indeed, by refocusing its energies, the community theater sought to repair the damage to the broken continuity that once existed between art and life.
>
> The energies were dissipated quickly. For all its eloquent motives, the community theater movement fell into the waiting hands of erstwhile amateur actors, ingenuous matrons and clubwomen, and zealous businessmen who believed, somehow, that selling plumbing supplies had a natural kinship with selling theater. I mean no disrespect to local amateurs, matrons, or plumbing salesmen; but what was once a professionally oriented program devoted to breaching the walls of a grimly unimaginative theater, degenerated—by the middle 1930's—into an inadvertently fatuous, artistically inept enterprise that reawakened all the negative overtones of the word "amateur."

Dr. Golden goes on to characterize the movement in the years just after World War II:

> No longer professional (except in aspiration) and much chastened by its failure to reinstate High Culture to a proper throne, the Community Theater more sensibly adopted the role of crucible for local social and artistic energies. This was not an especially easy role. To be, at one and the same time, a center for communal and casual good fellowship ("We'll have a lot of fun") and an arena for severe artistic principles and disciplines invites dangers of the most fundamental kind. Not the least of these dangers is an inevitable ambiguity of purpose. . . .
>
> Because of the impossibly vulnerable and frustrating position in which a dual-purpose community theater finds itself—an élite and exclusive art form floundering in a sea of democratic and all-inclusive operating principles—it does not, as a rule, possess the strength to become a dominant symbol of a community's character or to invade, on a more intimate level, the lives and actions of a community's citizens. As a result, the Community Theater is still woefully lacking in support—moral, physical, and economic. [It] is, however, still in the market for an operational ethic, one that might serve as a matrix for its opposing objectives. . . .[4]

NTC believes that the solution to Community Theater's dilemma of objectives—its key problem—is to raise its work and product to a consistent level of art. We have no quarrel with dramatics as a hobby, as a form of sociability, as a means of group therapy, or as a device for civic promotion—it can have many uses. But a community theater, to be worthy of the name, must devote itself to dramatic art; it must commit itself and its members to attaining the highest artistic standards of workmanship within its power.

To do so, it must first know what is meant by high (that is, professional) standards, and what they require of practitioners in every branch of the operation. It must have the kind of leadership which can be counted on to select a season of plays worth doing, and which can instruct, guide, and direct a corps of volunteers in effective, harmonious collaboration. It may or may not conduct acting classes, but it must devise some method of insuring that its performing artists are sufficiently skilled and trained to undertake the roles assigned them; that in rehearsals they work, and not just fool around; that in performance they interpret their roles, and not merely show off; and that, in general, they submit themselves to the discipline, and strive earnestly for the goal, of ensemble acting. Similarly with the scenery, costume, lighting, props, and make-up crews backstage, it must manage to impart both technical skill and a zeal for efficient cooperation, often under stress—the kind of workmanship that finds its reward in a production well staged. Again, in the front of the house and in the house itself, the management must see to it that publicity, reservations, ticket sales, ushering, refreshments, and so on, are handled in such a manner that the public will come, will find the experience rewarding, and will be eager to spread the word and to return for the next play.

Even earlier in its operation, the community theater must find the way to impart the spirit of its aims and objectives to those sectors of the town on which its immediate prosperity depends: on civic leaders who will support its initiatives and perhaps form its board of trustees or advisory council; on the local press and broadcasting station, on which it will rely for publicity and discriminating reviews; on all the potential playgoers of its public; very likely, too, on school administrators and teachers.

Every successful community theater has, in addition to its other tasks, an educational job to perform. Until we have audiences all over America who can appreciate the distinction between theater as a hobby or a social service and theater as an art, and are capable of making the distinction themselves, solely on the basis of quality of play and production and not on the presence or absence of a Broadway label, we are going to have difficulty achieving widespread recognition of theater as an art and as a profession. An audience whose theater experience is confined to careless, shoddy productions or to vapid plays will never demand drama of quality or productions staged by trained directors, actors, and technicians. Until audiences do, and until there are vast audiences who know and appreciate good theater, there will continue to be a tragic waste of countless highly-trained, gifted theater people. Despite the progress that has been made in many areas, those dedicated to Community Theater are still essentially pioneers with a pioneer job to be done.

## *Profile*

To learn the facts about today's community theaters, a questionnaire containing some 30 queries was sent by NTC to 677 established groups throughout the country. Replies were received from 341 of these, but not all answers could be used in the tabulation, and specific totals are indicated with each question. From this sample and from statements from directors, critics, and NTC members, we submit a kind of profile of the state of the Community Theater.

The oldest community theaters in our survey were established almost 100 years ago. The Aurora Drama Guild, Inc., Aurora, Illinois, and the Concord Players, Concord, Massachusetts, were founded in 1874. One other group from the NTC study was established in the same decade—the Footlight Club of Jamaica Plain, Massachusetts, 1877. There are other unsurveyed theaters existing today which were established in the 19th century and which illustrate the potential longevity of this kind of organization.

The Concord group was founded by Louisa May Alcott and, appropriately enough, the group's play for children in 1962 was *Little Women.* It was performed for a total of 2,100 people; their normal audience size is in the 400–500 range.

The Aurora group reports that, operating with 120 volunteers and no full-time, paid staff members, they grossed in 1962 over $2,800, and played before a total audience of approximately 2,300.

The Footlight Club correspondent reports:

> As I suppose most clubs of our type do, we consist of two groups of people—those who enjoy taking some part in the production, and those who enjoy viewing it. We produce three plays annually, usually recent Broadway successes. Occasionally, we vary this pattern with a standard classic, and on rare occasions, with an unpublished play. The club is in no sense an experimental theater, and although many of our active members are ardent students of the theater and would like to do more work along that line, the economics of the situation require that the plays we produce have an appeal to our general membership.

> The membership may be described as a neighborhood one—a middle- and upper-middle-class neighborhood. Our plays are selected with this in mind. In addition to the plays, we conduct workshops for our members from time to time and run social events (one or two a year) as fund-raising activities.

While these were the oldest groups in the survey, fully 37.9 percent of the groups reporting were founded since 1952. The following table and graph indicate the number of theaters and year of founding.

Post-1960 data for the accompanying chart and graph were incomplete. The authors believe that the full facts would show continued increase.

**NUMBER OF COMMUNITY THEATERS FOUNDED PER 5-YEAR PERIOD, 1870–1963**

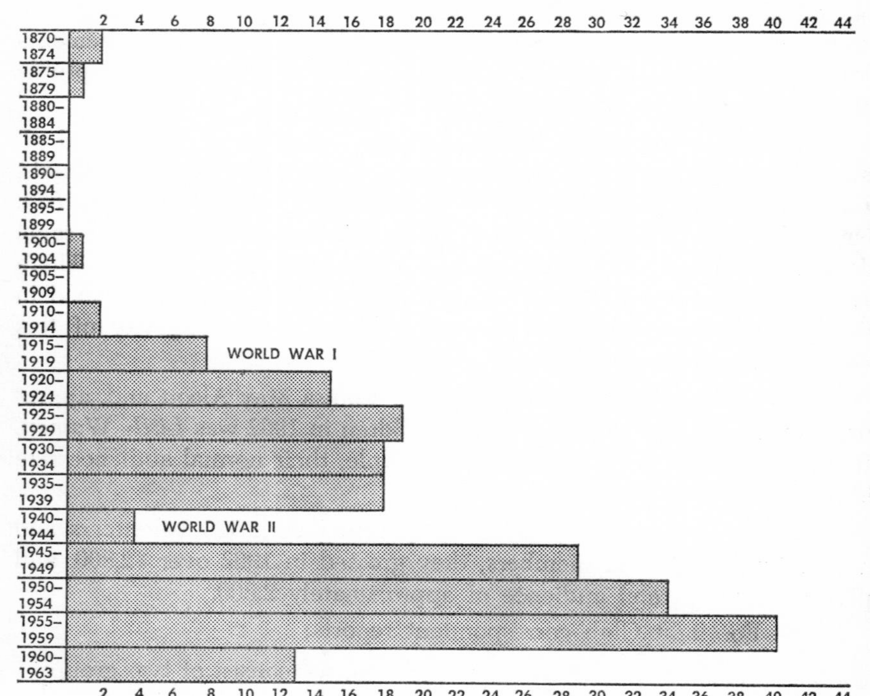


## *Building and Staff*

NTC asked many questions pertaining to the operation of community theaters. Most of the groups (48.1 percent) rent their facilities, with many rentals as low as $25 a year or merely the payment of janitorial fees. Of the groups who reported on this question, 33.2 percent own their own building or were in the process of building. The balance of

**NUMBER OF COMMUNITY THEATERS FOUNDED IN EACH YEAR, 1874–1962 (FROM THE SAMPLE OF APPROX. 200 QUESTIONNAIRES)**

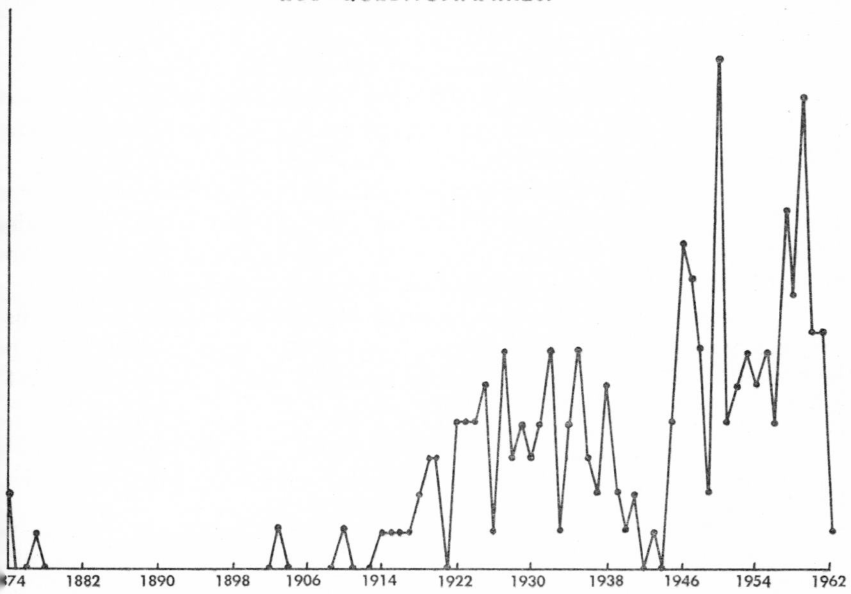


3.7 percent have their facilities provided free, or nearly free, by school oards, recreation commissions, or churches.

The average seating capacity of the auditoriums used is 454, with xtremes of 60 to 2,000. It would appear that the rental of facilities is ne major item of subsidy for many community theaters. However, for ne larger and more successful groups, with few exceptions, owning neir own building is an important factor in their strength, growth, and ermanence.

An increasing number of community theaters are building or re-nodeling buildings solely for theater activities. Very often, entire com-nunities support such enterprises. NTC expects that community the-ters, as a movement, will greatly benefit from this building boom, nd that many American towns will again possess a real "theater" de-oted to living drama. Space stages and arena theaters are in the plans f many groups.

The number of professional staff members employed by community neaters is very small compared to the number of groups. Out of 211 roups, 132 reported that they do not have a full-time paid director, and f these 44 said that they employed only part-time directors or other ssistants. The remaining 88 groups employ a full-time paid director and a combined total of 71 production staff members, including technica assistants, scene designers, etc. Among these 88 groups, an additiona 59 employees were engaged for box office, secretarial, or janitorial work on a full-time basis.

While the majority of community theaters do not employ a full-time paid director, either because they cannot afford to or cannot find one, the largest and most successful groups do. In the opinion of one NTC member, "the full service and full growth which can belong to a community theater will come best and soonest to the theater employing a community theater director." This has been proved again and again, particularly in those locations such as the Omaha Civic Theatre, where the same director has been in residence for more than ten years.

Unfortunately, the low pay scale of community theater work discourages young people who might want to become directors. But to those aspiring young people, one director and NTC member, Howard T Orms, has this to say:

> A community theater is a small business venture, but with no profit from that business—the dividends being in the form of growth and wider service to the community.
>
> Some of these theaters that are in precarious existence, because they lack continuity of leadership and clean-cut objectives, will not be in existence ten years from now. On the other hand, many now pilotless, can be among the most successful in the near future—with a trained director.
>
> The organization without a director must be convinced that it needs and can afford one. "Indeed," in the view of another director and NTC member, Art Cole, "it can't afford to be without one!" Obviously, the organization that has a good live director is not going to let him go, and pays him generously to stay. The salary in a going organization may reach $15,000 for a 9- to 12-month season, and seldom is under $7,000.
>
> But, the young man or woman, looking for a director's job, will seldom find one of the good ones open. They must start at the bottom, as most of the present well-paid directors have done, and must consent to be pioneers; go to a struggling group, offer to work for a bare living and grow with the theater. Or, better, they will get jobs as assistant directors on the staffs of successful organizations and learn the main job of getting on with people.
>
> We would also warn that they who would be community theater directors must acquire the most widespread training in acting, directing, scene design, costumes, lighting, promotion and business management; and more than a superficial appreciation of the other fine arts. They cannot be specialists in only one field, but when they do their job well, advancement can be rapid.

In the light of the increasing numbers of theater-trained college and university graduates, it would be natural to assume that many of these eventually find their way into community theater operations. Some, of course, do, but far too few. In his valedictory address as president of NTC, Theodore Viehman, long-time director of the Tulsa Community Theatre, pleaded with his academic colleagues: "Why don't the people you folks train in college come into the Community Theater?"

### Actors

Whether or not there are full-time Equity actors is a major distinguishing criterion between the community and the professional resident theater. Even so, there are some community theater groups which do hire actors occasionally either on a part-time or per-show basis. Eight groups included in the study reported a total of 62 actors hired on such a basis.

Even though the number of paid actors may be small, the number of volunteers participating in all phases of production, including acting, is tremendous. In reply to the question: "How many volunteers are there in your organization?" many groups reported "countless," "innumerable," or "entire membership." Of 191 groups giving a number, the total was 33,458 volunteers or an average of 175 volunteers per group. Of the community theaters in the survey, the Midland (Texas) Community Theatre, reported the largest number of volunteers—1,760!

The Stanford Research Institute estimated that there were approximately 500,000 actors in nonprofessional (educational as well as community) theater in the U.S.A. The U.S. Census for 1960 counted only 13,488 professional actors, and Actors' Equity Association reported, 13,500 members in 1967, so it is obvious that most of the acting in this country is being done by the volunteer.

### Management

Not only is the volunteer doing most of the acting in the country, he is also the one who runs most of the community theater organizations. Leadership may be through a small committee or a large board. In some communities, boards are composed of members whose presence is calculated to lend prestige to the theater. Other groups operate with working boards whose members are expected to undertake specific responsibilities. Some boards are elected directly by the membership voting by mail on a printed ballot; others are nominated by a committee appointed by the president.

In the opinion of many professional directors, the most successful formula for a community theater is to have an active board with built-in constitutional provisions for continuity and turnover in order to avoid deadwood, apathy, and regression. It is believed too, that gradual rather than sudden turnover of board leadership is a desirable objective.

One thing is very clear from NTC's findings: permanence of working quarters and continuity of leadership are supremely important to a local theater's morale and success.

### *Audience Characteristics and Problems*

The vast majority of community theaters perform for local audiences only, and do not tour. In the NTC study, only 9.9 percent of the theaters reported that they toured regularly, and 4.7 percent made only occasional or rare tours.

The majority of community theaters also address their work chiefly to adults. Only 30.6 percent reported playing "regularly," and 6.6 percent "occasionally," to audiences composed of students—mostly at the annual production of a children's play. Moreover, 64.9 percent of the theaters admitted to giving no productions for children and young people. NTC believes that children's theater is one of the most valuable services a theater can perform for its community, and that it is an immensely strengthening device for the group itself. Regular children's productions, whether acted by adults, by children and adolescents, or by a combination, win vast local support and lay an excellent foundation for future audiences. Drama that captures and engages the community's youth is a genuine social service that is also a theater's best life insurance.

What types of audiences attend Community Theater? Here we found a wide range and difference in responses. The directors or officers who answered the NTC questionnaires were asked to rate their playgoing public as to taste, intelligence, and discrimination in respect to live drama. In reply, 49.6 percent regarded their audience as "average," 22.9 percent as "above average," and 12.3 as "high." Only 9.1 percent rated their playgoers as "below average," and 6.1 percent as "low." In the opinion of these directors, the typical community theater audience is above the national average in discrimination and taste. This bears out the opinion of most NTC members (themselves directors of nonprofit, and for the most part nonprofessional, theaters), who consider the public that attends local plays to be well above the intellectual average of their communities' population.

Evaluating the taste and intelligence of an audience is of course a highly subjective and relative matter, and playgoers are already a self-selected minority. According to a special Gallup poll of February 1963, 18,000,000 adults, or 17 percent of our population, attended at least one theatrical production of some kind during the previous year.[5] The same poll further ascertained that 20 percent of American women attended theater at least once during the year, while only 15 percent of American men did so. Of persons attending, 51 percent had some college education.

No detailed analysis of the composition of the audience for non-professional theaters, comparable to the study on the professional theater by Baumol and Bowen, has ever been made, and NTC was in no position to attempt one. The present authors, however, believe that the average community theater audience, though a small percentage of the total local population and drawn in the main from the better educated sector, would represent a somewhat wider spread of the population in respect to income and occupation—and perhaps in other regards—than professional theater audiences.

Although audiences for Community Theater far outnumber those attending professional theater, the community theaters face a constant battle of attracting the public. NTC, from many opinion sources, lists the following reasons as most influential among those discouraging a larger attendance at plays:

1. For those community theaters in city centers, traffic has become too difficult. It is easier and more pleasant to stay at home.
2. With the disappearance of the large three-generation household, and grandparents and aunts living-in, the baby-sitting problem has become crucial.
3. A philosophy of "togetherness," which has created a lot of "do-it-yourself" projects involving parents and children, keeps many people at home.
4. Installment buying (TV sets and such) does not leave enough money for theater tickets.
5. Taxes and other payments withheld from salary checks cut down available funds.
6. The small exposure of the general public to live drama provides little chance of convincing them that the theater is more important or more interesting than other forms of recreation.
7. Many performances are given in uncomfortable facilities. Theater, at its best, flourishes in a climate especially created for its existence. Ineptly designed auditoria are almost the rule in the United States. The horrible "gymatorium" is everywhere.
8. General competition with other community events, and lack of coordinating arts councils to keep dates clear.
9. Puritan hangovers still, in many places, nourish a suspicion of theater groups.
10. Censorship of many kinds casts doubt on the choice of certain plays done by the community theater.
11. Lack of artistic ideals or educational motives in the group itself, which cannot bother to educate an audience or to bring them along to better things, results in stagnation.
12. A steady diet of poor-quality theater has an effect similar to bad food at a boarding house.
13. Conflicts in leadership within the group itself cause inferior work to be done and "unpleasantnesses" to arise.

14. Inferior understanding of goals and purposes by the group.

15. The "fun" motive in community theater, too strongly stressed, may lead to time unwisely spent in superficial social activities.

16. Failure to place or build community theaters in locations where people are: for example, in or near shopping centers.

17. Competition with television and spectator sports.

Of this list of factors accounting for the small percentage of Americans attending the theater, perhaps the single most influential is the last one listed. TV and night sports have contributed strongly to the destruction of the playgoing habit. Americans, though the most mobile of people, are not accustomed to displacing themselves in the evening for the sake of seeing a play. They can see shows on TV "for free" and without effort, without dressing up, and without having to sit through what they do not happen to like. This relatively new evening habit of countless millions of Americans—plus the lowered standards of taste in entertainment that it has induced—constitutes, in our opinion, the community theater's most formidable obstacle for attracting a larger audience.

After realizing the problem what can Community Theater do about the low standards of taste of audiences?

Respondents in the study were asked to check the ways in which their community theater organizations have tried to educate audiences to an appreciation of better plays, raising their standards of taste. The methods most often employed were playreadings, classes, discussions, and lectures. About one-fourth of the respondent groups, however, used none of these methods. A dozen groups added "workshops" to the suggested list, and an equal number said they "try to produce better plays." Producing better plays is, of course, the best and most natural way to educate audiences so that their standards of taste are raised.

NTC believes that the chief difficulty in producing better plays is that Community Theater particularly has not developed enough men and women in its own ranks with an intellectual grasp of theater's nature and possibilities, hence many of the people involved lack aesthetic sense or scope. Their concept of the theater is not to produce better plays but to attract larger audiences with popular plays—good or bad. But there is a conceptual aspect in all art, which cannot be overlooked.

This tendency to produce sure-fire plays instead of "thinking" plays calls attention to the lack of training opportunities for community theater leaders to assist them in developing the right concept of theater. With so few professionals who are trained in good drama operating in Community Theater, how can the enthusiastic but untrained volunteer director acquire both skill and the correct stimulation?

## *Play Selection and Subject Matter*

Conformism is a national trait of Americans, reinforced by merchandising, advertising, television and radio media, books and magazines, and all the other concerted and big-spending disseminators of ideas and products. Among the "culture consumers," to use Alvin Toffler's apt term,[6] the theater and its public have not escaped this vast and penetrating influence. Indeed, its own industry (commercial producers and theater owners, play publishers, record manufacturers, etc.) has developed particular methods of effecting what Gorelik calls *Gleichshaltung*, or homogenization. The publishers' catalogues of plays, freely distributed to amateur groups, tend, with their come-on blurbs, to stress the advantages of doing sure-fire pieces. Since they generally publish only plays that have had a professional production—and never designate the ones that flopped—the faraway, playreading committee of a community theater is apt to assume that anything they recommend in a given category is safe to undertake and sure to be popular. Inevitably, the play which the committee has heard or read the most about receives the first attention, unless the group's leaders know enough good drama to look beyond the recent Broadway successes or the inferior copies of Broadway trends.

Conformism, in the selection of plays for a community theater, is the safe way out, since running with the herd involves the smallest risk of disapproval. It is also the easy way, since those who choose the plays for the group very often find the classics, or "thinking" plays of any period, difficult to read, and therefore tend to select those in which meaning is readily comprehended. The group's membership, the audiences, indeed the community as a whole may also influence the play selection. Most modern community theaters are not especially class-conscious, but they do generally tend to produce with some type of audience in mind, and they all seek public approbation; therefore, they bow to a community's taste.

But how does one know the present taste of the American community in regard to theater? One way of estimating the taste of community theaters and their audiences is to use as an indicator the actual plays selected for production. NTC, in 1963, asked the two most influential publisher-agencies catering to Community Theater to list the plays they handled that were then being most frequently performed by community groups.

Samuel French, Inc., supplied the following list:

*The Miracle Worker*
*The Mousetrap*
*The Cocktail Party*
*Come Blow Your Horn*
*Five-Finger Exercise*
*J.B.*

*Look Homeward, Angel*
*A Majority of One*
*The Matchmaker*
*All the Way Home*
*Blithe Spirit*
*Our Town*
*The Rainmaker*
*Rhinoceros*
*Send Me No Flowers*
*The Skin of Our Teeth*
*Ten Little Indians*

Dramatists Play Service, Inc., listed the ten plays from their catalogue which had proved to be the most popular among community theater groups during the calendar year of 1962, together with the approximate number of performances given of each play, as follows:

*The Pleasure of His Company* (525)
*The Glass Menagerie* (470)
*My Three Angels* (455)
*Harvey* (370)
*Visit to a Small Planet* (312)
*Auntie Mame* (310)
*Bell, Book and Candle* (280)
*Critic's Choice* (270)
*Bus Stop* (250)
*Born Yesterday* (240)

In June 1961, the Special Projects Committee of the New England Theatre Conference (NETC), representing six northeastern states, published the results of a survey covering the stage productions from 1956 to 1961 of the member groups in the NETC's five divisions (University and College, Community, Professional, Secondary School, and Children's Theaters). Of the plays produced by more than four groups in the Community Theater division, the titles recurring most frequently were:

*My Three Angels*
*The Solid Gold Cadillac*
*The Teahouse of the August Moon*
*Harvey*
*Bell, Book and Candle*
*Separate Tables*
*The Silver Whistle*

Some critics accuse Community Theater of performing nothing but "warmed-over Broadway," and these lists tend to substantiate the accusation. On the other side of the scale, however, NTC found some evidence of attempts to change this situation. Samuel French, Inc. noticed a marked increase of popular interest in avant-garde plays and playwrights, as shown by the following figures (given in reverse order).

For Beckett's plays:
45 productions from January to June 1963
42 productions in 1962
16 productions in 1960
2 productions in 1958

For Ionesco's plays:
200 productions from January to June 1963
280 productions in 1962
60 productions in 1960
42 productions in 1958

The NETC survey desired to learn more about the community theaters' own reactions to the plays they had produced. It asked them which plays, of all those done, had proved the "most satisfying." The results were illuminating. Here are the authors who topped the list, with the plays done:

1. Maxwell Anderson: *Anne of the Thousand Days, Elizabeth the Queen, Joan of Lorraine*
2. Arthur Miller: *All My Sons, The Crucible, A View from the Bridge*
3. Thornton Wilder: *Our Town, The Matchmaker*
4. Tennessee Williams: *The Glass Menagerie, Summer and Smoke, Cat on a Hot Tin Roof*
5. Bernard Shaw: *Arms and the Man, Candida, The Devil's Disciple, Don Juan in Hell*
6. Oscar Wilde: *The Importance of Being Earnest*

There was also a sprinkling of plays by O'Neill, Hellman, Fry, Eliot, Anouilh, and Giraudoux in the list.[7] The classics and new works, however, were noticeably absent.

NTC finds that by and large American community theaters choose the most popular Broadway hits. It also finds that many community theater groups would prefer to present plays of a more serious nature and of a greater dramatic stature than their audiences are yet willing to accept.

The problems and views involved in both play selection and audience taste (for the two are intertwined) are expressed in various ways in the following quotations from correspondents.

From the standpoint of the nonprofessional participant, the president of a community theater says:

> The problem of "good" plays as against "entertaining" plays is constantly before our board, and the board is by no means in agreement. It is my experience that our associate members (our audience) come to the club for an evening of relaxation and entertainment. They do not enjoy a play that preaches a moral or that forces undue mental activity to catch the meaning. When we do a more serious play, and we do produce one at frequent intervals, audience comment is invariably "well acted, but I did not care for the subject matter." Since we need to keep our associate members to exist, the majority of our plays are selected with the view of entertaining.

Kendrick Wilson, for many years the successful professional director of the Omaha Playhouse, sees another dimension in the survey:

> One factor affecting "public taste" in Community Theater, I believe, has not been seriously considered. It may supply some answer to the fact that the ten most popular plays of a given period will basically correspond aesthetically with the most popular of today. This factor is the increase in audience during recent years. This increase is bringing into our theaters more and more theatrically untrained individuals who have not had the advantages and taste-raising opportunities of years of theatergoing. Mixed with the old-time diehards, they help make up a resulting audience at the same average taste level as we had 15 years ago. The basic difference now is that the audience is twice the size.
>
> In Omaha, in 1953, we helped pay the bills for doing *Abe Lincoln in Illinois* with a bit of fluff called *Remains to Be Seen*. In 1962, the bill-paying-fluff was *Come Blow Your Horn*. The literary merit of the two plays is about the same. The majority of the audiences liked both of these plays. The difference is that in 1953 we played to 3,000 and in 1963 to 7,000.
>
> About the only clear statement that can be made is that in Omaha the taste *for* theater is improving; the taste *in* theater is proportionally static. But, with the larger attendance, a larger number of persons want good theater.

From a staff member of the Little Theatre of Charlotte, North Carolina, comes the following point of view:

> The mores of a community affect the decisions to present various plays. *Cat on a Hot Tin Roof* can play here, but not there. Shakespeare may go over yonder, but not in the hill country. But, mores change, develop, maybe even grow. Intelligent community theaters do not blast through the moral attitudes of the area. These Thespian organizations treat mores as a large pond. First, a toe is stuck in. Then, if it is not frozen, they try the foot, then the calf—and so on. A problem that we have is that of the old-time members who have been with us 20, 25, 30-odd years; their background, exposure,

thoughts are often quite different from those who have created the attitudes of the present generation. So, a careful advance must be made so as not to drive away the old-time patrons, and yet so as to attract new ones.

There are other play selection considerations besides the mores of the area and character of the community theater audience. These would include facilities at hand, costs involved, and plays or musicals available. The use of many classical plays might also be limited by a lack of trained performers. Enthusiasm and interest on the part of volunteer actors are not sufficient assets to carry off a performance of the more difficult classical roles.

Community theater play selection, as seen through the eyes of some critics not directly involved, is quite different. Writing in the Des Moines, Iowa, *Register and Tribune*, Ogden G. Dwight says:

> Community audiences subsist in massive apathy, hooked in addiction to massive entertainment. The narcotic equation that health equals satisfaction equals amusement has become, by steps of false artistic and economic logic unnecessary to elucidate, the spurious *Q.E.D.* of the average community theater.
>
> Choosing bad plays, debasing taste and intelligence, is an abdication of community theater's duty and purpose in the community which comprises its audience. Since the choices are made by a committee from that audience, the selection group must be members who have good knowledge of repertoire, high ideals and standards, an acute and questing sense of responsibility, principle and stubborness. They must resist continual adult child-cries for never-ending fun and frolic.

Robert Summers, a playwright from Philadelphia, told NTC:

> To date, Community Theater has been particularly backward in recognizing new and original talent, and has relied heavily upon cues from Broadway and off-Broadway. My experience indicates that Community Theater is largely as hit-happy as Broadway . . . and seems to lack even Broadway's courage, when the investments between the two are compared.

A criticism from playgoers, some directors, and participants pertains to the subject matter of the newer or "avant-garde" plays that have been dominating the serious theatrical scene. A Midwest volunteer-president expresses the view that too many of the excellently written plays of today reflect a sick philosophy in their portrayal of negation, and that this is a philosophy not generally held by the American people. She and others feel that faith, hope, and courage are not dead at the grassroots, and that there is a yearning for plays that can be considered testaments to man's courage, love, integrity or nobility. It is a widely held view.

"Let's stop taking an old burlesque routine and making an enti play of it," pleads a noted community theater director from the Sout "Let's stop being afraid of the big emotions—love, hate, fear, ambitio ecstasy. . . . The homosexual, dope addict, and sexually inadequate ca be portrayed rarely on the local (or 'hometown') stage."

One of the present authors, in an article published over ten yea ago, expresses some still-relevant views on this problem of subject matte

> It should be clearly understood that we are concerned with good entertainment and also with good "box office," and that the kind or rather kinds of plays we would urge Community Theaters to seek out and produce have no more to do with pollyannaism than with pessimism. If we accentuate the positive, it is not from ignorance of the negative; it is because drama's great role is to illuminate life, not befog it; to exalt and not to depress the spirits of its beholders.
>
> This distinction has nothing whatever to do with categorical differences between tragedy, comedy, melodrama, farce, or even the modern serious drama. Plays of every one of these kinds may enhance or may belittle life, according to the insights, outlook, and powers of the playwright. The deeper these insights, the broader the outlook, the stronger the artistic powers of the dramatist, the more likely are his plays to quicken and enlarge the lives of all, players as well as public, who give their talents, time, and attention to his work.
>
> We believe that too many plays being put on by community theaters are not worth their talents and efforts, not worth the time, money, or attention of their public. We believe this state of things is due not to any preference for life-belittling plays, but to other causes. One of these is, of course, sheer laziness in play-selecting: taking the nearest thing to hand. Another is timidity, whether from box office fright or hesitancy to try something different (or "new" or "old"), or from fear to face greatness in drama—as if the great play did not always bear up the players and public rather than bear down on them. A third cause is ignorance: not knowing where to look for truly fine plays, or not knowing how to handle them, or perhaps not knowing with confidence the difference between plays that belittle and plays that enhance life. Whatever the cause—and there are others, less excusable—the effect is to "see small" and so to lose the splendor that theater exists to give.[8]

Initially, of course, subject matter is a playwright's problem. I attempting to articulate some of the problems of American playwriting Samuel Selden[9] wrote NTC the following statement:

> The most prized factor in all kinds of storytelling now appears to be the "kick." Not the portrayal of a deep love, or a healthy hatred, but whatever can be manipulated for immediate shock value. At one time, the literary artist's ambition was to win for his product the sound of applause. Now, he feels that he has failed unless he hears from his spectator or his reader, a gasp. Not long ago, we saw the

review of a new novel. It appeared prominently in one of our most reputable literary magazines. "The author's talent," said the critic, "is one of the greatest I have encountered in 40 years of reviewing. . . . His knowledge of man's nature is profound, and in the depiction of character he is a sorcerer." Then, to give point to his remarks about this writer's particular genius, the critic added, enthusiastically: "His description of sexual acts matches in vividness anything that can be found in American novels, and in one passage he has dared to do what no other American has, so far as I know, hazarded."

Are we, in our advancing age, becoming tender-minded about what should be regarded as sober criticism? We don't think we are. We believe only that we are beginning to get a little tired of a lack of proportion.

When the question is asked why literature and the theater are obsessed by themes of depravity and hopelessness, the ready answer is that the people of our country, buffeted by the storms in the world today, really think that way. And so, the artists are just mirroring their spectator's minds. The artist—so goes the argument—serves his function never more faithfully than when he shows outwardly—honestly and frankly—what would, otherwise, be locked with pain and a festering of the soul in men's interiors.

We find ourselves wanting to challenge this reply. It is too easy, too glib, and therefore suspect. Have we actually lost our interest in, our trust in—our admiration, and affection for—the American values of loyalty and courage, and the regard for the feelings of other people viewed both realistically and poetically? We do not believe it. We look at our friends, our colleagues, our neighbors next door, our students and their families all around, and we find that the fundamental virtues are still being practiced daily. They are practiced quietly, generously, and with assurance, as they always have been. They are not boasted about, it is true. The reason why they are not boasted about is because they continue to be taken for granted.

The same values are still vigorously defended in public life. Before we go to the office in the morning, we read a paper with many of whose policies we heartily disagree. Yet, the editorials have integrity. They argue with other men's points of view loudly, and sometimes a little crudely perhaps, but honestly. Our national life is filled with greed, fear, and ignorance—it always has been—but, it also contains a wonderful amount of decency, bravery, and wisdom. We are not, so far as we can see, tottering on the edge of the gutter. As citizens, we are vigorously hopeful and we care.

But, the artists tell us that we are looking at deceptive exteriors. Underneath is where the rottenness exists. They, the artists, are the perceptive ones. Those of us who are hopeful are sentimentalists—blind to the truth. The sores which exist below the social surface are surely there. We wonder, however, if they really do represent the basic truth of our lives, or are they, rather, the special, the limited, truths. We would be better prepared to accept the broad judgment of the pessimists if we could free ourselves from a nagging suspicion that they—at least some of the most vocal of them—are lazily trying to take a shortcut to theatric effect. The human proclivity to express oneself in sadistic or masochistic terms is with us always. It takes very little cleverness to stir these tendencies into action. The results are stunning, but the memory of them tends to be short-lived.

The sensation produced by an act of kick-and-run makes us think of the "needled" beer many of us had to drink during the wonderful days of Prohibition. Spiked with ether instead of alcohol, it produced a terrific wallop for about 20 minutes, then its effect vanished. When it faded, it left behind a feeling of depressing flatness. After taking a mug of that needled beverage, we were never convinced that we should stop drinking. We just wanted better beer.

What we think we regret more than our leanings toward synthetically produced tears is our loss of ability to laugh. Where are our comedies? We haven't seen a really good one for a long time. It is true that we still have the musical comedies—let us be thankful for them!—and an occasional piece of light witticism. But, no good farces. No good satires. We need to laugh once more. We need to forego the sniggers and to laugh with our whole beings, loudly enough and vigorously enough to shake ourselves free from the "mulligrubs" that possess us. We need, once more, to have fun in the theater.

Our finest drama has been our musical drama and our social drama of the 1930's. The former, was perhaps inevitable, and we think, in a sense, we can take no credit for it—it is grand American fun and gusto and humor and escape. May it wave on, but let us not suppose it is serious drama. The latter, the social drama of the 1930's, fed partially by the Federal Theatre Project, almost booted us off dead center, almost gave birth to a valid central organic American Drama (capitals ours!). And now Broadway is, let's face it, a stew of commercial ventures, derivative, adaptive, chaotic, bloated by the carbonation of the hard sell.

The impoverishment of playwriting in this country is manifested by the spate of imports and dramatized novels in recent seasons. In playwriting, as in production, there is an increasing tendency today to substitute novelty for value, to substitute sensationalism for meaning or gimmick for thought, to let experimentation become an end rather than a means.

NTC believes that the views expressed in the passages just quoted speak for the vast majority of thoughtful Americans, and in particular for those who are the playgoers, actual and potential, of Community Theater.

## *Experimental Drama*

The vitality of the community theater movement has not been applied to the production of new plays, or for that matter to new staging methods; hence it misses most of the excitement of genuine creation.

The early Art Theater in America and the best of the Little Theaters were dedicated to experimentation; modern community theaters are dedicated to experimentation very rarely. Realizing Community Theater's untapped potential as a catalytic agent in the development of new dramatists, NTC asked two questions: "Has your group ever considered producing a new, unpublished play?" and "How many new or previously unpublished plays has your organization done?"

Out of 202 responding theaters, a total of 94 replied that they had done one or more new or previously unproduced plays. An additional 14 groups have considered or would consider doing a new play. The two groups together represented only 53.47 percent.

The number of new plays per group varies from one to 68; but the value of these figures is dubious, since some groups listed productions during the past season, and others presented a total covering several years. Doubtless a large number of the new plays, too, were one-acts. Many directors did report that, while they produce Broadway hits for box office purposes, they also attempt to produce some drama that may be experimental, more difficult, or more daring.

The fact that 46.5 percent of the groups responding admitted that they had never attempted to produce a new dramatic work of any kind is an indication of how far Community Theater has departed from the Art Theater's dedication to experimentation and the fostering of new dramatists. In extenuation, some will argue that Community Theater, by nature, cannot be experimental to any significant degree. They remind us that theater is a part of the general cultural milieu, in which conformity is the rule, and that a community theater must be expected to address itself to the local majority—although it is obvious that the majority neither supports nor attends the theater. They also tell us that fear of community disapproval, or even censorship, is an awesome force prohibiting theater groups from attempting very much that is daring or experimental—yet the only way any art can grow is through experiment, which may or may not be daring.

Even within this context, however, there can and must take place a continual discovery of fresh sources and resources. A world-wide, rich theatrical heritage in drama is virtually unknown to the average community theatergoer. That should be one kind of discovery. Another awakening, just as exhilarating, can come from close collaboration over several weeks with a guest playwright in the creation of a new dramatic work. (Producing a première, incidentally, is not only a good way to achieve distinction for the group; the publicity it furnishes can more than offset the financial risks, and as a learning experience for all concerned it offers unparalleled rewards.)

## *Newspapers and Community Theater*

What is the attitude of the press toward Community Theater? NTC asked the question: "Do the mass media in your area take your organization's work seriously on a cultural level?" Amazingly, 280 groups replied "yes" and 45 "no." It would seem that the theater groups are satisfied, for the most part, that their efforts are being adequately noted in the local news media, both newspapers and broadcasts.

But perhaps our question was too broad, or even ambiguous, since to "take . . . seriously on a cultural level" does not necessarily imply critical discernment. Other contributors to the NTC appraisal have observed that in the majority of American towns there are but two types of drama critics: those who are inept or poorly qualified to judge, and those who are overly kind and applaud any local theater performance simply because it is a community effort. Neither type of critic can stimulate constructive growth in the group or in the public, any more than the critic who damns every show because it is only local talent. A community theater's health depends almost as much on sound and honest criticism as on capable performers and an enlightened public.

## *Finances*

What is the economic picture of community theaters? One hundred-eighty-one groups reported a total income from all sources of $2,888,356 or an average per group of $15,957. Of the total, $1,390,077 (or an average per group of $7,680) came from box office receipts and $1,349,469 (an average of $8,762 per group) from subscriptions and membership The total income from gifts was reported at $158,811 or an average of $2,443 per group. Therefore, approximately 49 percent of income comes from box office receipts, 49 percent from membership subscriptions, and less than 2 percent from gifts. While the highest income reported from box office receipts was $48,000, the highest number of groups (33) had incomes of $2,000 to $3,000.

The authors believe that this sample is too small to make any authoritative statement on the economic state of Community Theater Generally speaking, however, we believe that the number of prosperous community theaters is comparatively small and that most groups just "get by."

Groups were also asked whether or not they received any subsidy The vast majority of community theaters receive no cash subsidy. An indeterminate number receive an indirect subsidy in the form of rental facilities, such as school auditoriums, from municipal organizations Eight groups reported cash subsidies from chambers of commerce and other civic groups, ranging from $50 to $20,000 for a total of $23,380

One group reported the receipt of $48,000 in a special drive for building funds, and another received $10,000 as a participant in an Arts and Science Fund Drive. Five groups reported the receipt from individuals of a total of $2,800. Subsidy from foundations and philanthropic associations was reported by only five groups. These subsidies ranged from $1,800 to $24,000 for a total of $47,800.

Since the establishment of the National Endowment for the Arts and its subsequent stimulation of Arts Councils in most states, a new avenue of possible subsidy has opened up. It is impossible to gauge the extent of this subsidy to individual groups, but it is undoubtedly very small.

By far the largest indirect subsidy to Community Theater is the time and effort expended by the volunteer. If calculated in dollars at one dollar an hour, the total value would run over a billion dollars. (6,000,000 volunteers donating 5 hours a week at $1.00 an hour). There is an army of workers here which could potentially lift the theater to new heights of excellence. Training and education of such volunteers is, as we have said, one of the chief jobs the Community Theater has to accomplish.

## *Overview*

The concluding questions of the NTC survey asked: "What, in your opinion, is the present state (vitality, prosperity, usefulness, public esteem) of all types of theater in your area?", and, "What are the prospects for community or resident professional theater development in your area for, say, the next five or ten years?"

Granting that the respondents were those most interested in and dedicated to Community Theater, the replies to these questions were fairly encouraging: "excellent," 40 percent; "growing but uneven in some areas" (usually reflecting problems of finances or public esteem), 3 percent; "average or holding their own," 25 percent; "not healthy" or low," 12 percent. As for the prospects for theater, 22 percent said "excellent," 32 percent "good," 17 percent said "hopeful or promising," 11 percent "fair," 12 percent "poor," and 6 percent said "unchanging."

Theodore Viehman, former president of NTC, who directed the Little Theatre of Tulsa for 30 years, gave NTC this overview of the situation:

> Undoubtedly, in America the most important theater activity, potentially at least, is the Community Theater in all its forms from dramatic club to partly professionalized big business. The variations in quality of production, however, are many, usually, but not always, due to the degree of experience in the company, particularly in direction. The poorer and lower levels of performance—and

many times they are almost unbelievably uninspired—are usually in the smaller communities where contact with good theater is infrequent or impossible. There are many of these, with only inexperienced volunteer directors and actors, no patterns to follow and no imagination displayed.

Many community theaters come and go, having no sense of continuity or real purpose except to express themselves, usually miserably. They are ridiculed by their own meager public and by professional theater alike. They deserve it, and probably deserve only an "E" for effort. Some rise out of their miserable years after they find subsidy or means to hire an experienced director.

Perhaps the healthiest of our community theaters are those hundred-odd in communities of 100,000 to 300,000 population, where skilled directors and staffs have built up the quality of performance to near-professional levels, and a good-sized, discerning and appreciative audience has been attracted to membership and attendance. Even in those organizations, the bigger the attendance on each production, the lower the average taste IQ of the audience, and the greater, consequently, is the pressure to lower the caliber of the plays chosen for production.

NTC solicited another statement from a director who sees the Community Theater from a different vantage point and urges the steady inclusion of minority opinion. NTC member Ted Kehoe writes:

The American Community Theater is, in its finest flowering, grandly representative of the best and worst in America. It is pragmatic. It is independent in attitude. It is responsive to its constituency—the membership. In Community Theater we have come to know that a determined response to all minorities in the membership, including the entire range of taste, will result in a balanced fare and in theaters that continue. . . .

In the American system of free response, such a determination of fare is both natural and productive whenever one is able to ferret out the balance of taste and interest. There is room for any taste, room for any faction, if the right balance is achieved. . . .

Those who wail, who castigate, who bemoan the low state of theater are, I think, simply trumpeting their own inability to find and hold an audience. Or, if one looks closely, they are venting a desire to change people by some method still undiscovered. They do not accept the facts. The conditions of our theater, when it succeeds and when it fails, relate to things as they are. We cannot change them by wishful thinking, by complaint, or by law. If we seek change in the relationship between the public and the theater, then we must make the theater more of an intoxicant, more irresistible. We must slip in a piece of life that will intoxicate along with our gaily ribboned package of claptrap.

Repeating a plea made earlier, the greatest need of Community Theaters would seem to be for more better-trained leaders. Too much of the work is being done by persons without any formal training. Too many of those with university training lack sufficient knowledge of the technical aspects—designing, painting, lighting—or else are impatient with makeshifts, and therefore do not make efficient artistic use of the meager facilities often available to them at the community level.

NTC urges that schools, colleges, and universities help provide a steady flow of new leaders into the nation's theaters, including the community theaters, which are, after all, of, by, and for the people in a very true sense. Where Community Theater is stagnating, education alone can do much to raise the people's sights, dissolve old prejudices against the stage, open doors for the young to new vistas of public service in the arts. Theater is not only a matter of literature; it is also an art, a science, a business, a profession, and an institution within itself—and Community Theater offers opportunities and challenges worthy of the young talents that must be found and trained.

Movies, television, and traveling theatrical companies are sometimes seen as being rivals to Community Theater. NTC believes that more good theater, more good films and better television drama help the whole idea of theater in the community. The presence in Minneapolis of the Guthrie Theatre, for example, has greatly increased public interest in Community Theater in that city and area. A good community theater, in turn, stimulates interest and develops appreciation for professional theater; it can actually bring about the acceptance and success of touring troupes, which have always had difficult times. The key seems to be that healthy competition at a level of excellence improves the quality of all productions and heightens public enjoyment of good theater.

The trouble is, Americans as a whole have never seen enough good drama in any medium. Movies have indeed been getting better and better; but they are as near as millions of people ever get to a dramatic performance. Commercial television networks have been exceedingly slow to present plays of any stature to their countless viewers, and the live performances of even the ones they have shown are still inaccessible to people living at some distance from major cities. As for traveling professional companies, and even touring troupes from college theaters, they scarcely begin to reach the vast public that has, or might have, an appetite for fine drama well performed.

We have termed the responses to our queries on the present and future state of Community Theater fairly encouraging. We think they are, as one would expect, generally optimistic. But theater people as a whole are optimistic; they have to be. We looked for stronger evidence of Community Theater's prosperity and vitality than our respondents gave us; and we shall continue to look for it—hopefully.

Kendrick Wilson expresses the optimism which many directors and leaders feel:

> For 30 years, I have worked steadily in a branch of the theater that has grown healthier year by year, even as the professional theater (in New York) has sickened. I have watched audiences grow in my theater from 600 per production to over 6,000. I have seen a city, stimulated over a period of years by careful attention to detail in acting, staging, and a wise selection of a wide variety of plays, raise a half-million dollars to build a complete modern theater seating 520, with parking for 210 cars. I have watched the attendance at that theater grow to double that of the professional road companies doing the same productions in the same city. I have seen the professional staff of the community theater grow from one person (the director) to six—executive director, designer, technician, associate director, box office secretary, and custodian. A business manager will be added. I have reason to believe in Community Theater as the future hope for theater in America.

At NTC's Convention in November 1967, Art Cole, a highly successful Community Theater director, was asked to comment on theater audiences. We quote his concluding remarks:

> Audience-building, indeed the whole theatrical experience, begins with theater for children. High school theater is its logical product. College theater is the inheritor of high-school audiences, plus the knowledge and insight it is supposed to give. Community Theater is, for most, no more than the end result of all three; and Professional Theater is either the victim or the beneficiary of all four together—even as the excellence of professional football is the end-product of a process that now starts with YMCA Pee Wee football.
>
> Today 400,000 people can see live pro football in *one* league on *one* weekend—*live,* not televised. That's an average of 60,000 spectators per game. They go to watch *excellence!* They know excellence because they have spent a lifetime watching football. We don't leave sports appreciation to chance in this country. We work hard at it. Why, then, must we leave art appreciation, especially theater appreciation, to chance? Let's get off the professional theater's back, and attack the problem where it starts—with us, in our communities, with our own leadership, and with our enormous potential for audience development.

One thing, NTC believes, is certain: for *most* Americans the country over, better theater will come to them—when and if it does come—through Community Theater. Whether it comes within the next decade, or two, will depend on the quality of its leadership.

# III. IN EDUCATION

# In Education

## Educational Theater

AN EPIC STRUGGLE of this century was the effort of a small group of realistic idealists to create an educational theater. It was not easy to bring this sprawling, suspect, and often misunderstood bastard within American college halls. There were no foreign precedents, no prototypes, to serve as models or give the foundling academic sanction. University faculties and presidents held out against inclusion of the study of theater as long as they could; and when they could hold out no longer, they charily conceded a tiny spot in the curriculum for dramatic literature.

In the wake of earlier studies in Shakespeare at Harvard, theater was introduced into English department offerings in 1890 in the form of a course in the history of English drama to 1642. It was taught (from then until 1921) by George Pierce Baker, who, as his biographer reports, "read each play as a script for an actor, not a text for a reader, and pointed out those things which could be appreciated only in terms of the stage" and through "audience effect."[1] Baker later added courses in modern drama and, most influential of all, in "dramatic technique"—

reinforced by stage productions and by the frequent presence in class of theater professionals. Ironically, this great teacher, the "father of American instruction in playwriting," was to be given small thanks by Harvard for his pioneering efforts, and he finally departed in the mid-1920's for the greener theatrical pastures of Yale, where he took his Harkness money and built himself a fine new theater.

Meanwhile other university teachers were taking up the cause of the "living drama." Brander Matthews at Columbia made playgoing into a fine art for his students. Alexander M. Drummond rose above difficulties at Cornell to found the Cornell Dramatic Club, which grew into a notable academic department of theater art. Thomas H. Dickinson, professor of English at Wisconsin in 1910, had to write a successful Broadway play, with Minnie Maddern Fiske in the leading role, before his colleagues would allow him to teach American drama.

Edward C. Mabie battled strong forces to create the Iowa University Theater. Thomas Wood Stevens at Carnegie Tech, Frederick H. Koch at North Carolina, Alfred Arvold at North Dakota State, Allen Crafton at the University of Kansas, Sawyer Falk at Syracuse, Marion Stebbins at Mills College, and others, worked their hearts out for a great idea: to instruct students in the history and art of the theater, to bring dramatic literature to life in stage productions, and to help to portray a new creative view of theater to the American people.

These men and women were truly giants in their way, and were revered and emulated as such by their students. Their work has borne plentiful fruit. Departments of drama, speech, speech and drama, theater art, English (which sometimes include dramatic art), and just college theaters have proliferated on campuses throughout the country. True, the founding giants have nearly all vanished now and their places have been taken by other men and women, idealistic for the most part and perhaps better trained, but often of lesser stature than their unforgettable predecessors. A race of giants, however, is not easy to reproduce and the men and women of smaller stature have, to their credit and sometimes their dismay, propagated a mammoth movement out of the first beginnings created by these landmark figures of the past.

The founders wanted acceptance of dramatic arts within the college, and this they have achieved in full measure throughout the higher education systems of America—although on some campuses theater is still an extracurricular activity. They wanted theaters, and colleges now have the best collection of working theater facilities in America. They wanted graduate programs to train better teachers and scholars for the field, and to produce professional workers to take places in the commercial and noncommercial theater of America. This, too, they gained

In the area of graduate study they have perhaps gained too much, for the doctoral degree fetish has feverishly invaded the American educational theater—some believe to its detriment. Research specialists may not necessarily be excellent theatricians, yet the universities feel bound to place a major emphasis upon research.

Theoretically, Educational Theater provides the most likely milieu for bold, creative experimentation. Operating with a built-in subsidy, educational theater is the only branch of theater with few financial worries. However, operating with student actors only, educational theater has seldom been able to develop a truly polished and mature acting ensemble, nor has it been as bold and creative as it might be. Neither has Educational Theater, until recently, been strong in creating professional attitudes.

Writing NTC on this last point, designer Howard Bay, now head of the Brandeis University Theater, made this comment:

> The main ingredient in short supply is an ingrained professional attitude—not a grubby showbiz veneer, but the intense concentration of the craftsman. . . . Also, more true-blue professionals should join up full time. One-shot lectures, guest appearances, and the festival bit lend a jazzy air to the college cultural scene, but long-term immersion in the producing company is what is called for. The degree fetish must be judiciously tabled to procure pertinent professionals for school theaters. I don't wish to make light of the doctorate industry, but I do feel that a George Abbott could lead drama students further than the author of a paper on a little-known aspect of Webster's collaborators. Not that campuses should be inundated by pros at loose ends, but a choice brain with a lifetime application to the drama of the marketplace could do a lot of instilling of that professional attitude and a consciousness of the customers out front. . . ."

Happily, a definite trend toward professionalization is visible in the establishment of professional acting companies on or near the campuses of American universities. George Freedley[2] considered this one of the most important developments in American theater up to the present, and believed that the presence of such professional companies will also have a strong effect on student acting standards.

NTC assumes that University Theater will never become the American National Theater, but that its chief purpose and function will always be as training ground, stimulater and experimenter, and preparer of theater leaders and audiences. As such, programs for advanced degrees must be one vital part of its objectives: to furnish colleges, schools, and the educational theater in general with a reservoir of trained teaching, directing, and research talent.

## *Theater Programs and Enrollment*

By "educational theater" the present authors are referring to all programs of instruction and production in drama and theater arts that are sponsored by and conducted within educational institutions. NTC's appraisal is intended to give both an overview and an in-depth view, wherever this is possible. It has been assisted in this study by work already performed by others, specialists in this particular field, most notably by the editors of publications of the American Educational Theatre Association. The AETA was founded in 1936 to encourage the highest possible standards of teaching, production, and research in the educational theater field. In addition to its quarterly, the *Educational Theatre Journal,* it publishes the *Directory of American College Theatre,* from which considerable information on the development and present characteristics of the movement is obtainable.

The editor of the 1960 *Directory (DACT),* Burnet M. Hobgood, reviews the movement's history in these words:

> Theater in U. S. higher education has known two major periods of growth. In the decades following World War I and World War II, when the nation's colleges and universities were expanding their range of instruction, extracurricular dramatic activity and formal theater instruction increased sharply in all parts of the country. . . .
>
> Until the 1920's, campus theater activities were mostly of an informal and limited kind. Beginning in 1919, curricular programs were organized and developed at an approximate [annual] rate of increase of 20 percent. During the early 1930's, growth continued but at a slower rate. Schools that had introduced new programs in the 1920's consolidated their gains, allowed elaboration of what had been established, and in some instances, added programs on the graduate level. . . .
>
> Toward the end of the 1930's, the introduction of curricular and new extracurricular programs resumed its earlier pace, culminating in the most notable period of growth the field has known: 1945–55. Up to that time, the inception or reorganization of extracurricular work had increased more rapidly than the inception of curricular programs. In the decade following World War II, however, instructional programs in theater subjects increased at a rate of 28 percent, and new graduate programs flourished at this time.
>
> From 1956 to 1960, the comparative growth of curricular and extracurricular programs returned to normal. There were in 1960 more than 300 college programs equivalent to an undergraduate "major" in theater, and almost that many "minor" equivalents. Less than half of these schools actually award degrees in theater as a field. Forty-two percent of the "major" and "minor" programs in theater were established after 1945, and more than two-thirds of them operate in schools with enrollments under 3,000. Larger schools are clearly more receptive to the study of theater, on the

other hand, and the likelihood of a curricular program in theater is twice as great in colleges with enrollments of more than 3,000. Development of theater curriculas in smaller schools is on the increase, being concentrated for some reason in colleges with enrollments from 500 to 1,500 students. . . .

This was the story in 1960. In 1967, the *Directory of American College Theatre, Second Edition,* edited by Richard Ayers, revealed significant changes. Burnet M. Hobgood analyzed the new study in a paper delivered at the annual convention of the American Educational Theatre Association.

One of the first things we wanted to know from this second picture was how theater education's rate of growth in the 1960's compared to that of the 1950's, which had been a phenomenal 25 percent in the first half of the decade and fell to a still impressive 20 percent as the 1960's began. Because the rate of growth of higher education itself was then only 15 percent, as best we could gauge it, we speculated that theater education would decline at that rate as well. Instead, higher education has risen to a growth rate of 20 percent, we find, and theater is keeping pace with it.

Consequently, more than half of the nation's 1,581 accredited colleges in June, 1966 (the date of the second DACT's picture), offer enough instruction in theater and drama subjects to lead to a degree, and 77 percent provide curricula in theater. In nearly 90 percent of our junior and senior colleges more than 10,000 productions of plays are staged annually in about 1,600 campus playhouses before an audience of approximately 5,000,000 persons. The report has it that 116,000 collegians attend theater classes each year, 100,000 of whom participate in featured or studio play productions for the public.

The statistics are impressive: theater majors—18,051; theater minors—8,045; degrees granted—3,311; campus theaters—1,610; faculty—3,332 (898 with Ph.D.'s, 2,123 with Master's degrees); total audience—5,007,457.

No longer does the avocational theater program or campus theater club dominate the scene. According to Hobgood, "the majority of our colleges now take theater to be a field of study in higher education, and three-fourths of the current programs find their home in the liberal arts college."

The 1967 DACT data further reveal a major trend towards more specialized curricula. The number of course offerings is 71 percent greater in 1966 than in 1960. More significant, perhaps, has been the amount of change in programs. Almost one-fifth of the schools offering degrees in theater have made partial or total revisions in their programs.[3]

At the graduate level, 20 more programs have come into existence during the 1960's so that more than 3,000 graduate degrees are conferred annually.

In contrast with undergraduate enrollment in theater, where the majority of students are women, at the graduate level two-thirds of the students are men. Graduate programs develop most often in large institutions which are in or near metropolitan centers. The two areas which lead are the West Coast and the Middle American East.

## *Goals*

Diversity is the rule in college theater programs—not merely in the program offering, but in the avowed aims and purposes. This diversity may be the greatest source of misunderstanding on the part of those viewing Educational Theater from the outside.

Only a handful of schools, and most of these nonaccredited, maintain that they are training students for a career on the professional stage. Instead, almost all the colleges and universities justify theater training on an entirely different foundation—a foundation related in one way or another to the aims and ideals of a liberal, humanistic, or cultural education.

The undergraduate liberal arts colleges deny any interest whatsoever in vocational training for the theater. They believe that such training should be left to the "trade schools." They maintain that the function of the liberal arts college is not to teach students how to make money, but to teach them how to live wise and worthwhile lives, with or without it. Their basic concern is to provide the student with time and incentive for reflective thinking. The true goal lies beyond the mere accumulation of facts and knowledge; it lies in the less tangible but greater area of wisdom.

Twentieth-century man has far outdistanced his ancestors in the possession of facts and knowledge, but in true wisdom, in the wise and thoughtful application of these facts, mankind today may be less advanced than he was at the time of Sophocles. In liberal education, therefore, lies one of our greatest hopes for understanding and survival in a dangerous world; and in the fine arts, especially in drama, lies one of our greatest hopes for a liberal education.

Except for the last point, these are traditional objectives, not only of the liberal arts colleges in America, but of most of the older colleges and universities throughout the world. Only in America, however, do universities view theatrical production as within the legitimate objectives of such a liberal education.[4] In fact, some administrators now see the theater as the very center of the liberal arts, because it provides a synthesis of all the arts, a corporate and creative effort for all concerned. When asked to justify a theater program, the vast majority of American colleges and universities answer generally as follows:

1. One of the chief roads toward a true liberal education lies in the study of literature.
2. The greatest form of literature is drama.
3. The best and most stimulating way to extract full value from drama is to see it honestly and effectively performed on the stage.
4. To perform plays honestly and effectively requires great skill in the various arts and crafts of the theater.
5. Therefore, the study and practice of these arts and crafts—acting, directing, scenic and costume design, stagecraft, etc.—while perhaps not justifiable academically in and of themselves, are fully justifiable as the necessary means to a desirable end.

This majority view, although not universally accepted, is well expressed by Frank M. Whiting, director of the University Theater at the University of Minnesota, who wrote NTC:

> In other words, if through the development of acting and technical skills we can enable young college students to present an exciting performance of *Hamlet*—a performance that will give new insight into the play, provoke discussion, and stimulate study—we will have provided an experience in learning that lies very close to the heart of a true liberal education. Such values, of course, presuppose an extremely high level of production. . . .

Indeed, one of Educational Theater's chief problems is how to achieve this extremely high level of production. The recent increase in universities' graduate programs in drama and theater arts, with the corresponding growth in the number of students seeking advanced training, is clear evidence of one attempted solution. Another—since "high level" means "professional level"—is seen in the present trend toward establishing professional acting companies on or near university campuses. Still another is found in the employment of professional actors, directors, and designers to work with the advanced students in theater arts. A fourth sign is the creation by universities of a strictly professional "institute" or conservatory of theater arts, such as the one just getting under way at New York University.

Speaking of theater as an extracurricular activity in a liberal arts college, Paul Barstow, director of the Wellesley College Theatre told NTC:

> As the theater's continuing purpose in the life of a college community, three things seem to me primary: the opportunity for

students to learn and practice the arts and skills of the theater; the chance for students to see in production good and important works they study in the academic program of the college; and the service to the wider community offered by an entertaining and artistic theater. . . .

Operating under such a philosophy, though not that one alone, schools adhering to it often administer their theater programs in conjunction with a department other than theater, such as speech or English. This pattern was strongest prior to 1950, and still obtains in some regions, notably the central states.

In 1960, 42 percent of the academic departments offering theater programs administered them in association with another field, usually English or speech. In New England and the Pacific states, the trend is toward autonomous administration in a Drama or Theater Arts Department, but that situation obtains in only one-fifth of the nation's colleges.

There are, of course, differing views of purposes. One view, opposite to that of liberal education, is that college and university programs should train students for the professional stage—a vocational aim. Another is that an excellent liberal education is not incompatible with excellent professional training in theater.

Hobgood lists five types of programs offered by the various schools: recreational, avocational, liberal arts-humanistic, liberal arts-vocational, and pre-professional.[5]

A study of graduate schools conducted by Hobgood indicated that the vast majority of graduate students across the country are training for and entering the academic theater. The programs of graduate schools either try to balance the academic and practical training or weigh more heavily in favor of the scholarly.

For strictly professional training, there are a number of private schools which grant no degrees. ANTA lists 22 in New York City and 8 outside, but there are others not affiliated with ANTA.

It is impossible to judge teaching effectiveness in quantitative terms. However, Richard Ayers, editor of the second DACT, attempted to make some appraisal of this subject on the basis of his studies. He used as a measure the Minimum Criteria standard set by AETA in 1960, and he estimated that only one-half of the colleges and universities offering the equivalent of a baccalaureate degree in theater meet this standard. Worse yet is his estimate that less than one-third of these same college programs appear to meet the new Minimum Criteria established in 1966.

The problem of how to teach as well as what to teach is a major concern of this decade. There is evidence, however, that teachers of theater are beginning to realize that their main concern should be to see that genuine learning experiences occur in the classrooms and playhouses. A number of conferences have taken place in Los Angeles, Minneapolis and Princeton which seem to indicate a new awareness of the problems of teacher effectiveness. The great issue of the 1960's—and very likely of the 1970's—is quality. We have quantity; it must be made better.

## *Quality of Production*

Opinion varies widely concerning the quality of theatrical achievement attained by college-university productions in America. This is partly because of prejudice and partly because of the fact that there is a wide variation in quality, from "inspiring" to "dismal." However, since these adjectives and many others can be applied to all theatrical performances, nothing much is to be gained by a discussion of so subjective a factor. Everyone knows there are many imaginatively-directed and well-acted campus productions, and of course some, perhaps many, "duds."

Equally variable in quality are the physical settings: some new, elaborate, and expensive theaters and some old, inadequate quarters. Numerous Broadway producers told NTC that, with the recent exception of certain professional resident companies' theaters, the finest playhouses in the United States are to be found on college and university campuses. A definite trend toward new, modern theaters for colleges is shown by an AETA survey in 1963, which revealed that 298 academic institutions were actually building or planning new facilities.

One factor which does come into any consideration of quality is that of play selection. AETA's 1963 survey indicated a strong shift away from Broadway hits to standard dramatic works. During 1961–62, for example, only 21 percent of college and university productions were of plays stamped "Broadway," as compared with an average of 48.6 percent for the period from 1950 to 1955. Conversely, production of standard works (classics, from ancient to modern times) increased from an average of 27.7 percent for the 1950–55 period to 52 percent in 1961–62. This was shown to be a continuous trend. Musicals, over the same years, were decreasing in popularity for college productions—replaced, NTC believes, by the newer forms of drama that have captivated students everywhere.

The evidence collected by NTC could allow us to make no absolute or definitive judgment about the artistic quality of college and university productions as a whole. Educational Theater has come in for some sharp criticism on the basis of shoddy, lack-luster performances; of pretentious attempts to do plays that are far beyond its artistic, or even physical, capacity; of unimaginative directing, clumsy designing, atrocious acting, and so on. But it has also achieved, occasionally, levels of creative design, resourceful directing, and inspired acting which have won the highest praise from exacting metropolitan critics.

For a particularly "disparaging word" on Educational Theater in general, we give here a quotation from Theodore Hoffman, now of New York University, writing in the *New York Times* on September 1, 1963:

> Students make up less than 25 percent of the audience. Sumptuous scenery conceals inferior acting. The inevitable spiral of rising production costs, increased admission prices, use of non-student actors, splashy promotion, more elaborate theaters (usually proscenium, to double as auditoriums), and, above all, safe plays provide the dominant pattern. Educational Theater is only another form of the commercial commodity theater, whatever its pretensions and whatever else its academic program may accomplish.

For a quite contrary view and experience, we quote a reply from an NTC member about recent work on his campus in which he was not personally involved:

> On student attendance at university productions, our experience is diametrically opposite to the impression given by Ted Hoffman. Our 200-seat arena theater is jammed twice weekly throughout the college year by over 300 students, with a sprinkling of faculty from various departments, to see student-directed one-acts and to stay and take part in an hour's animated critique session afterwards. These short plays are staged with the utmost economy by students of play directing; they are performed by graduate and undergraduate students alike, including "non-majors" from the general pool of campus talent. In the last week of this spring term, just before exams, we had productions of Ionesco's *Jack, or The Submission* on Tuesday afternoon, Beckett's *Endgame* on Thursday afternoon, and a graduate thesis production of Osborne's *Look Back in Anger* on Friday and Saturday evenings (which will be repeated as our summer season opener)—all packed and with people turned away. Excellent performances, all of them, by any standards.

One obvious difficulty in securing high quality in campus productions is the shortage of students' time, especially undergraduates', that can be devoted to rehearsals and shop work. When such participation is made a part of their major curriculum, the problem becomes less acute; but in large departments it may also be compounded by the heavier schedule of productions needed to provide experience for all the students enrolled in theater courses. For these reasons, all too many college productions open under-rehearsed, and only approach "concert pitch" after a succession of performances.

## *Curricular Problems and Solutions*

A number of other problems and criticisms of college and university theater were expressed by NTC members and correspondents. One member,[6] seeing in these institutions the great hope for the American theater, comments as follows:

> I think that we have made an error in the general design of our undergraduate programs in Theater Arts. Both as a university administrator, and as a professional theater operator and Broadway producer, I have found that the average B.A. in Dramatic Arts who comes to New York to work in the theater is so poorly educated that it takes at least ten years for him to become worth anything to anyone. You cannot converse with him, because his fund of common knowledge is limited almost exclusively to the techniques of the theater, with a minor spattering of knowledge about the literature of the theater.
>
> I have, consequently, redesigned the undergraduate curriculum in this university to place a major emphasis upon the literature of the theater and the development of theater criticism, with a minor emphasis upon the acquisition of technical talents in the academic program. Thoroughly aware of the necessity for a high level of production, I have reduced the faculty load of a director who directs a show in a given semester from twelve hours to six hours. I expect him to spend that time in individual work with the members of his cast, and in polishing toward technical perfection for a good professional production. . . ."

This same person expresses criticism of the well-meaning critic who, encouraged by his well-meaning publisher and editor, goes out to a theater where an incompetent and embarrassing production is half-done, and returns to write a glowing account of that production, thus doing "more disservice to the American theater than any single deed which I know."

Another NTC member believes that the chief inhibiting factors to a stronger growth are the smothering effects of attachments to other academic disciplines, such as speech and English. He believes that such alignments place theater courses and productions in subordinate positions.

Another participant and observer in the field of Educational Theater, sees the problem differently.[7] He writes:

> My real argument is that we have plenty of good artists for fine theater, but do not have audiences in sufficient numbers to appreciate their efforts. Our university drama departments, by policy, force of circumstance, administrative edict, or sheer failure to perceive the problem, are confining their activities to educating an extremely small percentage of their total student body to become actors and directors. The overwhelming majority of the campus

population supports athletics *en masse,* music to some degree, dancing, drinking parties and petting, but a very small percentage are ever found in the campus theater. . . .

After 40 years in the American theater, trying to work under a banner I could respect, I am sorry to say I think the one greatest weakness in the American theater is the audience—both its size and its taste level.

We must do something about those audiences, as educators, more than as artists, if our theater is to have health and cultural growth. We have got to change somewhat our view, our direction, our target.

He suggests, as one possibility, a course in theater appreciation for the entire student body. He also suggests trying to raise theater taste at the high school level.

Theodore Hoffman, then chairman of the Theater Communications Group established by the Ford Foundation, wrote in the *New York Times* cited above about some of the "dangers of educational theater" as he saw them, judging by the need for professional standards:

Two years of four-hours-a-week acting classes hardly provide technique. A production directed by a man maintaining a full teaching schedule and rehearsed less than 125 hours, which Broadway actors find inadequate, hardly probes depth of character. A run of five performances hardly gives one a chance to "grow in the part." At best, Educational Theater applies surface exuberance to an unrealized intellectual sketch of the play. . . .

The rapidly spreading professional resident theaters, by producing the most challenging drama, have exposed the poverty of amateur work, and captured the serious audience that Educational Theater has lost. . . . When university administrators awaken, Educational Theater may be forced to shape its programs to the standards of the professional resident companies which are steadily shaking the whole apparatus of amateur commercial theater.

Educational Theater needs most to become a genuine academic discipline which, like any other, trains qualified students to master the most advanced and demanding subject matter of its field. . . . To capture the best university audiences by competently producing plays worthy of the standards of a university, it must free itself from the box office, train students effectively, and judge the faculty that teaches and produces theater by its professional competence, not by degrees and publications.

If administrators deny that mastery of the arts of theater, rigorously applied to great drama by talented students, involves a process of learning as imaginative and intellectual as that of any other discipline, then let them admit that partial training and amateur improvisation are even less worthwhile, and subsidize resident professional theater on the same principles that the other arts are brought to the campus.

From all the information NTC has received, it appears that the most important problems facing the university theater are: to create a climate on the campus in which the arts, both the performing and the creative, can feel at home and can grow and prosper, side by side with the traditional disciplines—a climate in which the arts are recognized as disciplines of equal merit, complexity, and educational worth to those of the physical and social sciences and the humanities. In addition the university theater must instill in all those working in the dramatic arts an understanding of what the theater is capable of becoming, and an unquenchable zeal to help it reach that goal.

Two measures that might be taken to improve the present situation and make for a healthier and more vital university theater have been suggested:

1. The re-education of academic administrators, faculty, admissions officers, school principals and vocational counselors, parents and students to make them recognize the centrality of the arts in the formation of the Whole Man. This means abolishing the entire concept of the arts, including dramatic arts, as something on the fringe of education and of living, as a luxury instead of a necessity, as an extracurricular activity instead of the mainstream of one's cultural development and a mainstay of our individual and collective sanity.

2. For the university theater to meet its present and future challenge, it must get rid of its too prevalent defensive attitude, and adopt a strong positive stand and outlook. Instead of "theater in education," or merely as "educational theater," it must see theater as education—education for living, for life, for all of life. It must set and maintain the highest possible standards of workmanship in all that it undertakes, and not flinch from severe self-criticism, or from the criticism of others, when it falls short of those standards. Being a school, it has to allow learners to fumble and fail, and help them learn from their failures; but, it must forever teach and practice intolerance of mediocrity. Only in doing this will it deserve the respect and support it is gradually beginning to enjoy.

### *Projections*

Looking ahead, Gregory Falls, director of The University of Washington Theatre and an NTC member, made the following statement for this appraisal:

The future of legitimate theater in this country lies, I believe, in a grassroots movement toward regional theater. True, this has been the cry for many years, and many have attempted and failed. However, I believe in, or at least hope for, a growing recognition by the large state universities that they have a responsibility in being repositories of performing art culture—at the most professional level. The university theater has for some years been a repository and representative theater in terms of plays, but not in terms of real theater. An amateur theater (regardless of the plays produced) is, at best, a secondary kind of theater.

In short, I envision the large American university hiring a truly professional theater company that will serve as a regional theater: producing recent and older plays, and touring them for "seasons" in important population areas in their region. Because these universities are usually state supported, it will be a subsidized theater, but because the support will be channeled through regular university budgets, there will be a cultured and educated buffer between the theater and the government.

The general public feeling that theater is a kind of frill or unimportant (when compared to space research or city planning, etc.) will continue in this country until we have a wider spread of professional theater. It will require a tremendous battle to establish these regional theaters through universities, but once a few are established, others will join the movement quickly. One such theater established and successful is worth a dozen bills through Congress, speeches at ANTA Assemblies, or even lone voices crying in the wilderness!

Another dynamic director, Lewin Goff of the University of Kansas Theatre, had this to say on the subject:

University theaters are filled with eager, imaginative students; are fortunate in having well-equipped physical theaters, excellent libraries, and museums; and have the best of audiences. It seems to me that the logical step is for these universities to align themselves with community groups nearby (and where theater groups do not exist, to start them) and to work toward creating permanent resident companies in these communities. Here, the university graduates will have a ready-made laboratory and eventually an ever-increasing number of positions. . . . The university-established resident professional company is as inevitable as the college football team and will soon rival athletics in importance! I know, because it is happening at Kansas.

The late Campton Bell, former NTC member and director of The University of Denver's theater, made this projection for the present appraisal:

In the next decade, I look and hope for a continued decentralization of the theater in this country, with the university theaters providing the leadership through a closer cooperation with the commercial theater. Since, in the main, the university theaters are our only subsidized theatrical organizations, they have the responsibility of preserving our theatrical heritage, of creating new plays, new forms, and of bringing productions to every segment of American life. I am hopeful that these institutions will make use of professional actors, directors, designers, producers, and producing groups; that they will take the responsibility of assisting in the establishment of professional companies in their regions; and that they will use their staffs, resources, and techniques to make the theater the social and cultural force it should be in our society.

The men just quoted are not starry-eyed dreamers. They represent the highest leadership in Educational Theater today. Like the founders of the movement, they and their peers in other regions of the country are realistic idealists, carrying the key responsibility for bringing their projections to reality, while exposed to the blame that inevitably follows any failure to meet high goals.

### *Land-Grant Institutions*

In an attempt to ascertain to what extent state colleges and universities conduct a statewide or area-wide drama field service, over and above their campus-based dramatic curricula and activities, NTC sent a questionnaire to 69 land-grant institutions and received 53 replies. Of these 53, only 10 indicated that they have any field drama program at all.

Of these 10, 9 employed a total of 17.5 persons; the remaining institution was employing 13. These field drama services go by various names: Off-Campus, Extension, Agricultural-Extension, Dramatic Center, Drama Extension, High School Speech League, Drama Advisory Service, and Wisconsin Idea Theatre. Only four reported that all counties in their state share in a field drama program. The majority of participants in such programs are young persons, usually 4-H Club members.

Many land-grant institutions do conduct workshops on the campus for adult drama leaders, chiefly in acting, directing, stagecraft, and children's theater. In reply to the question: "Do you have a lending library of plays?" 20 replied "yes," 19 "no," and the other 14 respondents were silent. Also, of the 53, 20 conduct an annual drama contest or festival for their region, usually at the high school level. Ten institutions reported that their teaching staff in drama held joint appointments with English and speech. Fourteen groups maintain or contribute service to a conference or association of drama groups in their state, but at least 18 do not.

All in all, the picture obtained from all but a very few of the land-grant colleges and universities reporting, in respect to both field drama service and campus and curricular programs, does not suggest great vitality or imagination.

The largest field drama service reported was that of the Wisconsin Idea Theatre, operated separately by The University of Wisconsin Extension. It employs three full-time and ten part-time staff members, and conducts tours involving two directors and twelve actors. The tours reach into every kind of community, and play many county fairs as well as city locations. Six hundred performances of original musicals and straight drama were presented by or under the sponsorship of the Wisconsin Idea Theatre from 1962 to 1967.

All counties of Wisconsin participate in a rural young person's program which involves approximately 4,000 adults and 10,000 young persons.

About 25 workshops are conducted annually in acting and directing, pageantry, stagecraft, playwriting, costuming, children's theater, and playreading. The University of Wisconsin Extension has a lending library of about 30,000 plays, and the Wisconsin Idea Theatre conducts an annual drama festival for young rural people. An estimated 2,000 plays are produced each year in rural Wisconsin; another 550 in community theater. The Wisconsin Idea Theatre also conducts experimentation and research under a grant from the National Endowment for the Arts, in "Small Communities Arts Development."[8]

Lack of interest and leadership may be the reason why so few land-grant colleges have been dynamically concerned with the promotion of theater activity in their areas. Very often, too, campus theater departments do not share enthusiasm for statewide efforts and may actually discourage the development of any kind of field service.

In qualitative terms, the influence of the Wisconsin Idea Theatre throughout the years has been profound. In all its workshops and training programs the emphasis has always been on excellence. Young people's drama has come out of a doleful self-expression phase into a highly creative activity. The recent proclamation by the Governor of Wisconsin designating the Wisconsin Idea Theatre as the State Theatre of Wisconsin has added strength to the idealism with which it has approached the development of better drama.

### *University-Professional Collaboration*

At various times in this report we have alluded to the need and the potentialities of collaboration between the universities and the profession theater. This collaboration, so earnestly sought by both sides, is now actually taking place, and we may expect to see much more of it in coming years. We can illustrate what is happening by taking a few of the outstanding examples.

On the West Coast, the formation of the Theatre Group, a function of the Extension Division of UCLA (quite distinct from the Theater Arts Department of the University), brought a new dramatic force into the sprawling Los Angeles community. Under the administration of Dr. Abbott Kaplan, directors such as John Houseman have staged fully professional productions of classics and unusual modern dramas with superb professional casts. The subscription for these plays in the first season was a sellout, and only the heavy demands upon the UCLA theater facilities limited the number of performances. In 1967, the Group has been dissociated from the University, has acquired its own quarters, and is known as Center Theatre Group.

Brandeis University in Waltham, Massachusetts, has been developing over the past few years a professional theater company in addition to its undergraduate and graduate programs in dramatic art. In its new Spingold Theater with three available stages for different types of work, Howard Bay, as department head and designer, and Morris Carnovsky, as chief stage director and occasional leading actor, have produced two seasons of major classics, modern dramas, and experimental plays. In the spring of 1967 they gave the world première of Jules Feiffer's first play, *Little Murders.*

Michigan State University at East Lansing has inaugurated a Performing Arts Company to augment the University Theatre's program and to tour the state. The enlarged program provides M.A. and Ph.D. candidates with assistantships in acting, management, and technical theater in connection with the professional company.

For over seven years, the University of Michigan has conducted on its Ann Arbor campus a most successful collaboration with the Association of Producing Artists.[9] APA has produced a 20-week repertory season each year, and in addition to providing professional theater of a very high quality, has participated in a professional fellowship plan. Under this plan, seven fellowships were awarded to outstanding graduating seniors and graduate students at an annual stipend of $3,000 plus an opportunity to work with the professional resident theater.

Ellis Rabb, artistic director of APA, in a letter sent from Ann Arbor in 1963, tells why, from an artistic viewpoint, professionals on the campus are worthwhile:

> The theater has greatly benefited from the movement between campus and professional world. As director and performer, I have experienced the benefits of such association. Prior to the formation of the Association of Producing Artists, I was one of the original members of the Antioch Shakespeare Festival, sponsored by Antioch College in Yellow Springs, Ohio, eventually taking on the responsi-

bilities of artistic director. I was also in residence on the Wellesley College campus, where the Group 20 players had a summer season. After the formation of the APA repertory company, we accepted the invitation of Princeton University to initiate their professional program of theater, and we played on the Princeton campus for two seasons. APA is currently under contract to the University of Michigan in Ann Arbor as its resident company to produce 20-week theater seasons each year. These experiences have led me and my fellow workers to a firm belief in the value of such associations. For while serving audiences of students, faculty, and community, we have served the interests of the administrations of these institutions by giving them the distinction of a successful program. And all the while, we have ourselves grown and learned, becoming ever closer to the fulfillment of the promise of the program. Such patronage of the theater can be the salvation of the art form in this country. . . .

President Harlan Hatcher of the University of Michigan reported to NTC that the affiliation between the APA and the University has been most profitable. He wrote:

The University entered upon this ambitious program as a natural development, not only of its primary educational assignment, but also of the community service role into which many of our great academic institutions are expanding. The small amount of "seed money" not recovered at the box office is as usefully and appropriately expended as the subsidies for our libraries, museums, and laboratories. . . .

In addition to the educational and cultural benefits, there is the stimulus which a continuous professional example provides to the academic, extracurricular and community theater work. These nonprofessionals (and their audiences) learn to expect more of themselves, and also are helped to achieve that higher standard. The excitement created by a continuing series of professional theater events also encourages both "town" and "gown" audiences to larger participation and more knowledgeable appreciation of all theatrical performances.

Finally, on the larger, national scene, we believe a pattern is being established for the return of professional theater regionally on a noncommercial, institutionally supported basis. The best theater workers are anxious to enjoy the artistic rewards of repertory playing, great roles, and resident status; the theater organizations appreciate the new thousands of man-weeks of employment being created at this University alone; and numerous colleagues have sent representatives to the campus to study the operation with a view to creating their own versions, adapted to their situations and needs. Thus, we have the support of both the university and theater worlds.

Perhaps, we have here the way to a true national theater—independent and regional in management, yet sharing the cultural standards and solid administration of the university community. There is no question of public appetite or taste (5 percent of the Ann Arbor population are annual subscribers to the program). The need is to satisfy that appetite with a viable, professional theater related to all the best of "Broadway," but freed of its liabilities, enabled to pursue the ideal of all dedicated theater people.

To achieve these goals, the University of Michigan has developed, under Robert C. Schnitzer, a Professional Theater Program of which the APA collaboration is only a part. The other facets include a high school matinee series, an annual tour of the state, a series of best-of-Broadway tours, and a new play project which is devoted to the preferential production of new scripts in behalf of playwrights. To date one new play has been produced in the project each year, and most of these plays have subsequently gone on to Broadway. The director of this project is Marcella Cisney.

The professional theater program at Princeton University is somewhat different from that at Michigan. At Princeton the philosophy is to provide high quality professional plays as a "library of living theater," for the purpose of training audiences, rather than the training of student actors in the vocational sense.

The Princeton program was initiated in 1960 with the APA, at the McCarter Theatre. This building had been donated to the University, but was previously used on a very limited basis. The University agreed to cover any losses of the initial production of four plays with an upper limit of something less than $60,000. Since more than half of this sum went into the maintenance, overhead, and fixed expenses of the building, the actual production budget for the four plays was a good deal less than that of a Broadway show.

By being very careful about waste, by using a modified "Shakespearean" stage, which could be decorated and converted in various ways, and by expending energy beyond the call of duty, the program directors managed in three years to put the operation in the black.

An unexpected outgrowth of this successful experiment was the playing of special matinees for New Jersey high school students. In one year, over 50,000 public school pupils attended a winter season of dramatic classics performed by professional actors.

### *Apprenticeships and Fellowships*

In the earlier history of the stage, and in many countries of the world today, the traditional method for a young dramatic artist to learn his craft has been by apprenticing himself to one or more master-artists—particularly actors. In Educational Theater's search for means to raise the standards of its performers and its productions, it was natural for it to look to the method of the apprenticeship.

For financial and other reasons, the oldest and most common system used in American colleges involves a large number of "apprentices" working with only one or a few "master-actors" who are employed to coach and to perform as guest stars. At times, this system has worked quite well. Stanford University used it for years, but now has a full professional company. Some of the leading women's colleges—Stephens, Smith, Vassar, among others—have begun employing male actors, usually professional, as assistants in the theater program. Stephens College has recently had as many as six professional actors to assist the undergraduates in producing approximately twelve plays each season. Dartmouth College now offers a summer season of drama produced by the Hopkins Center Repertory Company, which is composed of four professional actors and actresses working with a dozen or so specially selected students from various schools. Such combinations of professionals with amateurs depend for success, of course, upon the individuals involved. Disadvantages may include inadequate rehearsal for the amateurs, unbalanced performances, conflicts of personality between "artistic temperaments" and "the academic mind," even bickering for authority. On the other hand, some disadvantages can be eliminated if the guest artist remains on campus for the season or academic year and functions as a teacher or lecturer, as well as a performer.

A different type of combination has been in use for a good many years at Boston University by the Division of Theatre Arts. This has involved staffing the theater faculty with persons having extensive Broadway experience and connections as directors, designers, choreographers, and so on, besides a leading drama critic and a prominent teacher of dance. Thus the regular staff comprises full-time teacher-artists working with others who may come there to teach or direct a few days a week or a few weeks of the term. The aim is to surround the students —who, for the most part are oriented not toward the liberal arts but rather toward the professional theater—with a distinctly professional environment.

The Yale School of Drama, practically since its founding, has maintained such a professional environment through the many close and constant contacts of its teaching staff with the New York stage. Under the School's new dean, Robert Brustein,[10] the professional climate is being intensified, not only by the addition of famous Broadway names to its faculty, but by the establishment at the University of a full professional acting company. In his first year, Dean Brustein introduced into the Yale Theatre several entire productions of New Theater works from off-Broadway and Off off-Broadway—not without arousing criticism among the older faculty and the community.

A still more radical departure from academic traditions is taking place at New York University, Washington Square, where "a unique school of the arts" is being developed by Robert W. Corrigan, Theodore Hoffman, Monroe Lippman, and others long associated with the *Tulane Drama Review (TDR)* and deeply concerned about the need to regenerate university instruction in theater arts. According to Hoffman's report of an interview with Robert Corrigan, appearing in the *TDR* (Winter 1965):

> Our theater program is unique in that it is not a bastardized paradigm of the liberal arts and in that it assumes from the start what universities are slowly learning about theater. The increasing range of responsibility to the arts that universities have taken on cannot be discharged under one roof. An unpublicized crisis is shaking educational theater. No single drama department, squeezed into the liberal arts structure, can be responsible for research and quality public performance, or turn out artists, scholars, administrators, and teachers. The artist-scholar has proved a fish-fowl who influences neither art nor scholarship. The would-be actor-director who seeks the 'insurance" of teaching certification neither performs nor teaches well. Soon, the fact will strike home that last year unfilled design and technical vacancies outnumbered all the educational theater jobs that were filled in all areas.
>
> But things are changing, and NYU may be only a step ahead of the pack. Resident theaters, on and off campus, are replacing amateur pretentiousness. The specialized "professional" programs in universities have long proved their superiority in training imaginative theater practitioners, and some major schools are edging toward separate "advanced" programs. Smaller schools are spurning the catch-all curriculum for concentrated experiment; the real educational theater innovations may come from Bennington, Pomona, Immaculate Heart, Evansville, Alberta, Calgary, Toledo, Webster Grove. We may soon see graduate programs that relate scholarship to theater without debilitating production work, and produce publishable articles and even dissertations.
>
> NYU will assume its responsibilities in theater through a variety of programs and projects, large and small, permanent and *ad hoc*, within and without the school. Administratively, we have a School of Arts, with enough resident faculty to award BFA and MFA degrees. Attached to it are a series of institutes in visual arts, design, probably film and television, and the performing arts, where the theater program ties in. . . .
>
> At the "institute" level, we will inaugurate and cooperate in needed research and pilot projects, especially in scene design and technology, primary and secondary school drama teaching, theater history, and social psychology. We want to work with educational theater in providing advanced professional training and experience for younger teachers. We want to provide resident theater with assistance in personnel recruitment, in testing original plays and

> translations, in establishing "intern" programs. Eventually, we hope to offer studio production facilities to experimental dance and theater groups. As a public service, the program will offer lectures, forums, and seminars in theater, establish necessary publications, and serve as a center to bring European artists, critics, and scholars to America. . . .

Among other points made in Hoffman's challenging article is that "our most important obligation is to do something about the biggest gap in American theater, the middle level of training and experience of which qualified young practitioners between 21 and 30 are almost completely deprived. . . ." The result is NYU's plans for extensive apprenticeship for actors in a professional company, and an even larger project for training in design and technical work under "Master Teachers."

A somewhat different way of training young people for professional theater is the approach developed by Wayne State University.

In January 1964, a repertory theater in a university setting was launched at Wayne State, located in downtown Detroit. Calling itself the Classic Repertory Theatre Company, it started with the performance of four Shakespearean plays in a 20-week program.

The company was composed of 34 students from 11 states, lured by teaching and semi-professional fellowships of between $1,000 and $2,600. Its executive director is NTC member Leonard Leone. Wayne State spent $335,000 to buy and convert an old church into a "classic" theater seating 515. The facility contains a multilevel open stage and an unusual ramp that circles from the ends of the stage around behind the audience to permit actors to work in dimensions before untried. The aim of the new repertory theater is "to keep alive for our students as well as the general public, the great plays of our past, and to provide an advanced training program for outstanding acting talent. . . ." Chiefly, the idea is "professional training without a professional company." In addition, Wayne State's Theatre Department runs the general University Theatre—at the 1,100-seat Bonstelle, in the downtown area—with a popular repertory, playing to 92 percent capacity. Taking its two theater operations together, Wayne State is not only giving its students a combination of professional training with a liberal education, it is also furnishing a wide variety of good theater to its large student body (about 32,000 in 1966), to high school audiences, and to Detroit's playgoing citizens.

Among other large institutions offering graduate fellowships for professional theater practice along with intensive training is Indiana University. Under the direction of NTC member Richard Moody, the department operates no less than three theaters: the Indiana Theatre

Company, which uses graduate actors and gives performances on tours of the state as well as on the Bloomington Campus; the Brown County Playhouse; and a Showboat theater on the Ohio River in the summer.

A very distinctive fellowship program has been developed at Minneapolis through a liaison between the University of Minnesota and the Tyrone Guthrie Theatre, with the financial support of a local industrialist, Mr. William L. McKnight. The McKnight Fellowships permit outstanding young artist-scholars to spend the first half-year in graduate studies at the University, and the second half-year and the summer working as interns at the Guthrie Theatre. A summer theater symposium also involves professionals from the Guthrie repertory company, who are in residence from May to November.

NTC member Frank M. Whiting, director of the University of Minnesota Theatre, views these developments as significant "bridges" between the University and the professional theater:

> It will be a great day for America if the best features of a great university (respectability, deep roots, and permanence) rub off on the theater, while the best features of the great theater (imagination, excitement, and its insatiable dream of perfection) rub off on the University.

Whiting also writes:

> The present-day trend toward professionalization is being realized in three major ways: (1) many college amateurs are evolving toward professional status; (2) some college theaters are adding guest stars to their ranks; and (3) some theater departments are fostering the establishment of full-fledged professional companies.

But for lack of space, the present NTC report would have included descriptions of a dozen or more other examples of fruitful collaboration between universities and the professional theater: at Washington, Dallas, Seattle, San Francisco, to cite but a few. In each case, the established institution is feeling its way, experimenting with the kinds of cooperation that seem most feasible and that prove most beneficial to all the parties concerned.

### *Inter-Theater Communication*

One of the problems arising from the growing trend toward educational-professional collaboration is the problem of communication. The Ford Foundation, dynamically interested in the improvement of theater in the United States, established in 1961 the Theatre Communications Group (TCG), with a central office and director in New York City. TCG exists specifically to facilitate a continual exchange of information among the permanent professional resident theaters, and between them and the university theaters that are becoming professionalized.

As we saw with community theaters, there is a similar tendency among professional resident theaters to work wholly independently, in a sort of vacuum; and, in addition to this tendency, there is a long tradition of total separation between theater professionals and educators. To close these gaps, to explore and exploit the advantages of intercommunication, and to raise the quality of both educational and professional theater, TCG was created. Among its other services it provides funds permitting theater directors to visit and observe the operation of other theaters associated in the Group; it conducts annual national auditions (in Chicago and other centers) for actors seeking employment in nonprofit theaters; and it serves as a clearinghouse for all relevant information.

Inter-theater communication was also established in February and May of 1966, when two important developmental conferences took place in Minneapolis under the sponsorship of the U.S. Office of Education. Lasting about five days each, the conferences brought together 20 of the American theater's leading educators and 20 of its leading professional practitioners, besides a small number of observers from major foundations, the press, and the government. The overall purpose was to foster mutually beneficial relations between the professional and the academic theater, with particular emphasis on improving actor education and training. As a full account of these conferences on "Relationships Between Educational Theatre and Professional Theatre" has been published in a special issue of the *Educational Theatre Journal* (November 1966), no more will be said of it here. Instead, we quote a statement made by Frank Whiting, one of the conference hosts and participants, summarizing the values inherent in the current movement:

> From a national standpoint, the most promising feature of the movement lies not so much in the interrelationship of professional theaters with colleges and universities, as in the fact that such a relationship is forcing the long awaited decentralization of Broadway. Perhaps, most important of all, these new theaters are being established on a cultural nonprofit basis rather than on the gambler's nightmare of showbusiness. The financial foundation of the Tyrone Guthrie Theatre, for example, resembles that of a symphony orchestra, rather than that of a Broadway musical.
>
> Viewing academic and professional theater in perspective, we discover a curious evolution. Roughly speaking, until the 1920's, the American theater was a professional theater without amateur roots. After the 1920's, it quite suddenly changed to an amateur theater with no place to go. Maybe a sane balance is finally beginning to emerge. Maybe the best of the 17,000 students now majoring in

theater will find a professional future; maybe professional companies will find themselves able to recruit a far higher quality of new talent than was hitherto possible.

We should remember, however, that systems are only servants. On either a professional or amateur level, any system will succeed or fail largely on a basis of the artistry, integrity, and dedication of those who operate it. And let me repeat that the final test of good theater lies neither in professional standing nor amateur standing, neither in this system nor that system, but in the depth and quality of the theatrical experience which a given performance induces in the minds and hearts of the human beings who make up the audience. All else is a means to this end. The greatest problem and greatest glory of the living theater is that the human factors can never be ignored.

## *Professionalization of Theater Activities*

Mergers with existing professional companies, the creation of new companies, or total revamping of academic curricula in theater arts are devices not feasible in every university situation, no matter how much professional standards may be desired. Since, along with systematic training, students in theater arts need both intensive and extensive practice, various ways to achieve this have emerged over the years. The most familiar include summer theaters, Shakespeare and other festivals, touring troupes, showboats, outdoor drama, and other kinds of programs involving professionals with non- or semiprofessionals.

Summer theaters sponsored or operated by colleges and universities are far too numerous to name here. Some of these use their campus facilities, but mount a six to twelve-week season of shows not usually performed during the academic year. These may be musicals and light comedies, Greek and Elizabethan classics, avant-garde and experimental plays, or first productions of new plays in collaboration with the authors. Some of the college summer theaters operate in vacation resorts, using such theatrical facilities as can be found, improvised, or remodeled. There, the bill of fare is apt to be "light summer stuff," and the quality of performance often far from professional. A number of colleges and universities offer productions by visiting professional or semiprofessional groups, such as those of John D. Mitchell's Institute for Advanced Studies in Theatre Arts (IASTA), which moves from New York City to the University of Denver for the summer months. Successful Shakespeare Festivals have grown up around the country, either sponsored by colleges or manned by companies recruited largely from colleges and universities. Antioch College had one of the first of these; others are located at San Diego, at Ashland, Oregon, and—in the form of a Shakespeare Institute—at the University of Bridgeport, Connecticut. Showboat theaters, another type of summer theater, are operated by the drama departments of Indiana University (on the Ohio River), the University of Washington at Seattle, and the University of Minnesota. The boats, old side- or stern-wheelers, formerly moved downriver, but now, because of costs and river regulations, they rest at dockside. With the entire company in costume, they entertain their audiences with old melodramas, romantic dramas, and comedies. A quite different type of atmosphere surrounds the performances at the little, gem-like Asola Theatre. Situated on the Ringling estate at Sarasota, and run by the theater department of Florida A. and M. University, it offers a perfect setting for elegant plays of earlier centuries. In still another kind of environment, the Tufts Arena Theater, at Medford, Massachusetts, has carried on annually since 1943 a high quality university summer season, usually including both classics and tryouts of new scripts.

A few university touring groups are evolving toward professional status. A program of the Catholic University of America, called Players Incorporated, is one example. In another context entirely, the Wisconsin Idea Theatre, mentioned earlier, paid 30 actors some $30,000 for the summer of 1966 to tour the state, taking plays to rural communities that otherwise saw no live drama.

The varieties of educational theater activities by which advanced students obtain practical stage experience of an intensive kind are, indeed, numberless.

One particular variety deserves special mention: Outdoor Drama. In its modern sense, this term refers to the presentation of open-air, panoramic historical dramas. It is a movement stemming mainly from the creative mind of the dramatist Paul Green at the University of North Carolina, where the movement is still centered. Green's "symphonic drama," *The Lost Colony,* has been staged each summer since 1937 at the specially built Waterside Amphitheatre on Roanoke Island, North Carolina. Its success has begotten many others, including *The Common Glory* (Williamsburg, Virginia), also by Green; *Texas* (Canyon, Texas); *The Stephen Foster Story* (Bardstown, Kentucky); *Unto These Hills* (Cherokee, North Carolina), etc. *Unto These Hills,* one of two dozen such historical pageants written by Kermit Hunter, is about the Cherokee tribe; it has been notably successful, bringing prosperity to an entire community. Actors and staff in Outdoor Drama are paid, though not always at Equity rates. Important for most of them is the fact that, through daily performances throughout the summer, they gain invaluable experience of a professional character.

Like other sectors of the Educational Theater, college and university theaters have national and regional affiliations open to all in AETA and the various sectional conferences. Some are united also in national dramatic fraternities such as Theta Alpha Phi, which has about 50 campus chapters in 25 states, and publishes a magazine, *The Cue*. In addition, various drama festivals are held which bring together in one place specimens of the best undergraduate productions under the sponsorship of the host institution. Thus, the Yale University Dramatic Association's annual Festival of Undergraduate Drama, initiated in 1956, draws college players and directors from near and far for two days of intensive performance, criticism, and discussion.

The University of Kansas Theatre, under the direction of Lewin Goff, has developed a notable means of giving its students a professional type of experience while serving different segments of the larger community. In addition to the regular production of plays, the Kansas Theatre stages a Drama Symposium for participants from all over the state. A director-loan program is aimed at helping to create at least one new Kansas community theater each year. Goff's players even perform occasionally at the Federal penitentiary, Leavenworth, and a campus workshop is attended by theater representatives from 16 communities.

The University of Kansas, responding to the growth of the resident professional companies, has concerned itself with specialized training for selected and qualified students in preparation for professional work. These students benefit from constant community exposure and training.

Inasmuch as the NTC Appraisal started in 1962 and covers such a wide area of activities, and inasmuch as new programs and changes have been continuously evolving throughout the country, this report cannot pretend to be all-inclusive. In Educational Theater alone, activity is so dynamic that we can only suggest the extent and variety of this rapid evolution. Thus, a most promising future annual event (Spring 1969) is the American College Theater Festival at the J. F. Kennedy Center for the Performing Arts in Washington, D.C.

## High School Drama

NTC believes that the situation regarding high school drama, while still far from ideal, has definitely improved since 1945. In 1945, the class play was often produced to raise money for some worthy cause and extracurricular dramatic clubs were the sole pattern in most high schools of the nation. There was a general apathy in a community's families toward theater in high school, except when one of the children from a family was in the annual class play; and when people did attend a production, they expected only the most popular offerings, ex-Broadway light comedies, melodramatic mysteries, or inane and innocuous plays such as *Tommy's First Tux*.

It is estimated that less than 2 percent of the high schools of the nation had full-time drama teachers in 1945. Most high school directors were teachers of English or other subjects who were assigned to coach the play.

There were some exceptions, and these few interested and qualified teachers began to push for better production and a healthier attitude toward theater in the high school as a meaningful and worthwhile educational process. The first organizations for teachers in the field were the Secondary School Theatre Conference of AETA and the National Catholic Theatre Conference, which helped teachers to work for higher production standards.

The National Thespian Society, primarily a student organization, provides another kind of link between efforts in high school theater. Mr. Leon C. Miller, executive secretary-treasurer of this organization, reported to NTC in January 1967, as follows:

> The level of drama directors and instruction is definitely improving in our high schools. School administrations are slowly beginning to recognize that the high school theater program is not merely a money-raising project (a frill), but a real contribution to the educational growth of those who welcome participation in the offered theater program. Secondly, there are more qualified teachers (drama directors) in high schools today, and these teachers are being recognized for their superior work.

The Thespian Society reports its own growth as evidence of the growing theater interest. In 1951, the Society had approximately 1,100 affiliated schools with an estimated student membership of 16,500. By June of 1967, it hoped to pass the 3,000 school membership mark with an estimated student membership of 50,000. The Society also estimates that there are about 15,000 schools not affiliated.

A summary of the 1965–66 Thespian season indicates, also, a considerable change in the play bills undertaken by these member high schools. Of the 2,891 Thespian affiliated schools (1,778 submitted an Annual Report), 3,566 full-length productions were reported. The ten most frequently produced major productions were: *The Mouse That Roared* (113), *Our Town* (98), *Arsenic and Old Lace* (77), *You Can't Take It With You* (68), *The Miracle Worker* (64), *The Diary of Anne Frank* (60), *The Night of January 16th* (60), *The Curious Savage* (57), *The Sound of Music* (47), and *The Tea House of the August Moon* (45).

In the view of Leon Miller, the "weakest links in our high school theater chain are the isolated rural high school, sometimes the consolidated school, where theater is nearly impossible because of the necessary use of buses, making after-school hours non-available, and the lack of adequate auditoriums, little theaters, scenery and lighting."

His suggestions for improving the picture are summarized here:

1. Unite efforts to improve drama programs on television, where theater makes its first impression.

2. Cooperate with the colleges and universities in each state to establish high school theater as a primary curriculum course, not secondary to speech and English.

3. Continue to prepare teachers to be good directors of high school plays. Separate the mentally and physically unfit from those who qualify.

4. Extend invitations from college and university productions to high schools within a 50-mile radius, with reduced ticket rates.

5. Exchange tickets between high schools themselves.

The only clouds I see on the horizon are financial. If school bond issues are defeated and cut-backs required to meet limited budgeting, high school theater may suffer. There is only one answer: we must convince school VIP's that a theater program is just as important as any other.

A primary goal of theater educators is the establishment of theater study as an integral part of the secondary school curriculum. Many theater educators believe that the solid values of theater in education will never be reached until this takes place. Identification of theater as a separate art form with special benefits, and its establishment in the curriculum free from involvement in other subject matter are the main objectives of secondary school theater education organizations.

Miller wrote NTC:

High School theater education has accomplished the improvement of content in its courses, so that actual theater values have come to the fore, and the classes are more than training grounds for production. Since the theater is the one art in which the medium and the final result is man himself, the understanding of oneself and of one's relations to others through the art of theater could make it a way for man to retain equilibrium in a more and more automated society.

Another strong organization in the development of theater at the high school level is the National Catholic Theatre Conference, formed in 1945. It counts a membership of 6,000 and, in qualitative terms, has developed an alert, progressive, and dedicated force. The Conference conducts workshops, festivals, and contests on a regional basis, plus an annual convention. A conference official assures NTC: "The programs of these events are challenging and fresh: the classics, avant-garde, originals and modern drama line up side by side. Critic judges are seldom embarrassed with the tawdry teen-age play of two decades ago."

Not only do drama directors in secondary schools work within established institutions, whether public or private, secular or parochial; they are also professionally grouped by themselves in national, regional, and state associations or conferences. Besides the National Catholic Theatre Conference with its Secondary School Division, the American Educational Theatre Association (AETA) has a special division known as the Secondary School Theatre Conference (SSTC), many of whose members also belong to the National Thespian Society. Regional conferences, likewise, have divisions devoted exclusively to the particular problems of theater in the secondary schools.

In many of the states and regions, moreover, annual drama festivals are held in which casts and crews from participating schools present short plays or cuttings of longer works. Such festivals generally operate much in the manner of debate tournaments: casts from neighboring towns first compete for a chance to perform in a state festival (frequently sponsored by a prominent newspaper, the Junior Chamber of Commerce, a businessmen's club, or a state Arts Council); then the state winners take their plays to an inter-state festival, and eventually, perhaps, to the National Thespian Conference. These contests and meetings afford excellent opportunities for high school students as well as their teacher-directors to exchange ideas, compare their work, and stimulate one another to better procedures and higher standards. To an outsider, all this activity may seem sheer busyness; but those who organize or judge such competitions know that this system brings out more and better-trained performers every year, and just as important, an ever-higher quality of plays are performed, despite an inevitable tendency toward conformity.

In spite of all the gains mentioned, however, many high schools, both parochial and public, are not theater-conscious. Too many schools, following a misinterpretation of James B. Conant's attack on the public school system, have jettisoned the fine arts as a frill. Too many guidance counselors and departments neglect the humanities and the integrated man, and regard theater study, particularly, as an extra. Furthermore, college admissions policies reinforce the pressures which deter talented students from seeking a career in theater. Every year some of the most talented applicants in the arts, including theater, are rejected because the College Board and other admissions tests fail to cover the subjects and qualifications in which the applicants are strongest.

While the picture of drama in the high school is healthier and stronger than it was in 1945, the colors are far from rosy.

## Children's Theater

Léon Chancerel of France, world-famous organizer of theater for young people (Children's Theater), spoke for perhaps the most dedicated group of theater folk in America when he wrote:

> There is in children a thirst for the wonderful—even more, a need of laughter and emotion and beauty. It must be fulfilled. Children who do not laugh become disillusioned men. Those whose hearts are not touched become men with hearts of stone. It is not to men that it is necessary to teach love, but to children.

Such teaching should, of course, be a function of the family, the church, the school through everyday contact with the young. It is also a chief function of the arts, and in particular the theater in its educative capacity.

The trouble is that it seldom begins early enough and the process is intermittent, not constant. Americans still tend to think of the arts as a luxury, as something for the few, the specially gifted, and not as a daily necessity for all. Consequently, our democratic society continues to relegate the arts to the periphery of its existence, to its idle hours, to the expendable fringes of its school curricula, and even there in late and broken segments. The National Council of the Arts in Education,[12] in its 1966 conference on "Education and the Expanding Arts," found unanimous agreement on the proposition "That education in the arts is necessary to develop the natural creative talents of all young people; that it has been neglected especially in the public schools; and that this education should start at the bottom—the elementary school, or even before—and not at the top." Drama is one of the arts it found most gravely neglected.

Recognizing that the chief victims of such neglect are the young—and the adults they grow up to become—a small group of intrepid pioneers, mostly women, started the Children's Theater movement in the United States. This movement has grown in volume, in momentum, in geographical extent, and in the variety of its forms, functions, and practicing groups. The present NTC report can undertake only a broad picture of this remarkable development.

Live drama for children falls into two main categories: Children's Theater and Creative Dramatics. In Children's Theater, dramatic works are presented by living actors for child audiences. The players may be adults, children, or both; their primary obligation is to the young audience. Creative Dramatics, on the other hand, is concerned essentially with the participants: children, under the guidance of an imaginative teacher or leader, create scenes or short plays and improvise characters, action, and dialogue. No audience is present as a rule, and no obligation to one is implied. The first requires devotion to the performance of a theatrical work of art; the second is chiefly an educational or therapeutic tool and an imagination-stimulater in the creative life of the child.

Mark Twain described Children's Theater as one of the very, very great inventions of the 20th century. When one considers its proliferation, its variety, and its refinement over the past 60 or 70 years, one is compelled to agree.

A few independent "progressive" schools were experimenting as early as the mid-1890's with a new pedagogical philosophy embracing the performing arts and dramatic play, as opposed to the notion that school is "just a place in which to learn lessons and acquire skills." But Children's Theater had its practical beginnings in this country not in elementary public school programs but in big city settlement houses. The Educational Theatre Alliance in New York and Hull House in Chicago were among the social agencies that initiated the movement in the early 1900's. Their leaders saw in the practice of dramatic arts a valuable means of teaching American ways and social communication to children in their slum communities. Settlement house directors in these and other cities soon took up the idea and developed formal theater programs. Lillian Wald's Henry Street Settlement House, Alice and Irene Lewisohn's Neighborhood Playhouse, and Franklin Sargent's Children's Theatre, in New York; Hettie Greenleaf's Children's Theatre, the Peabody Playhouse, and Roxbury House, in Boston; the House of Play in Washington; Karamu in Cleveland; the Community Theatre in Duluth—these were among the early centers applying dramatic arts to the purpose of social assimilation among children from many ethnic groups.

Civic and cultural organizations gave the movement its second impetus, toward art. The Drama League of America, for example, through productions of plays for children, sustained and advanced the effort in the direction of artistic appreciation. In some cities, such as Columbus, Ohio, in 1916, the Drama League was aided by public recreation commissions, boards of education, and chambers of commerce in establishing permanent children's theaters. The Association of Junior Leagues of America has given massive and continuous support to the movement since 1921, through the sponsorship and production of plays by its many local Leagues, through sponsored courses in theater with children (creative dramatics), through the leadership supplied nationally by its Children's Theatre Consultant and locally by League volunteers. In 1925 the Art Institute of Chicago set up the Goodman Theatre for Children.

Private theater companies and schools began spreading the concept of fine drama finely performed, not only in their home communities but all across the country by touring troupes. Stuart Walker's Portmanteau Theatre, an outgrowth in 1915 of the Christadora Settlement House in New York, was a veritable Johnny Appleseed of theater art. The King–Coit School of Acting and Design, founded in New York in 1923, took pupils from the age of five, taught them to dramatize stories, develop and envelop them visually, then produce them locally and on extensive tours. Clare Tree Major's professional theater for children, working in association with teachers of English, superbly played to countless audiences of American children from 1922 to 1954. Other professional children's theaters did likewise: Dorothy Gordon's, Adrienne Morrison's, Dorothy McFadden's, the Junior Programs, Inc., Grace Price Productions, the American Children's Theatre in New York, and Eva LeGallienne's Civic Repertory Theatre (notably with its famous production of *Alice in Wonderland*), to mention but a few.

Along with professional theater schools, drama departments in colleges and universities began in the 1920's to produce plays for children and to offer courses in children's theater and creative dramatics. Besides the Goodman School of the Theatre in Chicago, an especially noteworthy development was begun at Northwestern University: under its supervision, creative dramatics was taught in the lower elementary grades of Evanston schools. Numbers of high schools—even junior high schools—began producing plays for children. Children's Theater began to develop like the two sides of a coin: on the one side, theater *for* children; on the other, creative dramatics. In its efforts it enlisted many other civic and cultural agencies: the Child Study Association, the National Music League, museums of fine arts and of natural history, recreation associations, and so on.

Recreation departments introduced Children's Theater into their own programs. The most widely recognized municipal children's theater is that founded at Palo Alto, California, in 1932. Religious drama gained recognition in youth church programs and seminary curricula. It found uses for children's and young people's theater that had been unknown, not to say disdained, in former years. Creative dramatics was employed for older teen-agers, to bridge the gap between early and late adolescence, and to reduce the risks of juvenile delinquency. Dramatic programs, including instruction, became a regular feature of summer camps. Thus, at mid-century, Children's Theater presented a kaleidoscope of activity. Directing this activity were professionals and volunteers, recreation and religious leaders, high school teachers and university professors.

One of the greatest forces in charting the course of the children's theater movement in the second half of the 20th century has been the

Children's Theatre Conference. CTC was founded at Northwestern University in 1944 by Winifred Ward, Professor of Creative Drama at Northwestern and Director of the Evanston Children's Theatre. At the organizational meeting, it was decided that the children's theater should function as a committee of AETA, and in 1951 this committee became AETA's first Division.

Much experimentation with Creative Dramatics went on during the 1950's. University courses and classes in the subject increased, and trained graduates found jobs awaiting them in public and private schools. Authorities in education encouraged its use in teaching language arts and social studies. Earlier pedagogical theories about the role of playmaking in the growing child were dusted off, brought up to date, and made a part of teacher-training, to be applied eventually in public schools.

Theater *for* children likewise expanded in the 1950's. Numbers of university and community theaters added children's theater productions to their regular series. New professional companies were formed and extended the area of their tours. The number of Junior Leagues active either as sponsors or producers reached its height in this decade. In 1954 a second publishing company, the Coach House Press, joined the Children's Theatre Press, founded in 1936, in exclusive publication of children's plays. Standards in scripts are a constant concern of CTC; the demand for more and better children's plays mounts each year, and with it the number of playwriting contests and the effort to induce professional dramatists to look to this lucrative field. Also, since professional theater for children is a long-established tradition in Britain and Europe, CTC has been extending its horizons and contacts abroad through the International Children's Theatre Committee, first appointed in 1951. During the following decade, representatives of CTC took part in youth conferences sponsored by the International Theatre Institute.

Today, the parallel lines of theater *for* and theater *with* children are becoming more clearly defined. Theater for children is becoming more professional in character; informal drama (creative dramatics) shows a trend toward becoming drama education rather than child development.

The professional trend in theater for children is evident in both commercial and civic theater. The number of professional children's theater companies in New York alone has more than doubled in the last five years. The producers of these companies are taking an active part in Region XIV of CTC;[13] many accept responsibilities in national children's theater councils. Participation of CTC representatives in the recently formed international children's theater organization—International

Association of Theatre for Young People (ASSITEJ)— is influencing this trend toward professional productions. ASSITEJ has no counterpart for our informal theater *with* children. Children's Theater in Europe is almost completely a professional theater. Local productions here are becoming more professional in character. An increasing number of civic children's theaters are employing full-time directors. At the August 1966 CTC Annual Meeting, a panel composed of one director and two members of boards employing directors discussed duties, responsibilities, and salaries of full-time directors. A new vocation, director of civic children's theater, seems definitely in the making.

At present a survey is being conducted in colleges and universities to learn what children's plays are being produced and what courses are being offered.[14] If college and university representation at CTC meetings is an indication of the amount of activity in these institutions, however, there has been no significant change during this decade. This is another area of concern.

It should be noted that the trend toward professionalism has been accompanied by a decline in volunteer productions. One example of this is the reduced number of Junior Leagues having children's theater projects today as compared with ten years ago. Paid jobs are on the increase.

The objective of creative dramatics and its place in the curriculum and in community programs is undergoing careful examination. There is a developing interest in drama education comparable to art and music education, and, with drama, the related art of the dance. Creative Dramatics, both as a technique of teaching other subjects and as a means of child development, is being critically assessed. In community agencies, such as the Scouts, the emphasis seems to be now on cultural rather than psychological and social development. A study committee appointed by CTC is at present charged with defining the problem and with exploring the relation of child drama to the language arts. A long-term consideration is the development of a spiral curriculum for drama in the elementary schools.

The first half-century was a period of ebullient growth and development for Children's Theater. In the 1960's, this lusty infant of the 20th century is undergoing self-appraisal and close critical study. One seasoned director, stepping aside from his accustomed work, finds several flaws in the picture:

> Children's Theater in America has not begun to sense its own might, its own potential for altering the theatrical axis of the country, because it has not probed deeply enough into the peculiar nature of the child who comes to see the play; nor has it articulated fully

enough the transcendent objectives of putting on the play in the first place. In other words, Children's Theater has not yet assumed a major role in the formulation and pursuit of American cultural aspirations.

Certainly the theater can exert more influence than tableaux-ridden, superciliously moral, and grossly cute child drama would suggest. Yet for all its patronizing and conscientious airs, adult society has underrated the natural compatibility that exists between children and the theater, and has thus denied itself a potent instrument for inculcating firm and lasting cultural ideals. If it is important that society transmit messages relating to moral standards, to racial myth or national lore, let the messages be transmitted joyously. Let a genuine communion take place: if the child naturally turns to movement, color, dream, mimicry, fantasy, symbol, and conflict as unconscious devices to bring about a resolution of the raw and vital impulses that swirl through him; and if the theater naturally employs —as it must—movement, color, dream, mimicry, fantasy, symbol, and conflict as conscious devices to bring about a resolution of artistic problems, let the theater's methods of resolving a human crisis be fully applied, in an exemplary manner, to the unformed impulses of the child. Not to squelch these impulses, but to refine and dignify them.

So what have "kiddies' shows" got to do with the American theater? No conception of an American theater can be formulated until it begins at the beginning. There is no beginning better than children.[15]

Another experienced director, Art Cole, NTC member, Midland, Texas, lays it even harder on the line:

We have too long put children's theater on the shelf. It is absolutely essential that good live theater become warp and woof of every child's life if he is ever to have an appetite for theater and some demand for standards.

In America we have continually made the idiotic assumption that when one reaches 21 he will be struck by lightning, or pass over a magic line, or that some other magic transformation will turn him into a theater addict with a demanding taste for the best in theater.

When this doesn't happen (it never has and it never will), we bemoan the sad state of the Broadway theater. Broadway theater is exactly what grown-up children have made it.

We must have more and better theater for the young. Whose job is it? It is everyone's job. Theater for the young must become a part of the planning and programming of every community.

# IV. IN COMMUNITIES - THE PROFESSIONAL

# In Communities - The Professional

IN ADDITION TO the broad categories of Commercial, Community, and Educational Theater, there is another major sector of theater activity in the United States. This fourth sector is primarily professional in nature and operation, and includes the professional resident theaters, touring companies, summer stock, and a few other professional activities.

## Professional Resident Theaters

NTC recognizes the Professional Resident Theater movement as the newest and most promising development on the American theater scene. Variously called resident professional, regional repertory, permanent professional, or just repertory or regional, the movement expresses the long looked for trend away from Broadway and toward decentralization, away from the commercial one-shot, "show biz" complex and toward permanent establishments where the finest drama can find a home.

These professional companies differ from the commercial productions of Broadway and off-Broadway in at least two respects: (1) instead of being set up for the production of a single show and then dissolved at the end of its run, they are organized for continuity of management, of artistic policy and, in the main, of performing and technical personnel, playing extended seasons of 20 weeks or more; (2) they are, almost entirely, incorporated as independent, nonprofit organizations. While they may aim to be self-supporting, they are not tied fast to the profit-making goal essential to commercial theater.

The movement differs from Community Theater, too, in several ways. While serving the communities in which they live, these companies usually draw their top personnel, namely, managers, directors, designers, technicians, and actors from elsewhere—although they may find suitable talent locally and train it, when necessary, in their own theaters. Also, the companies are all professionally oriented, mostly professionally trained, and engaged on professional terms—though not necessarily at full union rates. In promotion, ticket-selling, ushering, and other functions, they frequently benefit from volunteer help, but their basic staffs and acting companies are all involved in producing good theater as a vocation, rather than as an avocation or for fun.

The movement differs from Educational Theater in that its primary aim is not to provide a formal broad education or a training ground for students, but to produce plays—in the best seasonal repertoire possible—and to provide a fully-achieved milieu toward which students may aspire, and where, occasionally, they may gain professional apprenticeship.

NTC has a special interest in this movement, having dedicated itself from the beginning to the decentralization of theater in the United States. Already in the present report, in discussing the APA-Phoenix Repertory Company, the Lincoln Center Repertory Company, and the Actor's Studio Theatre, we have cited three decentralized theaters in Manhattan. The others, across the country, are extensions of the same effort.

Not all the regional theaters are nonprofit. In the 1964–65 list of permanent professional theaters appended to the Rockefeller Panel Report on *The Performing Arts,* 19 of the 55 theaters mentioned are noted as commercial. In the same list, two theaters are designated as nonprofessional, but are included "because they have continuity of management and professional direction." Not all, moreover, are, operationally, repertory theaters, (including several which, like the Lincoln Center Repertory Company, use that word in their name), in the sense of producing several different plays concurrently and offering a change of bill two or three times a week during a season. But most of them have certain goals in common, which set them apart from the categories already described and which make them a part of what we have called a movement.

### *Origins*

This movement, in its present manifestation, is really less than 20 years old. Only an even dozen of today's resident professional theaters existed in 1950. These were:

- Alley Theatre, Houston
- Arena Stage, Washington, D.C.
- Barter Theatre, Abingdon, Virginia
- Cleveland Play House
- Erie Playhouse, Erie, Pennsylvania
- Goodman Memorial Theatre, Chicago
- Mummers Theatre, Oklahoma City
- Old Globe Theatre, San Diego
- Old Log Theatre, St. Paul, Minnesota
- Pasadena Playhouse
- Phoenix Theatre, New York City
- Pittsburgh Playhouse

By 1960, these theaters had been joined by eleven more:

- Actor's Workshop, San Francisco
- American Shakespeare Festival Theatre and Academy, Stratford, Connecticut
- Charles Playhouse, Boston
- Circle in the Square, New York
- Dallas Theater Center, Texas
- Fred Miller Theatre, now, Milwaukee Repertory Theatre
- Front Street Theatre, Memphis
- Institute for Advanced Studies in Theatre Arts (IASTA), New York
- La Jolla Playhouse, San Diego
- New York Shakespeare Festival
- Theatre Group (UCLA), now Center Theatre Group, Los Angeles

In 1960, several more theater groups began operation:

- Association of Producing Artists (APA), based at the Phoenix in New York, but playing several months of the year at Ann Arbor
- McCarter Theatre, Princeton University (host to resident companies)
- Playhouse in the Park, Cincinnati
- Professional Theatre Program, University of Michigan (host to resident companies)
- Vanguard Theatre, Detroit (disbanded)

Today, we have, depending on classification, some 39 more resident professional theaters:

Actors Studio Theatre, New York
Actors Theatre of Louisville
American Conservatory Theatre, San Francisco and elsewhere
Arena House, Harrisburg Pennsylvania
Arizona Repertory Theater, Phoenix
Asbury Park Playhouse, New Jersey
Center Stage, Baltimore
Eagles Mere Playhouse, Chicago
Free Southern Theatre, New Orleans
Hartford Stage Company, Connecticut
Hawaii Repertory Theatre, Honolulu
Inner City Repertory Company, Los Angeles
John Fernald Company, Rochester, Michigan
Kansas Circle Theatre, Kansas City, Missouri
Lakewood Civic Theatre, Ohio
Long Wharf Theatre, New Haven
Magnolia Theatre, Long Beach, California
Millan Players, Detroit
Morris Theatre, Morristown, New Jersey
National Repertory Theatre Foundation, (touring, but based in New York)
Negro Ensemble Company, New York City
Peterborough Players, New Hampshire
Pocket Theatre, Atlanta, Georgia
Repertory Theatre, New Orleans
Repertory Theatre of Lincoln Center, New York
Repertory Theatre of Loretto–Hilton Center, St. Louis, Missouri
Seattle Repertory Theatre
Stanford Repertory Theatre, California
Studio Arena Theatre, Buffalo
Syracuse Repertory Theatre, Syracuse, New York
Theatre Atlanta, Georgia
Theatre Company of Boston
Theatre East, Rochester, New York
Theatre of the Living Arts, Philadelphia
Theatre St. Paul, Minnesota
Trinity Square Players, Providence, Rhode Island
Tyrone Guthrie Theatre, Minneapolis
Virginia Museum Theatre, Richmond, Virginia
Washington Theatre Club, Washington, D. C.

Like the Theatre Guild, which grew out of the old Washington Square Players in 1919, several of the metropolitan resident theaters listed above evolved out of off-Broadway groups or status. The Circle in the Square was formerly (1951) known as the Loft Players. The Phoenix Theatre, in its early commercial phase, was considered as off-Broadway, and the National Repertory Theatre was organized in 1961 by the Phoenix to perform its work beyond New York.

Similarly, a number of the resident theaters began as summer groups. Two examples are the Old Globe Theatre, of San Diego, with its summer seasons of Shakespeare; and the Peterborough Players and Playhouse in the Park, whose work in the summer months is widely known. Although the Tyrone Guthrie company performs its repertory from May to November, the Guthrie Theatre is in use the year around.

Also, from the list, it is evident that many of the resident theaters sprang from universities and theater schools, and quite a number still retain some affiliations, or even maintain an academic function. To name a few, we cite the Goodman Memorial Theatre, IASTA, the American Shakespeare Festival Theatre and Academy, the Center Theatre Group in Los Angeles, and the Stanford Repertory Theatre. Many more were started by groups of former fellow-students of university drama departments.

The new regional professional movement also has much in common with the older Community Theater movement: in organization (non-profit), in technique of promotion, and in the common goal to present fine theater to "neighborhoods," large or small. Indeed, the origin of the new movement, taken as a whole, is rooted in the older Little Theater and Community Theater. Among the resident theaters that began as amateur community groups are the Alley Theatre, the Cleveland Play House, the Erie Playhouse, the Charles Playhouse, the Pasadena Playhouse, and the Pittsburgh Playhouse. The last one has only recently changed from a semiprofessional to a full Equity basis.

In Community Theater, the organizations range from a totally volunteer, and hence amateur, group to a volunteer membership group with a professional administrative staff, and possibly a few paid actors per production. In resident professional groups, there is a range from the totally professional (hence, paid and full-time) company to a primarily professional acting staff using volunteer assistance in supporting roles. Of the professional groups replying to the question: "Do you use volunteers?" five groups said they used volunteers as both actors and workers, nine used volunteers as workers only, and only six used no volunteer assistance.[2]

The evolution of a strong professional theater from within the community, and starting at an amateur-volunteer level is not unusual. As a typical instance, the Mummers Theatre in Oklahoma City, directed by Mack Scism, started in a tent with a $600 debt. Through energy and imaginative programing, Scism has developed the group into a full Equity company producing a rounded repertory. The Ford Foundation has helped the Mummers construct a new theater building, for which the community has contributed matching funds.

The Mummers' evolution from the spark generated by a single, highly motivated individual to the inclusion of a similarly inspired, dedicated, and selfless group working toward the achievement of a professional, hence accomplished status, may well be the healthiest and most promising pattern emerging on the American theater scene. This pattern, when successful, can inspire the formation and development of yet more amateur groups.

## *Responsibility to Theater and Community*

The goals and rationale of the Professional Resident Theater movement were stated by Sandra Schmidt in her series of articles on regional theater published in the *Christian Science Monitor*, July and August, 1964.

> [They] have to do with the general growth of culture in the United States. More people, more money, more education, more mass communication, and more leisure time have created a vast reservoir of people who are vaguely, half-consciously looking around for something to do, for something to broaden and enrich their lives. The professional theater has a distinct role to play in relation to this, at the community level.
>
> The role of the regional theater is to present first-rate professional productions of distinguished and significant plays that audiences might not see under normal commercial auspices.
>
> Within this role, certain of its goals are to provide an acting vehicle for, as yet, unrecognized talent; to supply a training ground for all types of theater personnel; to create an atmosphere in which playwright and director can work together in the production of original works; and to stimulate, educate, involve, and entertain its audiences.

A commitment to the theater above and beyond the call of making a living or a profit is certainly an essential and integral part of any thriving or striving professional resident theater group. Talk with any of the directors, and the note of unapologetic idealism and dedication is sure to be sounded. Said one director a few years ago: "It may be that we achieve the ideal too rarely. Perhaps, thus far, not at all. It is a fact, however, that after 11 years we exist. In our American theater, we have a right to claim a plateau. We may not make it, but we plan to try for the peaks."

There is plenty of evidence, too, that a climate exists in America today in which "trying for the peaks" is conceivable. Zelda Fichandler, director of the very successful Arena Stage in Washington, D. C., writes:

> When the power of men and the power of the moment come together, anything and everything can happen. It is possible that the American theater is on the edge of such a time, or already within it, and that this is the time when our theater is to come of age.
>
> The immediate "moment" is described by economic well-being, a general inclination away from acquisition and towards inquiry and search, and a political climate that at least admits that the arts are something worth stirring up.

All the professional resident theaters, generally speaking, cling to "the power of men and of the moment," while knowing that their destiny is linked to that of the community they serve. And the responsibility is reciprocal.

Brooks Atkinson once remarked: "To be fully alive to ideas and beauty, every large city needs its own theater as it needs its own library, music center, forums, and art museums." The resident theaters are striving to fill the theater needs in their cities. Some of them have been at it for a long while.

In 1915, a group of nonprofessional drama enthusiasts gathered in Cleveland to create a theater in protest against the stereotyped commercial theaters then active. Meetings were held in attics, living rooms, and coach houses to read and discuss new plays and new ideas for "the art of the theater"—ideas which were beginning to filter through from Europe. From this beginning the Cleveland Play House evolved—but with difficulty.

The group was strictly amateur, as were many such groups during the era of World War I. In 1917 it converted an old church into a theater building. A number of persons in the group had dreams of a professional theatrical career, but were otherwise engaged in their occupations. In 1920 the group ceased to function, but in 1921 Frederic McConnell was engaged to assume professional direction of the new theater. The goal was to develop a theater, professional in nature, rooted in a community, rather than a community theater with professional assistance. This was a milestone in the development of regional professional theater. The Cleveland Play House has long since become a completely professional theater, outstanding for the quality and continuity of its work.

An entirely different evolutionary pattern is illustrated by the Tyrone Guthrie Theatre in Minneapolis. This regional theater was conceived primarily by Sir Tyrone Guthrie, who believed that America might be ready for a first-rate repertory company in some city other than New York. A number of cities were considered by Guthrie and his fellow producers, Oliver Rea and Peter Zeisler.

The Minneapolis–St. Paul area of about 1,000,000 people seemed to them to have the hunger for, the need for, and the means to provide and support so ambitious a theatrical undertaking. A beautiful theater building was erected with funds raised by an enthusiastic young local board. The Minnesota Theatre Company Foundation, as it is now called, with a company of about 40 players, has been offering an outstanding repertory of classic and modern plays from May to October for the past four years.

An audience analysis report of the Guthrie Theatre revealed that 70 percent of the audience of 193,000 which attended the 1963 season came from within 100 miles of the Twin Cities. The report said that "Eighteen percent of our audience from Minneapolis were people who had not seen a play of any kind during the previous year. But only 4.7 percent of our audience came from the category of clerical and secretarial workers, which indicates we have an informative job to do there."

This sense of responsibility to the community and audiences is typical of all the existing regional theaters, and is clearly revealed in the replies to the NTC questionnaires. We quote some of the replies of directors to the question: "What are your specific objectives?"

*Theatre East,* Rochester, New York. Mrs. Lee Kheel, Executive Director: "We expect . . . to present good theater to the public and, through the school, to the children."

*Studio Arena Theatre,* Buffalo. Neal DuBrock, Executive Director: "We want . . . to develop a permanent acting company of the highest order; to develop an audience large enough to support the theater. . . ."

*The Center Theatre Group,* Los Angeles. Gordon Davidson, Executive Coordinator: "We desire . . . to achieve a high artistic level of theatrical production, to develop new plays and playwrights, and to create a high critical level in the community."

*Arena Stage,* Washington. Zelda Fichandler, Director: "We . . . expect to maintain high artistic excellence, to encourage new playwrights, and to achieve a successful economic base for a performing arts institution."

*American Conservatory Theatre,* New York, and *Geary Theatre,* San Francisco. William Ball, Director: "We expect to extend American

Conservatory Theatre into the mainstream of community cultural life; to provide training for students, scholars and associates; and to create a large universal repertory performed in two major cities. . . ."

*Repertory Theatre,* New Orleans. Stuart Vaughan, Director: "We want to develop a lasting theater of high excellence for New Orleans; to provide continuity of employment for staff and company, and to develop rapport between our educational and general audience policies. . . ."

*Playhouse in the Park,* Cincinnati. Brooks Jones, Director: "We will provide fine theater for a continuing audience. . . ."

*Washington Theatre Club,* Washington, D. C. Davy Marlin–Jones, Director: "We provide important, excellent theater with increasing emphasis on the American playwright; and expect to create a school from which the professional theater may draw actors, and to aid the other arts. . . ."

*Barter Theatre,* Abingdon, Virginia. Robert Porterfield, Director: "We desire to be able to provide better theater; to sell all our seats, and to hire better actors."

*Cleveland Play House.* K. Elmo Lowe, Director: "To mount and do worthwhile plays with a good company, to develop our audience and pay our bills!"

*Loretto–Hilton Center,* St. Louis. Michael Flanigan, Director: "We do quality productions of good plays, and try to develop audience support for good theater. Also we try to train worthwhile young artists. . . ."

*Pittsburgh Playhouse,* Pittsburgh, Pennsylvania. Richard Hoover, (then) Managing Director: "To provide quality theater experiences for our audience. . . ."

*Actors Theatre of Louisville.* Richard Block, Director: "To provide better productions for an increasing audience. . . ."

*Professional Theatre Program,* University of Michigan, Ann Arbor. Robert Schnitzer, Executive Director: "To provide theater fare of the highest professional quality for campus, community and region. Also to provide a bridge whereby the highest caliber theater students may become professional. . . ."

*Milwaukee Repertory Theatre.* Tunc Yalman, Artistic Director: "We desire to help keep mankind's mutual heritage in the art of the theater alive for today, and thus enable it to extend into the future . . . to stimulate audience members to a greater awareness of themselves as living human beings, and to open new realms of experience for the mind and senses by presenting exciting old and new works of the theatre. . . ."

*Arena House,* Harrisburg, Pennsylvania. Thomas H. Prather, Manager: "We want to provide good theater, whether it be *Mary, Mary* or *Macbeth.* Also to produce original plays, and to be financially solvent rather than dissolved!"

*Center Stage,* Baltimore. Douglas Seale, Artistic Director: "We aim at better theater productions for a broader-base audience."

*Hartford Stage Company.* Jacques Cartier, Artistic Director: "We are after the support of the community at large, and the development of meaningful community relationships. Naturally, we expect to do good productions of good plays. . . ."

*Front Street Theatre,* Memphis. George Touliatos, Director: "We want to find out where and how to guide the theater; we expect to educate present and future audiences. . . ."

The statements just quoted—and they could easily be multiplied—are honest and typical expressions, NTC believes, of the new movement's objectives; and they all show a sense of responsibility toward the community. What, now, about the community's responsibility toward the Professional Resident Theater? What kind of community deserves such a theater? What kind of community has the potentiality for maintaining one as well as for benefiting from one?

### *Community Support*

Hopes, high aims, and good intentions are all very fine; but more than these are needed if a town is to have and to keep a permanent professional theater company in its midst. Besides a devoted, skilled staff and troupe—hard enough to assemble and organize in the first place—a number of *sine qua non* factors concerning the local community must exist or be developed. From the experience already accumulated by leaders and observers of the new movement, here are some of these factors:

1) A city with a population of at least 200,000, preferably larger, having a higher-than-average level of income, education, and cultural enlightenment;
2) A history, or at least solid evidence, of broad, popular interest in matters intellectual and artistic, as shown by its support and use of schools, libraries, museums, musical organizations, etc.;
3) A strong, stable nucleus of civic-minded professional, business, and industrial people;
4) A citizenry eager and discriminating enough for first-rate drama to support a public drive for a theater building costing over $1,000,000, and to maintain its operation year after year

with generous donations, popular subscriptions, and word-of-mouth promotion, even in the face of inevitable deficits;

5) Local business, industrial, and municipal support, based on an open-eyed recognition of the cultural and practical benefits of having a professional resident theater;
6) Local educational, cultural, social, and civic organizations that will give united and continuous support to the resident theater for the common good of the community;
7) Local press, radio, and television media that will supply adequate publicity for the theater's events and discerning, fair-minded reviews of its productions;
8) A general determination on the part of the public, the municipality, and all the supporting agencies, groups, and individuals, to protect and defend the theater management's autonomy in its operation, personnel, choice of plays, and modes of production.

No matter how much outside subsidy the resident theater will require and receive for its building and its continued operation, local support, both moral and financial (as in the case of matching grants from foundations), is indispensable. In the most common daily and year-to-year terms, this means buying subscription tickets and keeping the house filled.

As we have stated, the American public cannot be considered, as yet, a vast and powerful ally of the theater, in any of its forms. This is partly a result of the failure to instill in the public a continuing sense of the great excitement and identification which theater at its best can stimulate.

What are the resident professional theaters doing to develop this sense of theater enjoyment in their public? The repertories of these theaters certainly indicate that their aim is to involve the audience in a meaningful theatrical experience rather than a mere amusement. Play selections include fine classics and the best of modern drama.

According to the replies NTC received, audiences for good plays are increasing. The directors of regional professional theaters reveal a deep respect for their audiences and an awareness of how to stimulate them.

Zelda Fichandler of the Arena Stage in Washington, D. C., expresses this attitude and process very well:

> Washington, D. C., is a metropolitan area of about 2,000,000 which has grown almost 40 percent in the past ten years. It is the

second fastest growing city in the United States, and its population is expected to leap another 60 percent in the next 20 years. It has a higher percentage of professional people in its population than any other metropolitan area in the country, an extremely high percentage of college graduates and people with advanced university degrees, and many people with average and above-average incomes. Its population, contrary to prevalent opinion, is chiefly permanent and not transient.

While Washington is a city of many and fascinating faces, the most fascinating and, hence, news-getting of these is not the most typical. For example, in a city of about 2,000,000, what is called "political Washington" is numbered at about 15,000; "diplomatic Washington" at about 25,000; "military Washington" at 60,000, and Washington's "residential society" at about 15,000 to 20,000.

The balance of the 2,000,000 are our customers—doctors, lawyers, teachers, scientists, government workers, students, businessmen, craftsmen and cab drivers. This is an oversimplification, of course. Many senators, congressmen, ambassadors and members of society's echelons attend productions frequently. But when they come to us, they come on their "night off" from their formal duties, in their private roles, and to see and not to be seen.

It is an ideal audience for which to produce good theater—for it is alert, responsive, creative, deeply human and, though not rich, solvent. It is typical of our city and our audience that 80 percent of the money raised in the community for our building came not in the form of gifts, but in the form of subcriptions to 6 percent interest-bearing bonds, and that 75 percent of the total amount of bond purchases was in units of $200 and less.

Ours is an audience attracted by two elements: vibrant, original theater; and prices as low as we can get them. And, we have done our best to cater to these twin interests.

Our subscription series (sold for a 25 percent reduction in the spring and again in the fall at a 15 percent reduction) appeals to 8,000 of our 10,000 subscribers at the greater reduction. Our second plan (you can buy all eight plays or, if you prefer, you can select seven out of the eight) acknowledges the great amount of traveling done by our patrons. And the privilege of exchanging tickets for other than the regular subscription night also takes the community pattern into account.

Our subscriber rolls have grown from 2,300 to the present 10,100 since the beginning of the subscription idea at a particular low point in our fortunes in 1956. We consider that the success of our institution is truly based, above all things else, on the subscription system which makes concrete Jean–Louis Barrault's credo that "there is only one way to create a real theater: to strive unbendingly to attract the devoted adherent as opposed to the transient public interested only in the hits."

Drama is the best medium for making people think, because it is a creative interpretation of their own experience. A classic theater

> aims to take avantage of this fact and to fulfill its organic function by being, openly and admittedly, *education.* The word "education" is not used here in the sense of "propaganda." Theater is a bad set for propaganda—for, by the laws of its own art, it deals with the imitation of a human action. The classic stage is, at root, a tribunal where the rigorous and beautiful laws of logic and human behavior must be obeyed. Theater audiences can only be persuaded of what they already "know," but did not know they knew. That is, truth can only be revealed to them, not preached at them. Since life itself makes man aware of human motives and human causation, a false note in the imitation of life is quick to be detected. Behavior that is oversimplified, behavior contrary to life, stacking the emotional cards to prove a point, a climax that is not made inevitable by the chain of preceding events—all these an audience is quick to spot and to dismiss.

It must be abundantly clear from Mrs. Fichandler's remarks that alert directors of professional resident theaters understand their public and know what audiences want and need, and also how they respond.

### *Management Guidelines*

A few years ago John Reich, director of the Goodman Memorial Theatre in Chicago, told NTC members how, over the previous five years, his organization had built its audience from 35,000 per season to the point where it had 5,922 subscribers and 156,000 playgoers, and was playing to 90 percent of capacity for an average of 260 performances per season. This record (doubtless now surpassed) was accomplished, he said, by the following seven-point program:

1) *Judicious selection of plays:* an eclectic repertoire chosen from the best drama, old and new, including, "for the younger and more vital subscribers," some avant-garde works.

2) *Careful casting:* combining some guest actors of repute with the regular company, including students, but offering the guest players only parts they have not previously performed, and screening them judiciously for their human qualities and potential influence upon the company as well as for their artistic talent.

3) *A subscription drive:* begun early and energetically pursued.

4) *Press releases handled by professionals:* a full-time press staff (of two), and a working understanding that the director should not talk to the press and that the theater's press representatives should stay out of the theater.

5) *An imaginative effort to make theater-going enjoyable to the general public:* the necessity for courtesy and calm in the box office, for comfortable seating in the house, and for an adequate, well-managed, inexpensive parking lot adjacent to the theater.

6) *An occasional bonus or special treat for subscribers:* making them feel they are favored persons, by offering them choice seats, in addition to a 20 percent discount (six tickets for the price of five), and by extending the discount to include special attractions added to the regular season.

7) *The creation of an image of a friendly theater in the life of the community:* making it a place to learn and think about drama—free talks before performances, dress rehearsals open to the press and selected members of the community, benefit performances at a low fee, a bookstand offering current paperbacks on theater, a neat announcement board for all local cultural events, etc.

NTC believes that every theater management, professional or otherwise, can find these guidelines useful.

## *Subsidy*

Directors report that a favorable climate for good drama is building in the communities served by resident professional theaters. Of the 25 respondents to NTC's questionnaire, 23 stated that their level of public support was rising, and the same number consider their theaters to be artistically successful.

Additional evidence of the changing climate toward the arts is seen in the very substantial sums of money which foundations, such as the Ford and Rockefeller, and, more recently, the United States government have been contributing to theater arts, and in particular to the development and support of resident professional theaters.

NTC queried 42 professional resident theaters regarding subsidy as a factor in their financial status. Of the 25 replying, 15 said they considered themselves financially successful, and 10 said "No" unequivocally. Of the 15 financially successful groups, only the Arena Stage and the American Conservatory Theatre stated that they had received no subsidy and were entirely self-supporting.[3] Nine theaters were depending on funds from private subsidy for at least 20 percent of their support, and three groups for 40 percent. Eleven of the groups depend on public funds for partial support ranging from 2 percent to 75 percent.

The subsidies listed came from a variety of sources, including the Ford and Rockefeller Foundations, the National Endowment for the Arts, the U.S. Department of Health, Education and Welfare, university sources, local fund drives, state Arts Councils, individuals, industry, and municipal governments.

The addition of full Equity companies has posed many tough financial problems for regional professional theaters. At times, these problems would have been unsolvable without the aid of philanthropic foundations.

The resident professional theaters to date (1967), including most of those listed previously, have received a total of $10,742,113.61 in subsidy from the Ford Foundation alone, as well as considerable subsidy from other sources impossible to identify with accuracy.[4]

The factor of subsidy has helped to solve some problems, but has raised others. The question arises: Can the resident professional movement survive and thrive without subsidy funds? The experience of the commercial theaters, of European professional theaters, and of the present American resident theaters seems to indicate clearly that without substantial subsidy only a small portion of these professional theaters can exist. On the other hand, national subsidy has been known to result in diminished local support.

Some directors, recipients of foundation largesse, have expressed certain fears regarding their future. While grateful for assistance in building new and needed facilities or in developing full Equity companies, they recognize that this financial support is going to end. They wonder if the increased costs of production incurred by this expansion will be offset by increased income after subsidy ends. They further worry whether they will be forced to retreat from production of the classics and return to the more "sure-fire" box office hits.

Related to this worry is another: the danger of the theaters losing their independence, their autonomy in guiding their own destiny. If "he who pays the piper calls the tune" should at any time become the attitude of any of the large subsidizers, especially local and municipal ones, the theater managements would have no other choice than to knuckle under or resign. Already, the founder and artistic director of one of the very successful resident companies, the Theatre of the Living Arts in Philadelphia, has been forced out by influential pressures exerted upon and through his Board of Directors stemming from disapproval of his choice of plays.[5] Board members, not donors, tend to dictate policies.

In the case of a resident professional company that is evolving out of a community theater, the worry was expressed to NTC that professional status itself may create a local problem. It may discourage the dedicated involvement of the volunteer—a factor that was very important in a resident professional company's evolution.

At the present time all subsidies to the theater are dependent on the will, wishes, and judgments of large foundations and smaller individuals, plus a few government agencies. All subsidies are limited in objectives and in time. Amounts are, therefore, specifically geared to a particular plan or program or period of time: a building program, actors' salaries, a one-year special experiment, and the like. This method is quite different from the constant and continuous state and municipal government support common in most European countries.

The survival and growth of the regional professional movement must rely on one of two factors or both: a stabilized and continuous form of subsidy; and constant strong community support.

All of these worries indicate that the basic problem and, ultimately, the only solution lies with the public itself.

The public, in general, is still, even now, not at all really conscious of its responsibility to the theater, nor of the rewards to be derived from it. Most people are very happy to allow foundations to assume responsibility for subsidy, and, unfortunately, have the erroneous impression that the foundation subsidies are wholly adequate for the entire country.

### *Actors*

The regional theaters have made the decentralization of theater in America a reality in more than one way—location and personnel. Broadway is no longer the only site and scene of good professional theater. Regional theaters have the task, and readily admit it, of developing their own community of producers and performers. These groups are seeking and selecting those plays, both ancient and modern, which will once again appease the hunger for experience and meaning as only excellent productions can.

Professor Richard Moody of Indiana University writes NTC that he believes there is now a much more sophisticated awareness of the strictly commercial nature of the Broadway stage. "Even for the visitor to New York," he says, "Broadway doesn't seem to have the same fascination it used to possess. There is a much more sophisticated recognition of Broadway for what it is. The signs of decentralization, spoken about for so long, are now really happening. There really is a theater of quality here and there, throughout the nation. This theater doesn't need an apology to go along with the ticket. . . ."

Hand in hand with the decentralization of site in the professional theater is the growing decentralization of the acting pool. The majority of the regional theater's professional actors come from the New York theater. The success in luring good actors away from New York is due chiefly to the challenging and varied roles available. An actor offered four or five roles per season which he has always dreamed of playing, and which would never be available to him in New York, becomes friendly toward the idea of a prolonged residence in another city. Any good actor is interested in improving his art and recognizes that roles in great plays enlarge his horizons and skills.

Conditions and pay in regional theaters, too, are quite favorable. These theaters employ actors both on production and on seasonal contracts. Of 25 regional theaters replying to NTC's queries, 12 employed on contract per production while 19 employed actors also by the season. Their actors' average salary is reported as approximately $200 per week —far better than the general average of $50–$65 a week for off-Broadway shows.[6]

The professional actor in regional theater, therefore, has greater security than he does on or (still less) off-Broadway, unless he happens to be continually in demand. This offer of security may be the strongest asset possessed by these theaters in drawing and holding talent and in building a cohesive ensemble.

*Variety,* on March 9, 1966, under its front-page headline, "Hinterland Legits Top B'way," published the results of a survey made in a typical midseason week of the previous January:

> For the first time since the heyday of stock, there are more professional actors working in regional theaters than in Broadway and touring productions. The turnabout is seen as only a hint of things to come in legit, as resident professional companies proliferate in the hinterlands. . . .
>
> Briefly, the mathematics show there were 1,194 professional actors at work in 49 regional theaters in the U. S. and Canada, as of five weeks ago. By contrast, 1,140 actors were under contract on Broadway and in roadshows.
>
> For purposes of comparison, the figures were placed side by side with those for a similar mid-January week in 1960. At that time, there were just 445 troupers at work in the non-Broadway orbit, in just a dozen or so regional companies. On Broadway and the road, 1,491 actors were under Equity contract.

To explain this change, the *Variety* writer said:

> Most of the regional theaters are more culture-oriented than entertainment-minded and more often community-subsidized than free enterprise. A few notable exceptions . . . specialize in light fare or in touring stock productions *à la* summer circuit. But they don't change the general impression that something big in legit is happening outside New York, with attendant grist for the touters of an American culture boom.
>
> If anything, the survey figures are conservative. For example, they don't include regional and festival theaters shuttered in mid-January. . . . Also, the non-Broadway total does not include 152 professionals at work in the 36 off-Broadway houses in New York. . . .

The fact that this survey was made by the director (Milton Lyon) of the Actors' Equity Foundation's new Department to Extend the Professional Theatre shows how significant in the eyes of the performers' own union is the shift of the "numerical focus" away from Broadway.

Actors, to put it mildly, have not been among the most affluent economic working groups. The 1960 U.S. Census shows that the median annual earnings of actors, dancers, and entertainers amounted to only $1,880—a fact that could largely explain the decrease of 26.2 in the number of actors, dancers, and entertainers in this country between the years 1950 and 1960. Out of the approximately 13,500 members of Actors' Equity, as is well known, only a small proportion are ever under employment contract at any given time (witness the total of 1,334 at work in that mid-season week in 1966).

In spite of the relatively good pay, seasonal contracts, and challenging roles in the regional theaters, managing directors report a considerable turnover of actors. Only about three-quarters of a typical company return each season; the rest drift away to other locations, usually back to the big theatrical centers. One of the major attractions of New York and Los Angeles for actors is, of course, the opportunity for lucrative work in films and television, including TV commercials. The actor who has spent a season in Memphis or St. Paul may well feel that he has "had it," at least for the time being, and may want to go where there is "more doing." The survey just cited, however, must be music to the ears of regional theater directors.

The hope has been expressed by these directors that an increasing number of actors will develop from the local region itself. As the resident theaters become stronger training grounds, opportunities for theatrical careers near home will naturally widen. The proportion of talent imported from New York should therefore decrease, in favor of a greater percentage of indigenously trained actors.

The present situation is that there are still many more actors aspiring to jobs than theaters seeking them. Most regional theaters receive a large number of job applications. A fair percentage of these are from actors of real talent and often of considerable reputation. This interest doubtless reflects both the decline in the number of Broadway and road productions and an increased awareness of the financial security, steady employment, and better roles offered by some of the regional theaters.

Few of these groups have yet attained really polished ensemble acting companies. It takes years to achieve this—as the experience of the Lincoln Center Repertory Company attests. Fame has indeed come to the Resident Professional Theater as a movement, and to certain particular theaters. The directors and actors of these pioneer companies are responding well to the exciting task of living up to all the fine things that have been said and written about them. It is, however, unfortunately true in some cases that standards are not yet high enough, and that harmonious working relations between the theater management, the board of trustees, and the surrounding community have yet to be established. Not every "Regional Rep" is first-rate, and not every community that has one has learned to take it on its own artistic terms.

### *Criticisms*

The severest critics of the Resident Professional Theater and of the conditions in which it exists today are the men and women who have most at stake in its success. This, NTC believes, is both natural and healthy, since they are the ones who feel and must cope with the local stresses and strains. It is also natural and healthy that those not directly involved, but who are no less concerned with the American theater's prosperity, should speak their minds on the situation as they see it.

One of the latter group, Ted M. Kraus, vigorous editor of *Critical Digest,* a weekly newsletter serving professional, educational, and community theaters, has suggested that "the solution to resident theaters" may be more emphasis on "resident." In his issue of March 20, 1967, he said (perhaps with tongue in cheek, but with a serious point to make):

> Suppose a given community had to wait to find a tenant for their new marble palace that included an entire staff of "residents." Managing director, artistic director, actors, staff, etc., would all have to be residents of the community for five years. If such a building were not built until a group of qualified theater-trained "residents" were ready to move in, and were ready to be supported by fellow residents, the current problems of resident theater would be nonexistent. The past manager of one theater stated that managers should live at least six months in the area to get to know the pulse of the community. He is no longer on the job. Six years may be a better figure to start with.

There is little doubt that one of the main stresses results from a lack of mutual understanding between the local public and the performing group, sometimes amounting to rivalry over who will win on a given issue, such as the repertoire of plays. The director of one leading resident theater said: "We are sustained by two establishments. . . . One is a rather large subscription audience. We lost 30 percent of that subscription audience last year when we did *Endgame,* but it was the most exciting time we ever had." Most American playgoers are not yet ready for the New Theater (when they are, it will be "old"), nor are they, as a rule, very keen for classics. Yet the conscientious artistic director of a resident theater, while trying to build an eclectic program of plays for his season, feels that he must give something of both kinds, if only to stretch and, if possible, raise the taste-level of his audience.

To bring into the open the most candid opinions of regional theater directors on what it chose to call, for baiting purposes, the "New Establishment," the ever-alert and critical editors of the *Tulane Drama Review* held a Theater Conference in New York on November 21, 1965, and published a report of it in their Summer 1966 issue. NTC quotes here some of the pointed remarks.

Acting as host, Theodore Hoffman, director of the Theatre Program at New York University's new School of the Arts, led off by saying:

> Yes, the resident theater is now facing stultification. The trouble with it is you cannot get to an operational level that is reasonably comfortable. If you're not paying mortgages, you can just about break even. It is difficult to expand and there is a temptation not to expand. The theaters were started by people who had good intentions; they wanted to become artists. But the truth is that when you get a theater you don't necessarily become an artist. A lot of the directors in the resident theater movement ought to become producers.

John O'Neal, one of the founders of the Free Southern Theatre, referring to the theater's dual commitment, to art and to life, said:

> There is no way for anybody—artist or non-artist—to avoid participation in terms of the place he lives in. A man's first obligation is always to the act of living. . . . I know some artists who have concluded that the most profound poetry in these times is poetry of action, not of words. . . . If there is a reason to do theater, the people who are involved have to forge that meaning. That means we begin to arrive at places in opposition to the society at large, whether in terms of its political, economic, or sociological character. We must meet that obligation and strike out to forge a new reality. I think that means that we set out from this comfortable home, and move out to an audience that waits to be approached—and there are millions.

Gordon Rogoff, a staff critic of Joseph Chaikin's experimental Open Theatre in New York, and associate dean of the Yale Drama School, discussed the problem of acting:

> Stark Young said that [Martha] Graham "scrapes back to the image." And none of us are doing that in our theaters today, though it is beginning to happen with the Open Theatre. . . . We simply have a very weak body of actors in this country. . . . The great Talma said it takes 18 years for an actor to reach the beginning stages, really, of performing his art. And our actors just leap from their wishes and their dreams right onto the stage without any preparation. . . . The preparation is very difficult, and this is where the money should be poured. [He also called for better trained producers.]

The strain and cost of building an adequate resident company of actors concerned André Gregory, speaking from his experience as director of Philadelphia's Theatre of the Living Arts:

We have a company that has advanced considerably in one year, but there are only ten actors, and I need seventy, and I will not get them. We work very well together, and because we have worked for one year we do not "putz" around with each other for two weeks of the rehearsal period; we jump in and work. But we can only work for five weeks, not for five months. . . . We need money, we need time. . . .

Paul Gray, head of Bennington College's experimental drama program, charged the professional theater (and its public) with betraying the experimental theater:

The professional theater is told:
of the need for new acting methods
of the need for ensemble
of the need for art, for epic, for Artaud.

Their answer is continually about their preference for:
self-indulgence
the personality *thing*
and above all an admitted *conceptual mindlessness.*

The current repertory companies are no more than advanced collegiate theater—an umbrella step when a giant step is called for.

Since the professional theater has ignored its dissenters, its projectors, its heretics—in a word its youth—it should not expect its experimental theater to speak to it with respect. It won't. . . .

And what does the American audience expect of American plays? No dramatic extremes—moderation—the peculiar paradox—entertain the nonthinking man! . . .

An audience must be made! Members of this audience must enter into the essence of creative experience themselves—working at making the images led by and participating with the playwright and the players. . . .

Building an audience and building an acting ensemble—these are clearly two of the toughest problems a resident theater must learn to solve. Edwin Sherin, associate producing director of the Arena Stage, Washington, said:

Arena is an institution—and I use the word institution advisedly—that has been fighting for survival for 15 years. It first fought the battle of the box office, and I believe succeeded because despite sincere, negative criticism the audiences are coming. Last season [1964–65] we did 93 percent of capacity. Now we are dogged by different problems. Because of the eclectic nature of our repertory it has been difficult to gather a company who shared anything other than attempting to make a living in the theater. In seasons past, Arena has done what I think most regional theaters have done: used New York as a central casting agency, brought actors to play specifically assigned roles, and operated more or less like a winter stock company. Recently we felt we could take certain chances, and I mean they are real chances, because the life of that theater at one time depended on how many people were in the house: we hired a company of 16 actors, detailed the parts that they were to play through a season and on through a summer and into the following season; suggested that if the work meant anything to them, their life in the theater might extend over a period of time which could allow continuous development, and the search for a point of view. To this end we chose actors who were as diverse in their methods of work as we could find, using their talent as the determinant. We have spent now several weeks in a workshop program where actors are required to come and participate; the workshop is part of the rehearsal process, although the workshop has nothing to do with the plays themselves. We have attempted . . . to find that which stops us from showing on a stage our intellectual and visceral comprehension of a play. The discoveries have been significant. . . .

The directors at the TDR Theatre Conference kept coming back, as professional resident directors always do, to the problem of how to make the theater a part of its community. Paul Sills, director of the Forty-Third Ward Game Theatre in Chicago, offered a radical solution that his group has worked out, or worked at:

. . . The job of theater artists is to unite the community with the celebrations of its life. . . . How do you do such a thing? Let's take the community where I live, which is a bit of Old Town fixed up with stuffy people who put on a bad art fair every year, and get 50,000 people to show up for it. You can get thousands of people out on the streets for anything. They are dying to do something. But we cannot get them into the theater. The theater in itself is meaningless. Theater in the community is meaningful. But how do you go into a community with a theater if they do not like it? If you want an American theater, start off celebrating the Fourth of July and put some artists in the middle of the thing to help control it, and some playwrights who can bring out all the beauty and terror, . . . because, God knows, it is there in the revolutionary period. Have thousands of kids running through the streets with American flags. Start thinking about a theater that involves the actual and whole life of a community on a celebratory basis. That doesn't replace the traditional theater, but it informs it of the spirit of actual life and play. . . .

With all the stresses and strains, the questions and the arguments, that attend the establishment and operation of any professional resident theater, the larger issue must not be lost from sight. Writing from Arena

Stage, Washington, Zelda Fichandler sums up the problem of the regional theaters:

> The conditions seem to be these: theater must be dug out of its New York jungle setting where it is buried under exorbitant costs and ticket prices, a real estate shortage, an expense account audience, and an hysterical, cutthroat, boom-or-bust atmosphere, and re-rooted in the various cities throughout the United States hungry for it and prepared to nurture it. Playhouses must be built that will restore to theater-going its ancient magic—that is, that will reunite the audience with the play in the same room, close to and surrounding it, and will involve the two elements one with the other, and make of them cohorts in the creative process. Theater people must—by sorcery and all other possible means—galvanize, hypnotize, inspire, cajole, and compel an audience into the recognition that, for exhilaration and delight, the experience of theater is second only to that of living, and that they must go, and go regularly, to the theaters created for them.

## *The Future*

Practically all the directors of the professional regional theaters replying to the NTC questionnaire are optimistic about the future of this movement in America. However, because of the financial hazards involved, the erratic nature of subsidy, the difficulty of forming and maintaining fine acting companies, and the slow growth of firm audience support, NTC does not expect a great increase in the number of professional resident theaters in the near future. What the "optimum" number will be—if there is such a thing—is impossible to guess. But, wildly optimistic statements about the proliferation of regional professional theater in "most cities"—and we have heard people add, "of 25,000 and upwards"—is glib talk without foundation and without any comprehension of the problem.

It is obvious, as Herbert Blau told the TDR Conference, that "the New Establishment is not yet established." Still, the Professional Resident Theater movement—and it is a movement—has broken the strangle hold of Broadway by planting in almost half a hundred cities across the land, and even in Manhattan, professional organizations permanently rooted and growing in their communities; also by demonstrating that it can attract good actors in large numbers away from the lures of the Great White Way by offering seasonal security, challenging roles in classic, modern, and experimental productions, and a chance to live more stable, normal lives—and even raise families if they choose—while expanding and perfecting their skill as artists. By bringing into American cities totaling many millions of people, fine drama professionally staged and performed, it has begun the process whereby countless theatergoers who had never before experienced such enrichment except by traveling may cultivate their appreciation for good theater virtually at home.

Organizationally, the professional movement is in far stronger shape today than it was even five years ago. Individual theater managements are benefiting not only from the liaison provided by the Theatre Communications Group, which was created by the Ford Foundation primarily for them, but which, as mentioned earlier in this report, serves also to keep them in touch with the gradually "professionalizing" university theaters. The independent theaters are also linked, for business purposes such as collective solidarity in negotiating with Actors' Equity and other unions, through their new League of Regional Theatres. They are further served in one of their most critical needs by ANTA's Resident Theatre Management Programs, the first of which was held for two weeks in November 1966, with 53 managing directors (including some from universities) receiving instruction and advice from a "faculty" of 28 theater specialists. Through ANTA, too, which is the U.S. Center of the International Theatre Institute, they have available an important tie with comparable theaters and organizations throughout the world.

In yet another organizational manner, the professional resident theaters have been forging links with the commercial, educational, and community theaters, not only through the existing regional theater conferences, but through such special, government sponsored conferences as the two already described which took place in 1966 at Minneapolis. The cross-fertilization of ideas resulting from meetings like these, with the recognition of the interdependency of all categories of theater in America, is certain, NTC believes, to bear fruit.

One conspicuously weak spot in the professional resident theater movement is only beginning to be attacked by a few individual groups; namely, the discovery, encouragement, and development of new playwrights. For reasons already apparent from statements quoted from resident directors, it is a very hard nut to crack—yet it will have to be cracked if the movement is to fulfill its obvious duty to the future American theater. The tenuous economy of offering professional productions of even established drama becomes far more hazardous in the case of new plays by unknown authors, and experimental work generally. Here and there a few of the resident theaters have taken the risk—usually with some foundation aid. Residentships for playwrights, playwriting workshops, festivals of new plays, or simply occasional productions of new scripts, experimental or otherwise, have begun to make their appearance. Examples of these can be found in Minneapolis, Washington, Boston, and some other cities. The little Forum playhouse under the main auditorium of the Vivian Beaumont Theatre in Lincoln Center was constructed expressly for trying out new work. The Theater Company of Boston—which, far from having a "marble palace," had to scout the inner city for its third abode in half a dozen years, having been twice dispossessed of its none too adequate working quarters—has had one successful festival of new plays and is planning another. But these are small beginnings, not the needed massive attack on the problem of fostering our playwrights of the future.

NTC closes its report on the professional resident or regional theater movement with some optimism, much hope, and many perplexing questions. The most encouraging fact is: it exists, it is here to stay—so far, so good.

## Permanent Professional Touring Companies

If, like Community Theater, the movement to establish regional professional theaters bears any relation to the decline of "the road" (Broadway's extension into "the Hinterland"), the development of permanent professional touring companies is even more relevant to that decline.[7] Indeed, if one totals the current number of separate nonprofit professional productions with repertories of resident regional theaters, touring companies, and festival theaters, the sum will be found to approximate if not surpass the peak number of commercial productions sent out by Broadway in the heyday of "the road."

Today's permanent professional touring companies, however, with a seasonal repertory of at most three plays each, and playing mostly in major cities, cannot fairly be compared on any quantitative basis with the hundreds of commercial road show troupes that formerly laced the United States, playing one-night or week-long stands in countless towns both large and small.

### *National Repertory Theatre Tours*

ANTA lists seven theater touring agencies, under whose managements approximately 15 companies tour. The agencies listed are: Columbia Artists Management, Independent Booking Office, Inc., National Performing Arts, Victor Samrock, Martin Tahse, the Theatre Guild, Inc., and the National Repertory Theatre Foundation.

Of these, the National Repertory Theatre Foundation has the only company touring a repertory of plays. It also is the newest and has the most ambitious program. Much in the spirit of Eva LeGallienne's Civic Repertory Theatre (1926–32), and, still more, in that of the American

Repertory Theatre (1946–48), directed by Cheryl Crawford, Eva LeGallienne, and Margaret Webster and actually taken on tour, the National Repertory Theatre (NRT) evolved a program with specific educational aims. In this, it may be assumed, its co-producers, Michael Dewell and Frances Ann Dougherty, have been assisted by Miss LeGallienne, who directs the company with Jack Sydow.

Their goal is to bring a truly vital theatrical experience not only to audiences in major cities but to college and university student bodies. Indeed, their practice has been to select a college having a suitable theater that is available for a number of weeks, and rehearse their season's three-play repertory there, virtually in full view of the students and faculty of the drama department. Minimal admission fees are charged for performances on the campuses, and lectures, lessons, and demonstrations are added benefits to the host schools. On tour, too, the company admits groups of students at low prices and frequently sends members to give talks at local institutions.

The producers of NRT believe that drama alone, of all the arts, has a bearing on all courses of study, yet professional examples of that art are all too rarely available to teachers and students. The repertory offerings of NRT's first season—Schiller's *Mary Stuart* and Maxwell Anderson's *Elizabeth the Queen*—were greeted with enthusiasm by faculties teaching European history, English history, English and American literature, German, and religion, as well as by drama departments.

The first tour of the National Repertory Theatre (October 1961 to April 1962) played to a total audience of 250,000, of which one-fifth were students. With ANTA sharing in the sponsorship, the company traveled 50,000 miles, using plane, bus, train, and station wagon as means of transportation. During the 1963–64 season, the company again toured, this time with Arthur Miller's *The Crucible,* Eva LeGallienne's adaptation of Chekhov's *The Seagull,* and the Anouilh–Christopher Fry *Ring Round the Moon,* ending the tour in New York. In 1964–65, the NRT toured some 20 cities, all of 200,000 population or over. Since then, it has reduced its itinerary, keeping to the "best theater towns." To wind up its 1966–67 tour, it scheduled a four-week run in New York, but had to cut this in half because of poor business—at its moderate $5 top ticket price. Fortunately, the National Repertory Theatre Foundation has obtained considerable financial assistance from the theater industry, from private individuals and foundations, and more recently, from the National Endowment for the Arts. If it is hard for resident professional theaters to make ends meet, it is far more difficult—in fact, impossible —for a professional theater that tours. Yet, as NRT has abundantly proved, the hungriest audiences for good drama are in the "hinterland."

### *Theatre Guild–American Theatre Society*

When it comes to knowing the American theater audience, few persons today can surpass Warren Caro, who made that his constant study in his capacity as executive director of the Theater Guild–American Theatre Society for 20 years. Without prejudice to the other touring agencies named above, we cite this organization, which has been in the business for 36 years, as our example of a successful management of annual subscription series for Broadway shows on tour.

This management sells subscriptions in 22 major cities from coast to coast for up to 12 shows per season, to be presented between Labor Day and the first of May. A typical series of attractions includes musicals (which have increased in recent years), comedies, and some (though fewer than formerly) serious dramas. Most of the shows are American, some are fresh imports. In Eastern cities like Boston and Philadelphia, there may be a pre-Broadway tryout on the list. Subscription rates are scaled according to location in the theater, day of the week, and evening or matinee performance, and they average, of course, below the price of individual tickets.

The problem this organization has to solve each year, working through its local offices, is how to sign up subscribers, starting in late spring or early summer, for an entire season of shows beginning in the fall and subject to change of bills. In Boston, for example, where pre- and post-Broadway shows arrive under their own managements throughout the season, and where two professional resident theaters also compete for the trade, the Theatre Guild–American Theatre Society strives to get at least 5,000 subscribers to pay in advance for as many as 11,000 seats for a 12-play season; and that, as Caro said, "takes some doing."

Prior to his resignation from the Theatre Guild in September 1967, Caro told NTC members: "Without the underwriting of some kind of national subscription, any touring production is in trouble. But selling advance subscriptions requires an intimate sense of what the public will buy on those terms. We have readers in all our cities to assist us in the selection of plays. As for service to subscribers and enlisting the support of audiences, the community and educational theaters have been the most important aids in furnishing chairmen for local committees." As an example of what a body of subscribers can do, he cited the case of the Broadway production of *The Visit,* which closed after a respectable run, presumably because there was no more audience in New York. The Theatre Guild took it on tour, then returned it to New York for an excellent run at the City Center. Caro added that student subscriptions at lower rates are "most important," and that among Toronto's 22,000 general subscribers many had never before been in a legitimate theater.

One may easily find fault with the steadily increasing "lightness" of the bills which the Theatre Guild has been offering its subscribers in recent years; but, since this organization survives by sensing what its public will buy, the real blame, NTC believes, should be directed elsewhere.

## Summer Theaters

We have already touched on summer theaters in dealing with outdoor historical drama, Shakespeare and other festivals, college and university drama departments' summer operations, the Tyrone Guthrie Theatre, and other topics. But Summer Theater as a whole is a manifold activity and, for professionals, a big business. Precisely how manifold and how big is not easy to find out. As with Community Theater, the available figures are incomplete and elusive and widely variant.

*Equity* magazine listed 96 "Dramatic Summer Stock Theaters" operating in the United States in 1966 (a drop of 21 from 1962), plus 44 "Musical Summer Stock Theaters" (the same number as in 1962). These were all professional, Equity-bonded summer theaters presenting shows by the method known as "stock"; that is, offering a single production for a limited period of time, usually one week, and then replacing it with another, and so on throughout a season.

But Equity's list by no means comprises all the summer theaters in operation, not even all the professional ones. Simon's 1967 *Directory of Summer Theatres* estimates the number of theaters doing mostly straight plays to be 325, plus 30 musical tents. The *New York Times*, in mid-July of 1967, in listing the summer theaters "Along the Straw Hat Trail"—including only the states along the Eastern seaboard from New England to North Carolina—names 148 that present only or mainly plays, and 26 that specialize in musicals. Of the former, 27 are summer theaters operated by educational institutions (some of these in repertory), six are Shakespeare festivals, five are outdoor historical (or, to use Paul Green's term, "Symphonic") dramas, and five more are special types of productions, ranging all the way from New York City's Theatre in the Street to the Swansea, New Hampshire, Potash Bowl's annual revival of *The Old Homestead.*

Both apprentices and stars participate in this prolific activity of summertime dramatic performances, and the varieties of fare offered to playgoers are too numerous to describe here. In general, as one might expect, there is a marked leaning toward plays of the light, undemanding sort, especially in the stock theaters; but there are many notable exceptions. Among these, of course, are the Shakespeare festivals: in New York's Central Park; at Stratford, Connecticut; at Ashland, Oregon; Woodbridge, New Jersey; Burlington, Vermont; San Diego, California, and elsewhere. Most of the educational summer playhouses, also, whether on or off the campus, incline toward classics, old and modern, and include some avant-garde or experimental pieces, occasionally original scripts. The weekly bills of a good many commercial stock theaters, too, including some with star performers hired for the show, contain a fair scattering of serious plays by living authors like Miller, Williams, Albee, Anouilh, and Pinter. The director of at least one professional company, at Williamstown, Massachusetts, desiring to produce "great" drama but feeling that Shakespeare has had his share of festivals, has been offering successful seasons of Chekhov, Pirandello, Shaw, and comparable authors. The playwright William Gibson has set up a festival program at Stockbridge, Massachusetts, that brings out original plays by new writers. Some of the regional professional companies move their operation, for the summer months, to vacation resorts or university campuses. The variety of summer theaters (and their kinds of work) is almost limitless.

The summer theater began to stir in the 1920's, when Broadway theaters customarily put up their shutters from Memorial Day to Labor Day and "the road" was idle. A few actors found congenial employment for the three summer months in the vacation atmosphere of Skowhegan, Maine; Elitch's Gardens, Denver; Westport, Connecticut; Newport, Rhode Island; Dennis, Massachusetts, on Cape Cod; or Stockbridge, in the Berkshires; or Woodstock, New York, in the Catskills—but most professionals were left to their own devices. The potentialities of profitable summer work in pleasant surroundings had only begun to be explored and exploited when the Great Depression struck a massive blow at the entire entertainment business.

By the mid-1930's, summer dramatic activity had resumed and rapidly became dynamic, with playhouses opening in resorts and rural villages across the country. Barns, carriage houses, town halls, schools, disused "opera houses," railroad depots, and fire stations were converted into "straw hat" theaters by the hard physical labor and small capital of enterprising actors and directors, often with financial help from foresighted local tradesmen.

In those years, each stock company produced its own plays, with or without a visiting star to head the bill, usually for a season of 12 weeks, at the rate of a play a week. The importing of star actors and actresses, though expensive, increased business at the box office and brought the theater into nationwide prominence—and the practice grew. Most of the great names of the American stage appeared on the billboards of playhouses made over from country barns and lakeside granges. As summer playhouses prospered and multiplied, the supply of Broadway stars fell behind the demand, and lesser players were engaged and given top billing. Then Hollywood names—Joan and Constance Bennett, Boris Karloff, Arthur Treacher, Bette Davis, Edward Everett Horton, and many others—were drafted for the summer stage. Not all of these movie stars adjusted successfully to the strain of rehearsing by day and performing each night with a different resident company in each place. Legend has it that one summer Ethel Barrymore discovered that a number of the larger theaters were willing, for the sake of her name and talent, to hire the entire supporting cast she had been playing with in *Whiteoaks*. Thus, with a solid 12 weeks booked (and no lost time for rehearsals), Miss Barrymore created the "package show," replacing the lone touring star.

But packaging, in a short time, broke the back of the big resident summer stock companies. For one thing, it took away the local theater jobs. In 1959, for example, the Lakewood Theatre in Skowhegan, Maine, founded in 1901 and the oldest summer theater in the East, dropped its resident company entirely. Said its production director, Henry Richards, to a *New York Times* writer in 1964: "Casting a season of 11 different plays was impossible, with transportation costs and high rehearsal pay. This way, we get complete shows with stars, and share with others [that is, other summer theater managements] in the pre-production and transportation costs."

With the "star package" system continuing to spread, important consequences have changed the summer theater picture. The local playhouse has become, as one commentator puts it, a "roadhouse," and the local management, a rental agency. The summer theater has become the summer circuit, and around it goes a succession of names; some good, some fair, and some just plainly odd. The old line manager, who had been happy to produce and in many cases direct a hand-picked locally popular cast, and in so doing develop acting talent, now finds himself as creative as the local picture-house manager who took what was coming to him "out of a can." Inevitably, too, Equity and other craft unions have blocked the path to Broadway for young talent that used to find its apprenticeship working with seasoned experts in the resident companies. Television celebrities, disk jockeys, and nightclub entertainers—anyone and everyone with a name that will draw the curious—now tour the country in the guise of actors and actresses. And central booking agencies in New York, far (in every sense of the word) from the audiences they purport to serve, make up the "packages" as they see fit, and ship them out on the circuit.

Fortunately, not all the professional summer theaters have gone the way of the big ones—and not even all the big ones have. One of the biggest, in the sense of most justly famous, is the 28-year-old Bucks County Playhouse, at New Hope, Pennsylvania. Although the town itself has a population of only about 1,000, the theater can draw its playgoers from an estimated 5,000,000 people living within a 50-mile radius in Philadelphia, Trenton, Allentown, Princeton, and other cities, and New York is but an hour and a half away. In its building—a remodeled 17th century grist mill, on the banks of the Delaware—the directors, and particularly Michael Ellis, who controlled the theater's destinies for about a dozen years beginning in 1954, have produced successive seasons of some of the finest drama seen in America. Not only that, but Ellis made the Playhouse and himself famous by his revolutionary policy of trying out new dramatic works before audiences sprinkled with Broadway producers. Setting a mark worthy of emulation by any courageous theater director, Ellis produced over 50 new plays there, in defiance of all the Cassandras who said it could not be done. As he explained to Emily Coleman, the *New York Times* writer referred to above, "Ten years ago you could hardly get a good play to try out. Now, it is no loss of prestige to an author to try out in the summer; it costs $7,000 to $9,000 to try out a play here; it costs $110,000 to $150,000 to try out in New York. Most other summer theater producers claim they cannot do new plays, that people will not come to see them. That just is not true." In recognition of its accomplishment, the Bucks County Playhouse was made the official State Theatre of Pennsylvania: ". . . recognized throughout the nation as a leader in its field, maintaining an artistic tradition that brings great credit to itself and to the State of Pennsylvania." Michael Ellis himself received the 1962 Margo Jones Award for being the producer who had done the most to encourage new playwrights.

Among summer theater directors who both admire the Bucks County Playhouse achievement and fear that unionization and the central-booking, star-package system will prove the downfall of even this kind of theater, the hope is often expressed, not too unrealistically, of a return to the old resident company. When one sees the excellent work being done by small summer theaters, Equity and non-Equity, all across the country, such a prospect renews one's confidence in the problem-solving genius of a people that is beginning again to love the living drama.

# V. THE CHALLENGE

# The Challenge

NTC IS AWARE of the many problems in American Theater, but also sees a great challenge to persons involved in any one of the country's four great scenes of theatrical activity. The potential is tremendous and can be realized gradually if definite steps are taken once the weak areas are recognized.

# To The Commercial Theater

It is well to review the needs of the commercial theater first for it has a noticeable influence over the other areas of theater in America.

### *Broadway*

. . . Broadway (and off-Broadway) continued to get along as an old established permanent floating crap game of individual judgment and risk. There were problems and disappointments, but . . .

Fortunately for *all* theater in America, Broadway continues to discharge its creative responsibility, even as it bears the weight of

> its own excesses. It is deceptively strong; it has no secret weaknesses, its weaknesses are all on the surface for any detractor to see. It is its strength that is hidden, like the power of a magnet. Every September the New York theater turns itself on and draws to itself every alloy of playwriting creativity until its minimum needs are filled. . . .[1]

That Broadway, to say nothing of off-Broadway, resembles a "floating crap game" is a truism. That its strength is "hidden, like the power of a magnet," is a shrewd observation of a fact too often ignored by persons whose favorite metaphor for referring to Broadway is the "Fabulous Invalid." That "its weaknesses are all on the surface" is open to question; if they were, it would not have needed a Rockefeller Panel Report or a Baumol-Bowen survey of "the economic dilemma" to expose some of the worst of them. But the other statements—that "Broadway continues to discharge its creative responsibility" and that it "draws to itself every alloy of playwriting creativity" (even with the reservation "until its minimum needs are filled")—these NTC cannot accept.

For one thing, Broadway's minimum needs are far too minimal (and becoming more so year after year) to substantiate its claim that it is the theatrical and artistic capital of the world's richest and most powerful nation. For another, its "needs" in "playwriting creativity"—to judge by what it uses—consist mainly of musicals (dismal stereotypes when they are not blockbusters); of light comedies (titillating but vacuous, clever but boring); of based-ons (unoriginal attempts to squeeze a play out of a popular novel, film, TV show, or another musical); of adaptations of European works (seldom doing justice to the original play); and of pre-tested imports from England and Ireland. With the exception of some of the foreign drama and an occasional serious native play, Broadway's total annual output—amidst a world and a nation in ferment—has little urgency, relevance, significance, or lasting value.

Moreover, while Broadway may be exploiting what little playwriting creativity it thinks it can use, one has a right to ask, "What is it doing to develop *more* of that creativity?" And it will not do to reply to that question by turning about and asking, "What are the regional professional theaters and the universities doing to develop it?" They are not doing enough either; but they are not proud of it, and their consciences hurt. They are aware that the most salable scripts bypass them and go straight to Broadway (where they get lost); but in 1966–67 the professional regional theaters alone presented at least 25 new plays, and university theaters probably many more than that. For Broadway to discharge its *full* creative responsibility—and the same goes for the television, film, record, and other industries that profit from the work of playwrights—it will have to put a lot more money than it has to date into fertilizing and cultivating the seedbeds of American drama.

No one wants to see Broadway diminish—quite the contrary. That it continues to "get along," even as a floating crap game, is indeed fortunate for all theater in America. It draws by far the largest annual attendance at professional theatrical performances in the country (for example, 7,000,000 in 1963–64, compared with off-Broadway's 900,000 and the regional theaters' 1,500,000). New York alone, we are informed, accounts for over half (56 percent) of all theatrical receipts; and New York theatergoers, in 1963, spent per capita 9.5 times the national average ($17.94 compared with $1.88) to see professional performances—partly because metropolitan ticket prices are the highest in the nation.[2] Yet, doubtless for the same reason, Broadway's percentage of playgoers under the age of 20 is considerably lower than off-Broadway's and far below that of the professional regional theaters. Clearly, Broadway is leaving to other professional theater sectors, and especially to the nonprofessional theaters of America (educational and community), the supremely important task of cultivating the theater audience of the future.

In earlier times, students were often admitted to Broadway theaters at nominal rates whenever a house was certain not to be sold out. The motive for this bygone practice was perhaps that it is better for the performance to have a full house than a half-empty one; but the undeniable result was to rear a generation of young people in the habit and love of seeing live drama at its best. This practice has virtually ceased both on Broadway and on "the road." Today's "twofers" are no substitute.

NTC believes that Broadway producers, and commercial theater owners generally, have a clear responsibility to youth, if only in their own interest, and it would like to see some concrete sign that this responsibility is recognized.[3]

## *Broadway and Noncommercial Theater*

In the same spirit of helping to foster, instead of merely exploiting, this country's theatrical potential, the theater industry, NTC believes, should commit itself to a firm, broad-scale, permanent policy of collaboration with the noncommercial sectors of the American theater, particularly the resident and touring professional and the university theaters. It should be obvious that these theaters are doing a job that must be done and from which, if it is done well, Broadway cannot fail to be a major beneficiary, along with the public. For one thing, they are building and training audiences for good theater; and, with the speed and relative ease of travel, with more and more leisure and longer vacation periods, with a greater amount and broader spread of affluence, Broadway stands only to gain from this enlarged playgoing public. Even more specifically, it is from the colleges and universities, and to some extent from the resident theaters, that Broadway is now drawing practically all of its best talent: playwrights, actors, directors, designers. To help these institutions improve their product so that everyone benefits is in Broadway's own self-interest.

A splendid beginning was made in the two developmental conferences held at Minneapolis in the spring of 1966 under the sponsorship of the U.S. Office of Education, bringing together selected leaders from Broadway and other sectors of professional theater and from Educational Theater to consider what their respective sectors and the theater as a whole can achieve through mutual understanding and cooperation. These conferences were essential, yet they were only ground-clearing sessions; they explored and roughly mapped the areas of potential collaboration. It is now essential, before the goal becomes lost to view and the will to attain it wastes away in lip-service, that solid foundations be laid and the actual collaboration begun.

## *Off-Broadway*

It has been noted in this report and in many other commentaries that the off-Broadway theater appears to have drifted into the doldrums. Over the past decade it seems to have acquired many of the less desirable characteristics and most of the ailments of Broadway, and to have lost or abandoned much of the vision and drive that set it apart from the rest of the American theater in the early 1950's.

NTC believes that the off-Broadway theater still has a distinct role to play, and that if its leaders can stick to that role, it can have a distinguished future. This role, in NTC's view, lies in developing precisely those areas where off-Broadway has always been strongest and, conversely, in avoiding those areas where it has in effect attempted, and usually failed, to overlap Broadway—also those purely experimental areas now being explored in the "Off off-Broadway" coffeehouses and lofts.

Off-Broadway's highest achievements are all a matter of record and so need not be enumerated here. They came about, and can be matched and surpassed in the future, by pursuing certain objectives: (1) to be the first to introduce new kinds of dramatic work (one-acts and full-lengths, native and foreign) to the American public; (2) to produce plays, musicals, and revues that deserve performance but are not big enough or otherwise suitable for Broadway; (3) to show how to bring old classics to fresh life; (4) to give new American playwrights, and older ones who are developing a new line or style, the opportunities they must have to see their work faithfully and imaginatively produced. Most of these goals can be urged equally well for regional and university theaters, but in the commercial sector they are "naturals" for off-Broadway.

Economically, off-Broadway has become the victim of its own success. It originally sought a limited public; now its public is limited by the 299-seat capacity of its houses and the reduced number of its productions. Actors, directors, and designers who were willing to work for nominal salaries 15 years ago—and in effect subsidized the theaters—now demand wages commensurate with the other union rates imposed there. Higher production costs led to safer choices and fewer shows—the road to mediocrity. Off-Broadway's renewal must come about through readjustment of its thinking, its way of doing things, its vision of the goals it is peculiarly competent to attain. It performs a necessary function in the American theater. It will need courage, daring, to fulfill it.

## *Professional Acting*

The 3,000-mile separation of our stage and film capitals has developed two distinctly different breeds of actor, and the difference has been magnified by the vast disparity of financial rewards offered to performers in Hollywood and in New York. Actors in England and all over the Continent can readily combine careers on stage and in cinema to their own artistic and material enrichment and to the mutual benefit of the two art forms. In America, very few actors find this possible. As professional theaters in Los Angeles grow in number and quality, the gap may lessen. Television drama, so long as it is produced where stage actors can participate, offers the only practical alternative short of continual jet travel.

NTC has no solution for this dilemma. It must come, if it ever does, from a recognition by the several vested interests of these industries that the art forms they control suffer from this separation, and that the stage is not the only medium that is penalized. American cinema and television have both failed to make full use of the artistic potential available to them. Art films of high quality continue to come mostly from abroad; first-class television drama—even the slight amount produced—is still inaccessible to the majority of Americans owning sets. Our people want and deserve better films, better television plays, *where they live,* just as they want and deserve better live theater.

### *The Negro Actor*

We have room only to broach this vexing question, but with cities all over the land torn with racial strife the question must be raised: Where is the Negro in the American theater picture? What is the theater doing, what can it do, for our Negro citizens?

As performing artists, the Negroes have brought remarkable gifts to every branch of music, from jazz to opera and the recital platform. In the dance, too, they have excelled. As entertainers, alone and in groups, they have reached pinnacles of success. In the theater, despite the great talents and achievements of individual actors and occasional all-Negro companies, the story is different. A superb Negro actor and leader, Frederick O'Neal, has for a number of years been the elected president of the Actor's Equity Association. By his presence and through his efforts the status of the Negro actor has been much improved. Equity itself has instructed its members to refuse engagements in segregated theaters. Yet we know that the policy is far from airtight, if only for the reason that many performers do not belong to Equity. Meanwhile, *Variety* reports that fewer Negroes acted on the professional stage in 1966–67 than in previous years.

Casting is part, but only part, of the cause. Colored actors and actresses have played "white" roles with distinguished success, even in these years of social unrest. In the summer of 1965, Ruby Dee made a fine Katherina to John Cunningham's Petruchio in the American Shakespeare Festival's *Taming of the Shrew*—although it may be mentioned that one newspaper critic based his entire review of the production upon the "racial anomaly" of Kate's parentage! True, there are very few plays specifically requiring Negro actors, and fewer still involving only Negroes. Yet sooner or later the color-line in casting is bound to fall. It has already fallen in many festival theaters doing repertories of classics, where type-casting is not required; likewise in some regional and many university theaters. As more trained Negro actors and actresses are graduated from drama departments, places must, and NTC believes will, be found for them in professional theater.

Meanwhile, we applaud the spirit and the work of the Free Southern Theatre in taking fine drama to audiences throughout the Deep South from its base in New Orleans. More groups of this caliber are needed in all our cities with large Negro populations if the American theater is to do its part in the task of cultural integration. At present, for audiences as well as for actors, the "culture boom," as Alvin Toffler points out, "is still very much a white man's affair."

# To The Community Theater

Most of NTC's recommendations to the Community Theater sector come under the heading of raising the sights and extending the horizon. Community theaters need to adopt a truly professional stance regarding their work. Unless they are content with the old image of the dramatic club doing plays for fun and fellowship, they must gear themselves to professional standards of workmanship and discipline, and tolerate nothing less. They should also gain an outlook that is not merely local or regional but national and even international. They should know and feel that they belong to the *whole* of theater, not just to their own operation. They can start, if they have not already done so, by making contact with the American Community Theatre Association (ACTA) and with the American National Theatre and Academy (ANTA) for valuable assistance.

Community theaters should also aim high and then, as the advertisements say, s-t-r-e-t-c-h. It is not by repeating sure, easy, shopworn plays that they will grow as artists or build discerning audiences. The best drama within their capacity should be their target; it will lift the level of the group and the community faster and higher than any amount of mediocre stuff. It will expand their capacity.

NTC would like to see all community theaters learn, too, the excitement of trying new things: new plays, new procedures, and (at least intramurally) experimental kinds of theater. To produce an original play, each season, for example, with the author as guest of the community, can transform the group's whole concept of the artistic process. It places the group at the growing, the creating point, instead of merely at the using end of the line. It also helps a playwright up one rung of the ladder in his career.

When we ask the community theaters to take a professional stance, we neither ask nor expect them to become professionals in the sense of joining guilds and hiring union people. They do need, as their artistic head, a salaried, professionally trained director, and if they can afford one, a designer-technical director who is in essence a professional. Such persons are available and looking for opportunities to put into practice what they have learned in the universities. Many already have found their artistic home and have sunk their roots in the fertile soil of American communities. For them, theater is "a faith that one professes, rather than a profession in which one has faith." The special challenge of Community Theater, as recently expressed by Archibald MacLeish, is that it "preserves, in the all-enveloping anonymization of the U.S.A., the human dimension and the individual person's identity," both necessary conditions for the creative artist.

# To The Educational Theater

## *Training Talent*

It may be somewhat less imperative today than ten years ago to urge upon universities the need to take a more professional view of the theater and of the theater arts they teach and practice. Professional companies are already in existence on a few campuses, and more will come into being year by year as the advantages of collaboration between the university and the professional theater are recognized and the inevitable problems of adjustment find solution.

Many drama departments, however, are still very far from viewing their work as an integral part, an indispensable function, of the theater as a whole. They teach their courses, produce their plays, graduate their students entirely within the context of a liberal education. There is nothing wrong with that so far as it goes—up to the Bachelor's degree. The trouble comes at the advanced levels, where older, selected, self-motivated students are supposed to be *trained.* In all too many graduate departments the same relaxed liberal arts climate and amateur outlook prevail. The students are sent out with their Master's degree, but are masters of nothing—yet. They still have not performed or produced plays under conditions, disciplines, or standards recognized by the profession they hope to enter. They still lack anything that could be called a career apprenticeship. They still need to acquire what we have called a professional stance. And the worst of it is, they do not even *know* they need these things, and do not know where to go next or why their talents are not wanted. All they know is that they have taken courses, worked on shows, have a diploma to prove they passed the requirements, and are all fired up to go into theater.

NTC believes it is high time for every college and university theater department to take a close, hard look at its program in the light of this situation. Let it ask itself *why* it is offering each of its courses and to what end or ends its students are taking them. What will they do with them when they graduate? What are they equipped to do? What further preparation or training will they need, and where can they get it? What can the department do to give its students more than they now get, and send them out more fully prepared? These are questions that need to be asked and answered even in the context of undergraduate studies; at the graduate level they cannot be avoided.

Now, there exist outlets where the drama M.A. can find employment, usually in teaching and directing in a secondary school or junior college, sometimes in a community theater. But his prospects are not brilliant if his graduate training consists only of a year or two spent on a variety of studies and tasks in an atmosphere largely dominated by undergraduate laxness and the dilettante spirit. If he aims higher, whether as artist or as teacher, he will have to acquire not only special skills but also professional discipline, concentration, intensity. His university *could* have provided these. Why did it fail?

## *Professionals on Campus*

Since drama departments have become a major source of trained talent for the professional theater, and since the best kind of apprenticeship is obtained through working with experienced professionals, it behooves the leaders of university and professional theater to explore all the ways and means of bringing professionals into daily working contact with advanced students seeking theatrical careers. Acting is usually the first area to benefit from such collaboration, and it was the one primarily considered at the 1966 Minneapolis conferences referred to above. To have on the campus a company or at least a nucleus of good professional actors prepared to share their skills and experience with the ablest students—even for limited periods, such as a term or a summer season—can do immeasurable good. Such a group, by presenting the kind of plays and the quality of production with which the students in the department are not yet quite able to cope by themselves, can provide the needed apprenticeship for the ones who are ready to take advantage of it; it can also set an example by its work for all others involved in theater arts—to say nothing of its contribution to the whole student body and the community.

Acting, however, is only one of the areas (albeit the most conspicuous) that the university theater department is called upon to serve, and the one which, along with those of production, can benefit most directly from the presence of a professional troupe. The two most neglected artists in academic theater—we mean the playwright and the director, the fundamental creators—need a different sort of program to bring their talents to fruition.

Samuel Selden, a wise and seasoned teacher whom we have quoted before in this report, explains why this is so:

> It takes the writing of five, or six, or more full-length dramas to mature an author. . . . It takes the experience of handling all the details of an equal number of productions to develop a director. He must try and fail and try again. The more promising is his talent, the longer in all probability will it take him to develop the whole of it. The university will (with great patience perhaps) help these men and women through the stumbling creation of their one, first,

product. If these individuals turn out to be persons of genius, the professional playhouse may present the playwright's seventh play or the director's eighth show. Where, however, and how, are the two artists going to sharpen up their faculties in the long interval between the university education and the finished performance?

Selden, who said this in 1963 in the course of an address on "Future Directions of Educational Theatre" given at the University of Texas,[4] offered what NTC believes to be a most cogent proposal. He envisages the university's "image of its opportunity" in respect to theater arts as consisting of five elements, each having its proper place and function in a series. "At one end . . . is the student, the potential artist; at the other is the audience. In between are three agencies which bring the two opposites together. Next to the student stands the present curriculum," equipping him with the essential groundwork of general education, discipline, dramatic techniques. "At the other end of the picture, the audience must be served by that kind of agent which will provide . . . the most imaginative, the most stirring, the most inspiring entertainment possible, . . . something *good in itself*—not something good because of, or in spite of, something else." This agent, in Selden's fourth position, is the professional group, "looking straight to the spectator whom it must please and from whom it must draw a continuous supply of box office revenue to survive," hence using nothing that is obviously amateur. In the middle, the third position, to bridge these opposites, he would place an "experimental stock company" ("stock" because it would produce one play at a time):

> It would be a loosely organized group of theater workers who have already obtained their degrees and want to extend their experience. . . . They would receive no academic credit for their work. They would be bound by no term of attendance, be limited by no deadlines, and be governed by the very minimum of university regulations. All the members of the company would be volunteers. Some would be recent graduates, some would be alumni, some would be visitors from other parts of the country.
>
> Their place of activity would be a large room with a few lights, perhaps a platform or two and some movable chairs for whatever audience wished to come to see the products. That would be all.
>
> The purpose of the group would be to provide both directors and playwrights with an opportunity to prepare, in the simplest forms possible, one play after another. The author would experiment. The director would experiment. However, no one would be penalized for failure. Since no credit toward a degree was involved, no participant would have to play safe about pleasing a teacher. Since no one's monetary investment was involved, none of the authors and directors would have to conform to box office rules. . . . The showman who boldly tried to work out what he thought was a great idea, and fell flat on his face doing it, could pick himself up and bravely try again.

If there were not enough scripts available in the group, I would solicit some from authors elsewhere. There are many promising plays floating around. They need production. Some plays presented once need to be revised and tried again.

I would urge that the program of the Experimental Stock Company consist of two kinds of presentation: "finished" plays and plays "in progress." The "finished" plays would not necessarily be those which the authors and their associates felt were ready for unveiling on a professional stage, but works which had been carried as far as the authors were able to take them in the frame of their present experience. These would be rehearsed carefully in detail and performed in full, one each month. The plays in progress would be given in the form of readings, with the actors seated in a semicircle at one end of the room—once a week. After both the full performances and the simpler readings would be critiques. All the members of the Experimental Stock Company would participate. The spectators also would be urged to express themselves. In the light of this criticism the authors, the directors—and with them the actors—would be able to evaluate themselves. Thus all would have an opportunity to develop their creative talents from script to script and performance to performance—looking to the day when their skills would be of such value to the associated professional group that it would adopt them as mature craftsmen.

While the university theater department was aiding the Experimental Stock Company, the company would be rendering an equivalent service to the department. It would help the beginning students to see their preparatory work in the right proportion. It would help them to grasp the difference between first and second steps. It would give the more gifted of the students something to look forward to in the way of postgraduate experience. It would remove from them in the college stage of their work the feeling of a frantic need to try to complete their training in one giant stride. Those who were really serious about their desire to learn could plan to labor with the Experimental Stock Company, not for just one, but for several years—as long as it was necessary to mature thoughts and to achieve a really professional skill.

The primary advantage of an association with this group would be to the playwrights and the directors. However, the company could be of service also to the developing of another person who has been neglected by our universities. He is the dramatic critic. The critic who worked continuously in the body of the Experimental Stock Company would be able to exercise his analytical faculties on a wide range of creative efforts week after week, and to have his opinions challenged repeatedly by the judgment of the artists themselves and the spectators attending the critiques.

What Selden has described here is an expansion of the procedures originally devised by George Pierce Baker and used in his famous "47 Workshop," but applied now in the context of a fully developed department of theater arts. We quote him at length—although, for lack of space, omitting his rationale—because he gives what we believe to be the most promising university program yet conceived for developing playwrights, directors, and critics.

## *Innovational Function*

If the words "new" and "experimental" seem to have been repeated *ad nauseam* in this report, it is because NTC believes them to be the keys to the theater's healthy growth and development, particularly on our campuses. A few years ago the director of the Ford Foundation's program in the humanities and the arts. W. McNeil Lowry, charged that universities have "in the main" sacrificed professionalism and have "drifted along with the society in the perpetuation of the amateur and the imitator." In university theater, we know this to be true; and we know equally well that it must not be allowed to continue if our highest educational institutions are to pull their weight in the American theater.

At the close of his excellent chapter on "Culture on the Campus," in *The Culture Consumers*, Alvin Toffler quotes two distinguished educators on this point: Dean Birenbaum of the New School for Social Research, who declares that "it should be the function of the university to be the 'cutting edge'—the promoter of the avant-garde, the innovational"; and Harold Taylor, former president of Sarah Lawrence College, who has said, "The university is the exact place for the exploration of the new." NTC, more than half of whose members direct college and university theaters, fully endorses these statements and urges their application.

In our opinion, the innovational function does not impede but rather completes the artistic aims of a culturally conservative institution such as a university. Indeed it supplies the missing link in the theater's chain of past-present-future. It makes possible, moreover, what Joseph Golden calls "an intrinsic ethic of operation, virtually the only positive ethic in operation at the moment either in the universities or out of them." The university's very conservatism, he says, inculcates three major ideas into the growing numbers of students (20 percent each year) in instructional theater programs:

> First, that the inheritance of classical drama provides not only the intellectual satisfactions of reflecting on the living continuum of human vision, but also a practical source of vivid theater that should be exploited regularly and freely; second, that there are rational processes available—drawn from literature, science, and art—that can endow the theater with a sense of coherence and purpose; and third, that effective and satisfying theater depends heavily on a continuity of ideal and leadership.[5]

University instruction and practice in dramatic art make the "living continuum of human vision" most real and vital when they induce the student to see and participate in an art that is still going on.

### *Related Performing Arts*

It is perhaps too much to expect departments of drama and theater arts, on top of their immediate duties, to involve themselves in any formal or systematic fashion with cinema, television, dance, and musical theater; yet in the over-all picture of the performing arts each of these has its place, and each of them has a role to play in the formation of the theater artist, the student of drama, and the discerning spectator. Television and films are so much a part of Americans' everyday life that they have usually been taken for granted; the study of their history and current techniques, the comparative analysis of their products both in the United States and abroad, and the critical examination of these media as art forms have been so neglected in our schools that otherwise "educated" people—to say nothing of many who function as critics—lack the necessary foundation for informed judgment. The dance, too, has lately joined the ranks of our major performing arts; yet where do we find it in the colleges and universities? In probably 90 percent of these institutions today, dance, which is a part of every complete actor's equipment, is treated as an adjunct to the physical education of women—not of men. As for musical drama, so often hailed as America's supreme contribution to the stage, if not to the arts in general, it is indeed practiced in many a campus theater, but so little is it studied as an art form that few college graduates could trace its evolution, differentiate its varieties, or critically evaluate a given show.

This NTC report will not undertake to advise colleges and universities on how to deal with these theater-related performing arts. A good many institutions already offer classroom or laboratory instruction, or both, in one or more of these subjects—and this practice is certain to increase with the recognition of their importance not only for the performer in training but also for the ordinary educated person.

## To The Professional Resident Theaters

### *Prescriptive Suggestions*

Nearly all the members of NTC who are not directors of educational theaters or drama departments are the guiding heads and hands of community or professional resident theaters. Their collective knowledge has yielded for this report a tremendous amount of information of a diagnostic nature concerning the present state of theater in America. Their experience and insight have also furnished the authors certain prescriptive pointers for directors of regional professional theaters. We offer them here without editorial comment:

1. Attach yourself and your company by roots sunk into your local community, but keep a national view, a world view on theater at large. Be a part of your neighborhood and city as well as of the country and the world.
2. Neither impose on your public nor play down to it, but study it. Build audiences by understanding them—how they live, and think, and react in their daily lives as well as at the theater.
3. Remember what Robert Edmond Jones told us: "The theater is a source, a wellspring of energy. All our effort as workers in the theater must be to learn how to throw the energy, the sense of life, out across the footlights—more excitement, more beauty, more splendor, more and more energy."
4. Make your theater express your community, including its highest ideals. Make it express America today—its stresses and conflicts, yes, and its shortcomings, but also its aspirations, its potentials, its truths.
5. Be an ally of the community and educational theater groups and leaders in your locality and region. Take part in their conferences; share your knowledge with them and learn from them in turn. Go into the schools with talks, short plays, demonstrations, and bring the students into your theater to enjoy your full productions. Offer your playhouse for regional drama festivals and competitions.
6. Set up workshop programs for perfecting the skills of your actors, for developing theater skills in local people who want to learn.
7. Set up experimental programs in directing and playwriting, for testing original plays in progress, for completed new plays, for a playwright in residence.
8. Work toward the goal of a repertory policy, of rotating your plays through a season. This need not, should not, be done mechanically. Play it by ear, play from your strength: increase the performances of your strong bills, or add new ones if you can, as you retire the weak ones. Repertory takes more than stock—more of almost everything—but it pays larger dividends in a company's morale and performance.

### *Repertory Theater*

We have already noted that quite a number of American (to say nothing of British) professional resident companies bearing the name of "repertory" do not in fact have a policy of keeping plays in rotation, but are essentially nonprofit stock companies. Stock is a natural first step toward repertory; it makes smaller demands upon a new organization and permits it to feel out its potential and its public, develop its strong points and mend its weak ones as it goes along. If a company is fairly small and must job-in actors to play leads or character roles, or if it is short of storage or shop space for scenery, props, and costumes, then doing one show at a time may be the only feasible method of producing plays. The playhouse can still become a continuing and developing civic asset, as most of our American resident theaters have proved.

Artistically, however, the stock theater, even when it can afford to import stars, betrays certain weaknesses and invites certain risks, the chief of which is the risk of impermanence. The essence of a resident theater company is to be "resident," to reside in approximately the same community as the theater and its public over an extended period of time. The essence of a company is to work together as "companions" in a common effort, and by continuing collaboration to perfect their work and their product. So long as only, say, three-fourths of the members form the stable group and the remainder come and go with the successive plays, it will always be difficult to maintain a strong *esprit de corps* or develop strong and confident ensemble acting. Even when the entire company remains intact throughout a season, yet produces separate plays in succession, there is a danger of imbalance that can lead to insecurity. A good play that does not happen to draw is likely to be discarded before its full potential is explored, whereas in repertory it could be nursed along through further rehearsals and occasional performances until it does succeed. An instant hit, on the other hand, tends to be kept in continuous performance until the cast grows stale and the unused actors grow restless and the season is thrown off balance.

Repertory, too, runs risks, but they are chiefly financial. It costs considerably more than stock to set up and maintain. It requires a larger theater plant—for rehearsal rooms, shops, and especially storage. It also takes a larger acting company to play repertory. Hume Cronyn, summing up the experience of the Tyrone Guthrie Theatre in an article published in *The Best Plays of 1965–66*, makes some cogent remarks on this matter:

> In the season of 1965 the Minnesota Theatre Company presented five plays in repertory: *Richard III*, *The Way of the World*, *The Cherry Orchard*, *The Caucasian Chalk Circle*, and a revival produc-

tion of its first season's popular success, *The Miser.* The overall season was 39 weeks; the playing season—including three weeks of school performances—was 31 weeks. The acting company consisted of 32 actors, six of whom were McKnight Fellowship students. Local extras were employed in all productions. "Artistic," design, and musical direction involved six directors under the leadership of Dr. Guthrie, while Oliver Rea and Peter Zeisler as managing directors headed a production staff of 64 and an administrative staff of 26. The production and operating budgets combined to something over $1,000,000 and . . . there was a reported deficit in 1965 (the first deficit experienced) of $82,000.

After enumerating several "difficulties" encountered in the Guthrie Theatre program, including the wage scale, "which is generally too low to attract actors who have wives or husbands, children or leases, or who have been so improvident as to commit themselves to anything other than a part," he says:

> The professional acting company must be enlarged. Twenty-six actors plus six McKnight Fellowship students, no matter how gifted, should not be expected to carry a season of five plays over 30 weeks, rehearsing for the best part of five months in the bargain. Actors playing big parts in a classical repertory do not give good performances when they play six and occasionally seven times a week.
>
> Even more important, a continuing attempt has to be made to challenge, stimulate, and develop the company as a whole—in every department. There is a comforting but dangerous tendency everywhere to settle for known quantities, the amiable and familiar coworker. There is also the reassuring rationale that "the company must be held together," and that growth is only possible under such circumstances. This is an arguable matter of degree. Carried to an extreme, the Auld Lang Syne principle can make for arrested development.

Then, situating the matter of cost in its public context, Cronyn goes on:

> Development is not always a matter of money, but money helps. Large companies cost money. Training programs, touring, workshops, and better wages all cost money. . . . The concept of the theater as a cultural asset, an institution not less significant than a public library, art gallery, symphony orchestra, or the Metropolitan Opera comes hard. There seems to be an American tendency to build impressive theaters, spend a great deal on physical productions, and expect companies of equal magnificence to materialize on cue. . . . Perhaps the allocation of available money—never easily available—has to be reconsidered to the sacrifice of outward and visible signs, in the hope of an inward, and temporarily invisible, grace.

Is the repertory candle, in view of these vexing problems, worth the cost? Let us simply quote Hume Cronyn's conclusion:

> I believe that the repertory system, properly supported, properly developed, holds the best of all hopes for the American theater; the hope for better actors, directors, designers, all theater crafts; the hope for better service to the playwright and the eventual development of new ones. That hope will only become a promise with time, the nourishment of talent, and our continuing reach. We may exceed our grasp in these beginnings—but there is no alternative other than mediocrity.[6]

That others, both in the theater and in positions to help it, agree with this stand, share the same outlook, and are prepared to strive toward the same goal, is, NTC believes, self-evident. The decision of Washington's Arena Stage to adopt the system of rotating repertory in 1967–68 is only one of the latest signs that for the permanent professional resident theater in America repertory is inevitable.

### *New Plays*

We opened this part of our report with a truncated quotation from the editor of *The Best Plays of 1965–66* in which he was writing about Broadway's "creative responsibility." Let us now supply the omitted portion of that statement which, besides dealing with an aspect of theatrical decentralization—a topic that has engrossed the National Theatre Conference ever since its founding—raises the question of the creative power, indeed the staying power, of the regional professional theater:

> . . . those who look to decentralization as the hope of the American theater of the future are looking for a short way home that leads over a cliff. The regional theater's playscripts are not *really* brought by the stork or even by the Rockefeller Foundation or the National Foundation on the Arts, they are gestated the hard way in New York. To change the metaphor a little, the regional theater is a long, long way from being weaned. If New York goes dry, the regional theater must starve or worse; and by worse, I mean Ibsen and Chekhov.[7]

Leaving aside that last aspersion—since we can think of even worse fates, such as having to repeat endlessly the vapid comedy "smashes" of recent Broadway seasons—we would note that Guernsey does touch on a sensitive issue; sensitive because it is vital not only to regional theater but also to the future of American drama.

If Broadway can produce only a handful of new American plays a season—and, from these, only one or two of a substantial or serious nature—it is indeed going dry. We have, in this report, urged upon community theaters, upon colleges and universities, and upon professional companies sponsored by universities the responsibility to find and foster new playwrights and to help older writers carry their creativity to new levels of development. This same duty, NTC insists, devolves no less upon the independent professional regional theaters. Doubtless a playwright is, on balance, more helped than hindered by seeing a new work of his produced by amateur companies under college or community directors. Certainly this is true if he can see the same play produced —as under the sponsorship of the American Playwrights Theatre program—by 50 or more different groups. But the ultimate artistic success of any dramatic work depends in large part upon the quality of the director and the cast with whom the author collaborates; and it is of the highest importance that this quality be professional.

Producing a brand new script by an unknown playwright-in-the-making is always a major risk for everyone concerned. It is no wonder that the relatively new resident theaters, with all their other risks, have been loath to assume this one. But assume it they must, if they are to carry out their creative mission, merit the largesse they are receiving, and fulfill the promise inherent in their very existence. Otherwise they are doomed, to use Otis Guernsey's metaphor, to suckle at the shrinking breast of Broadway and become another lost hope in the annals of the American theater.

NTC has confidence in the spirit, purpose, and energy of those who are directing our professional regional theaters. It believes that they understand their responsibility to the American drama and dramatists of tomorrow and that, just as they are now coping with the problems of repertory, they will find ways to meet and discharge this greater responsibility. It would only urge that they give it the highest priority.

## To The American Public

Theater in America has reached a critical point in its evolution, a point at which it needs more than ever before the understanding and support of the public at large. In a broad sense this is because theater, or "the theater," in America has not yet fully evolved into an American Theater, still less into The American Theater. NTC's use of these terms, however, may be taken as expressing its faith in that eventuality.

Most of our theaters have traits which we and others associate with the United States, yet it would be risky to claim for them a national character comparable, for example, to that of the British, French, or Japanese theater. No one in particular is to blame for this; it is simply a fact—a fact which many have failed to recognize.

Our theater has come a long way from the colonialism that stamped its plays and performances until well into the present century, when we began to say it had at last come of age. (And indeed, between 1920 and 1950, we could say that with some confidence, if only because our best plays of those years had a noticeable effect abroad.) Nevertheless, the successive waves of avant-garde drama that have captivated our youth and strongly influenced the work of our newer playwrights and directors during the past one and one-half decades—notably the Theater of the Absurd, the Theater of Cruelty, and now the New Theater—are not of American origin but have come to us from France, Britain, and Central and Eastern Europe. This drama undeniably marks an international trend that cannot be ignored. What is regrettable is that its emulation (often its imitation) over here shows that too few of our younger playwrights are deriving their chief sustenance from the native soil and scene or speaking to the hearts of Americans.

In this connection it may be noted that as a people we seem to take the theater for granted—to take it, that is, or leave it. Americans need to learn that the theater, like the arts in general, has to be nurtured, cultivated, publicly sustained; it does not evolve all by itself in a vacuum, or on a shoestring.

Mention the word "subsidy" in connection with the arts, and an American tends to think first of the big philanthropic foundations (a peculiarly American institution), and (more recently, thanks to our belated acknowledgment of public responsibility) of the National Endowments for the Arts and Humanities. He does not, as a rule, realize that while some particular grants look quite large, the total sums allocated to the arts are extremely small (not over 4 or 5 percent) when compared with private and public subsidies to support science and technology (to say nothing of medicine, education, and welfare); or that out of the total foundation grants to the arts as a whole only a tiny percentage goes to the arts of the theater. Nor does he realize that all of the subsidy which the theater needs cannot be expected to come from one-half dozen major foundations and the federal endowments. It must come, in the main, from sources nearer to the localities in which it is to be used—that means, from the people who want good theater where they live, and who care enough to support it.

Another common misconception affecting the theater is the popular impression that America is undergoing a Culture Boom. The latest authoritative surveys of the so-called performing arts give little evidence to justify that impression. They show that while we have more theater activity than a generation ago, the proportion of Americans who see or take part in it on the professional level remains very small and narrowly restricted. Moreover, despite our national prosperity, as soon as we compare the over-all American theater picture with that of, say, France or Germany or England, our image shrinks. Our perspective is as short as our theater's history.

NTC believes this distortion of our national mirror has something to do with our American habit of impatience, perhaps with our inbred optimism. We read about projects for a new building or a development program, and already we see the work as an accomplished fact. Being impatient and overly optimistic, we easily become disillusioned when the fact is slow to materialize or proves less than we had imagined. Often our disillusionment leads to condemnation—seeking someone to blame—and from that to a rejection of the whole idea, which is discouraging to fresh efforts. This has happened with many a promising theatrical enterprise. "Art is long," the ancients have told us, but Americans are in a rush to get results. We do not seem yet to have learned that it takes years to mature an artist, to create a tradition, or to establish a resident repertory theater.

Americans, too, are prone to think in terms of machines or systems that can be designed, built, discarded, replaced, transported, reassembled. But the theater, as Robert Edmond Jones reminded us, is not a machine: "It is an organism. It is alive. It lives and breathes. It will not allow itself to be reduced to mechanical terms." Systems are only servants. In the last analysis, the theater is people—people out of the past, people here and now, and people yet to come.

Doubtless theater people are as impatient, unpredictable, and fallible as their public—but no more so. They may follow "a different drummer," but they respect their own discipline. They produce their best results when they are free of interference from the artistically unqualified, whether in Congress or the local P.T.A. As a nation we adhere to democratic principles, yet we defer to the expert in certain fields. We leave the scientist and technologist to work out solutions by themselves —indeed, we give them millions to spend as they see fit. Why, then, do we treat the theater artist, whom we support so feebly, as if we knew his job better than he does?

In the recommendations that conclude this report, a certain emphasis falls necessarily upon large-scale proposals calling for centralized action in behalf of the theater as a whole. Let us point out in advance that NTC, in urging these broad undertakings, does not for one instant abandon its faith in the inevitability of the theater's decentralization. NTC firmly believes, too, that sheer organization is no substitute for direct operation; or nationalization, for local autonomy; or institutions, for dedicated individuals. Given the present critical state of theater across America, however, it believes that only action on a nationwide scale by the strongest agencies available has a chance of carrying the theater over the threshold to its potential future.

We have dealt here with the theater in terms of its various sectors and segments, its facets and problems, the obstacles that impede its progress and the opportunities that challenge its leaders and public to greater effort and achievement. Despite this fragmentation of the issues, the final impression we desire to leave with those who read this report is that of the totality, the wholeness, indeed the oneness of theater in America. For, however diversified its forms and manifestations, the living theater is and must be one—one profession for those who labor and create in it, and a unique life-enhancing experience for those who find joy in the fruits of that creative labor. In NTC's view, it is an enterprise extending from coast to coast in which participants and sustainers alike have essentially the same purpose: to raise America's dramatic art to a stature befitting a great nation, and to make it accessible to all her people.

Is this goal beyond the powers of Americans to achieve? Not if our people share NTC's conviction that the future is what we make it.

# VI. RECOMMENDATIONS

# Recommendations

APPRAISING THE present state of theater in America and envisaging the theater's potential for growth and for service to the American people as a whole, the National Theater Conference offers the following broad recommendations:

1. *Intensified training of Community Theater leaders and directors.* It is suggested that a series of national workshops should be organized in various regional locations, under the direction of the American Community Theatre Association (ACTA) and in cooperation with other sponsors, including universities, state Arts Councils, private and industrial foundations, and government agencies.

2. *Planned development of Regional Professional Theaters.* There should probably be an organization plan under which cities desiring a resident professional theater could register with the National Council on the Arts. Subsequent feasibility studies could then be undertaken by the appropriate state Arts Council, under the general supervision of the Associated Councils of the Arts (ACA). When a project's feasibility is confirmed, the state Arts Council could undertake to bring together dynamic theater men and women interested in establishing such a theater with the local civic leaders concerned. Problems could be referred to a National Advisory Board for Regional Professional Theater—such a Board to be appointed by the National Endowment for the Arts. This is simply a suggested procedure.

3. ***Chartering of nonprofit professional State Theaters by the legislatures of the several states.***

In its search for a national theater, the United States has been unsuccessful in finding any kind of official status for such development. There is a national character latent in various fragmented sectors of the theater in America, but there is no entity representing the nation. NTC recommends the establishment or (in the case of existing dramatic companies of high artistic competence) the designation of an official State Theater in every state, with attendant support from public and private sources. These State Theaters would have the responsibility of illustrating the best standards of dramatic art in each state, and would give an official character, through their legislative charter, to the United States National Theater. The State Theaters would all be professional and nonprofit in nature and autonomous in management, and would eventually have approximately the same magnitude and prestige as the Tyrone Guthrie Theatre in Minneapolis. The District of Columbia would also be expected to designate an official theater, such as the existing Arena Stage.

4. ***Establishment of a National Theater Festival of America.***

In addition to the American College Theatre Festival already being planned to take place annually in the John F. Kennedy Center for the Performing Arts in Washington, NTC recommends the creation of a general National Theater Festival of America program to highlight the living theater in a multitude of locations throughout the country. The form of this Festival might be participation on the home stages by all community theaters, professional resident theaters, educational theaters—university, college, secondary school—and children's theaters. Each group would carry news of the Festival on its programs, and would produce one play each year as its National Theater Festival play. NTC believes this Festival would focus attention, both regionally and nationally, on the thousands of groups producing drama. Each group would contribute 10 percent of the gross receipts from its Festival production to a National Theater Festival Fund, to be administered by the National Endowment for the Arts in behalf of a National Theater. The National Endowment for the Arts would also appoint a National Theater Festival of America Committee to administer the Festival centrally and to advise and supervise local committees in the various communities.

5. ***Greater encouragement and support for outstanding nonprofessional Community Theaters.***
   Foundation grants to nonprofessional community groups have been extremely few and small. Grants from the National Endowment for the Arts have not yet touched this sector of the theater, and those from the U.S. Office of Education have necessarily been to school related operations. NTC suggests that a system, or some form of concerted action, that would enable excellent community theater groups to obtain greater consideration in the awarding of foundation grants—including grants from local municipalities, business and industrial firms, and civic organizations would be a signal service to the entire American theater. It would stimulate such groups to strive to provide theater at a higher level than at present and to stretch their artistic capacities by attempting the best, not just the easiest, dramatic works, as well as by lending their directorial and producing services to the authors of new plays.

6. ***A national program of encouragement to communities to establish children's theaters.***
   It is obvious that the United States must increase the opportunities in theater arts for its young people. These opportunities ought to begin at an early age—in lower elementary grades—and continue through elementary and secondary school years. A suggested approach to the development of children's theaters in our city neighborhoods and our local (including rural) communities across the land is through the existing schools. While the Children's Theatre Conference has done very important pioneer work, it is now time for all agencies—federal, state, and local—to combine in assuring the continuity and development of theater for youth. This is one area where local community theaters could also take on much of the responsibility of encouraging the establishment of theaters for young people.

7. ***A national plan to bring the professional theater into closer collaboration with college and university theaters.***
   Without question, the infusion of professionalism into academic theater—through resident playwrights, guest directors and actors, and full-time professional companies—is a major theater development of our time. But the evolution is only in the beginning phase. Two high-level conferences (those held at Minneapolis and described in this report) have already considered the subject with regard to actors. NTC recommends a carefully planned series of national conferences aimed at a thorough exploration of

the ways and means of university theater and professional theater collaboration in every facet of dramatic art. The ultimate goal would be to establish direct contact between university administrators and their theater directors on the one hand and professional theater leaders and agencies on the other, so that programs of harmonious collaboration can be instituted and successfully developed to the mutual benefit of the universities and the professional theater.

8. *Encouragement of playwrights to interpret America.*

A preponderant amount of the drama written by Americans in the past 25 years—to judge from what has been published or staged—is more reflective of foreign or international influences, when it is not directly imitative, than it is of the spirit of America and Americans. To be sure, the American theater, if it is to be strong and respected, must produce the best plays from many nations; but it must also export the finest and most representative American drama. NTC believes that our theater has not come near to realizing its potential in a body of dramatic literature created in contemporary terms and presenting a true picture of the United States and its people.

NTC's vision is of an American theater that is not attached to one stratum of society or of taste, but which joyously and fearlessly expresses the manifold life of America. This life ought to be seen and shown creatively, in its greatness as well as in its weakness, in all its ethnic variety and in its composite spirit, in the rich color of American folkways and in the flavor of American speech. Within this epic idea there is room and challenge for good drama of every sort: drama to be found in every region, in every kind of work; the tragedy and comedy of places and of people in places; plays about the variegated life of America seen big and seen small, but seen with understanding.

NTC addresses this recommendation to all playwrights (both those secure in their reputations and those just beginning their careers), to all teachers of playwriting, to all producers and directors, to all performing artists of the stage, to all drama critics and to all playgoers: that they encourage and foster in all possible ways a drama that reflects the vitality of our national faith —faith expressed without patriotic clichés—something that exists in the heart and may not be spoken at all, but that colors our way of saying and doing things—in such a manner that a deep and true portrait of us as a people may be conveyed creatively to other peoples.

# NOTES

## I. In New York

1. On the economic picture of Broadway, off-Broadway and other types of theater in the United States, see the recent survey by William J. Baumol and William G. Bowen, *Performing Arts: The Economic Dilemma,* New York: Twentieth Century Fund, 1966.

2. For further opinions on union activity in the New York theater, see Baumol and Bowen, *op. cit.,* pp. 230–235.

3. In resigning his position as consultant-director of the Legitimate Theatre Industry Exploratory Commission on June 21, 1967, after three years of service, John Wharton gave as his principal reason the Commission's decision to leave the campaign for ticket reform "to be conducted through other channels." He added:

   > I believe this decision was a mistake and will delay relief indefinitely. . . . In any event, the decision . . . removes from the Commission agenda the field of exploration which has interested me most. . . . I hope that our legislators will some day realize that the New York free enterprise theater sprouted to greatness when it was really free; that 50 years of harassment have been consistently hurtful and never helpful to anyone but the black marketeers; and that some day they will set it free once more. When and if that happy day arrives, I hope the then industry leaders will try a giant leap forward, and not struggle frantically to return to the ways of the 1920's. I would hope to see a whole new system of ticket selling worked out—it won't be easy to do—a system that could use automation, with a scale of prices that provided tickets for the least affluent and went up to a price that gave the theater the money now going into the pockets of speculators. When that happens, Broadway will be able to afford more productions, and more experimentation—although detractors seem to forget that Beckett, Ionesco, Pinter, Bellow and Feiffer have all appeared on Broadway.

4. Alvin Toffler, in *The Culture Consumers: A Study of Art and Affluence in America,* New York: St. Martin's Press, 1964, cites another reason for the drama critics' power. Unlike the symphony orchestra, he notes, "the profit-making segments of the theater . . . all present exact repeats of the same program night after night. They are engaged in what might be called 'quasi-mass-production'. . . . This . . . explains why the drama critics in New York are so much more powerful than the music critics. One or two bad reviews by the major New York theater critics can drive a play off the boards in 24 or 48 hours. A bad review of a concert by the New York Philharmonic will not put the orchestra out of business. For one thing, the orchestra sells seats by subscription, so that many of its listeners have paid in advance for the whole season. But beyond this, the concertgoer knows that even if Alan Rich of the *Herald Tribune* charged the orchestra with being slack when it played Beethoven last night, it might be superb in its performance of Brahms tomorrow. In contrast, if Walter Kerr . . . says that the script of a new play was

thin and its staging poor, the audience knows that these defects will be built into each subsequent stamping of the play," pp. 164–165.

5. Both Tennessee Williams and Arthur Miller have new plays scheduled for the season of 1967–1968.
6. Marston Balch is preparing a separate report in greater depth on the subject of the playwright.
7. NTC did not undertake a survey of the social, financial, or educational composition of the Broadway audience. For detailed information on this subject, the authors recommend two recent studies: Alvin Toffler, *The Culture Consumers op. cit.*, pp. 24–41, and Baumol and Bowen, *Performing Arts op. cit.*, pp. 71–97.
8. For a detailed history of off-Broadway groups, authors, and plays, the reader is referred to *The Off-Broadway Theater*, by Julia S. Price; New York: The Scarecrow Press, 1962.
9. It should be noted that a few off-Broadway theaters are organized as non-profit organizations: Circle in the Square, Theatre '67 ('68, etc.), and the American Place Theatre. The last two groups are specifically organized for the testing and improvement of new plays and playwrights and have received grants-in-aid for this purpose.
10. For further information on plays presented off-Broadway, see Julia Price's *The Off-Broadway Theater, op. cit.*, pp. 192–253.
11. The term "Off off-Broadway" is said to have been coined in 1960 by Jerry Tallmer, then theater critic for *The Village Voice*.
12. This excerpt from Michael Smith's article on Off off-Broadway appeared in the *Tulane Drama Review*, X, (Summer 1966) pp. 159–160.
13. Papp's January 1968 "stunt" production of *Hamlet* as a "shattered-focus Happening" seemed to most commentators to be a radical departure from the concept described by Judith Crist.
14. *Gleichshaltung* may be defined as "regimentation, bringing into line, elimination of aberrancy, homogenization.

## II. In Communities - The Volunteer

1. This rationale of community theater appears in Kenneth Macgowan's book, *Footlights Across America: Towards a National Theatre,* New York: Harcourt, Brace & Co., 1929, p. 20.
2. For further statistics on theater audiences, see William J. Baumol and William G. Bowen, *Performing Arts: The Economic Dilemma,* New York: Twentieth Century Fund, 1966, p. 96.
3. Earlier published surveys of the decentralized American theater will be found in *Advance from Broadway: 19,000 Miles of American Theatre,* by Norris Houghton, New York: Harcourt, Brace & Co., 1941; *A History of the American Theatre, 1700–1950,* by Glenn Hughes, New York: Samuel French, 1951.
4. The community theater movement is described by Dr. Joseph Golden in *The Death of Tinker Bell: The American Theatre in the 20th Century,* Syracuse, N. Y.: Syracuse University Press, 1967, pp. 164–168.

5. The Gallup poll figure regarding theater audiences is in wide variance with other estimates. NTC would rate 18,000,000 as presently very low, considering all kinds of theater productions. On the other hand, Baumol and Bowen estimate the total number of individuals attending professional theater in 1963–1964 (Broadway, Off-Broadway and Regional Theaters) at only a little more than 2,000,000. *Op. cit.*, p. 95.
6. More on the "culture consumers" will be found in Alvin Toffler *The Culture Consumers: A Study of Art and Affluence in America*, New York: St. Martin's Press, 1964.
7. For a complete listing of plays see *The "Most Satisfying" Plays of the New England Theatre Conference, 1959–1961*, Special Projects Committee, Frances Elder Chidley, Chairman, Winchester, Massachusetts, 1961.
8. For a discussion of subject matter in community theater play selection, see Marston Balch's "The Right Play in the Right Place: An Idea for Community Theatres," *Theatre Arts*, XL, (August 1956), p. 64–66.
9. Samuel Selden, whose comments on problems of American playwriting appear in this report, has been an NTC member and a leader in the American theater for 40 years. Now retired as head of the University of North Carolina Playmakers, and as head of the Theatre Arts Department at UCLA, he was a guest lecturer at Southern Illinois University in 1966–1967.

## III. In Education

1. This material appears in a biography of George Pierce Baker by Wisner Payne Kinne, *George Pierce Baker and the American Theatre*, Cambridge, Mass.: Harvard University Press, 1954, p. 39.
2. George Freedley, NTC member, and noted theater historian, was for many years Theater Librarian of the New York Public Library. He died in 1967.
3. 1967 *Directory of American College Theatre* (2nd edition) reports show: 39 schools offer graduate work through Doctor's level; 98 schools at Master's level; 45 schools offer graduate work but no degree; 13 schools offer theater minors at M.A. level.
4. In the past, only the American universities have accepted theatrical production as part of the liberal arts program. This viewpoint is now being changed in a few European instances: Bristol and Leeds in England, and the University of Helsinki, among others.
5. 1967 *Directory of American College Theatre* gives the following statistics on theater program aims: recreational, 237 schools; avocational, 323; liberal arts–humanistic, 557; liberal arts–vocational, 135; pre-professional, 44.
6. This criticism of university theater programs was expressed by John Caldwell, drama director, University of South Florida, Tampa.
7. The comment on audiences was offered by Theodore Viehman, former director, Tulsa Little Theatre, and former NTC president.
8. The Wisconsin Idea Theatre received a three-year grant in 1966, from the National Endowment for the Arts, for research in developing a cultural program in communities under 10,000 population.
9. An example of university–professional collaboration, APA prepares its repertory productions at the University of Michigan, Ann Arbor, and appears

there in the early fall. Under the terms of their merger with the Phoenix Theatre, APA then moves to New York to open at the Lyceum Theatre in November, remaining there until June. During July and August they play in Los Angeles, where they are under the management of Jimmy Dolittle. The company also performed some of its repertory in Montreal at Expo '67.

10. A detailed discussion of Robert Brustein's experience as dean of the Yale School of Drama may be found in his article "First Year at Yale," in the July 1967 issue of *Cultural Affairs,* published by the Associated Councils of the Arts, New York.

11. For information presented in the Children's Theater portion of this report, NTC is especially indebted to: Jed H. Davis, Director of the Children's Theatre Conference; Nat Eek, Associate Director of CTC (both men NTC members); Sara Spencer and Winifred Ward, pioneers in Children's Theater; Dorothy Thames Schwartz, a leader in the Children's Theater movement; and Nellie McCaslin, author of *A History of Children's Theatre in the United States,* unpublished doctoral dissertation, New York University, 1956.

12. The National Council of the Arts in Education was organized in 1958 as a federation of national associations to speak for the arts at all educational levels.

13. The Children's Theatre Conference, like AETA, is divided into regions and covers the nation.

14. In 1963 there were 295 colleges offering courses in children's theater.

15. These comments on American children's theater appear in Joseph Golden's *The Death of Tinker Bell: The American Theatre in the 20th Century,* Syracuse, N. Y.: Syracuse University Press, 1967, pp. 160–163.

## IV. In Communities - The Professional

1. One resident company difficult to classify is the American Place Theatre. Though located several blocks west of Broadway on West 46th Street and using the premises of St. Clement's Episcopal Church, it is regarded as neither "Off-Broadway" nor "Off off-Broadway" in its aims and operation. It is committed to the task of "making dramatists out of poets and fiction writers," and its notable success has won it both national awards and, recently, $500,000 in foundation grants.

2. For detailed factual information about 23 of the leading resident companies, see "The Regional Theatre: Some Statistics," by Sandra Schmidt, in the *Tulane Drama Review,* X, 1 (Fall 1965), pp. 50–61. For collective information about regional theaters as a class, see William J. Baumol and William G. Bowen, *Performing Arts: The Economic Dilemma,* New York: Twentieth Century Fund, 1966.

3. The Arena Stage (Washington Drama Society) has since received a Ford Foundation grant of $96,450 "to expand its production-intern program."

4. *Cultural Affairs,* a new publication of the Associated Councils of the Arts, in its first issue (July 1967), lists among 38 "recent foundation grants to the performing arts," 33 grants specifically for theaters. These 33 grants range from $10,000 to $1,400,000, and total $4,155,606. The same issue lists "Grants approved by the National Council on the Arts, 1965–67": eight grants total-

ing $1,028,500 to "Drama," of which sum Resident Professional Theaters received $483,500 for "Development of their companies." More recent still is the Ford Foundation's three-year matching grant of $900,000 to the APA-Phoenix Repertory Company.

5. For more information on the Theatre of the Living Arts situation, see the *Tulane Drama Review,* XI, 4 (Summer 1967), pp. 18–21.
6. The average salary for actors in these regional theaters is far better, too, it may be added, than the $80 average of actors' salaries (minimum $50–$125) cited for all regional professional theaters in 1964–65 in the Baumol and Bowen survey, *op. cit.,* p. 114.
7. According to Baumol and Bowen, *op. cit.,* p. 28: "By 1910, more than a decade and one-half before Broadway's major troubles began, a sharp decline occurred in the operations of the commercial touring companies. From a high of more than 327 companies on tour at the turn of the century the number had fallen to less than 100 by 1915, and since 1932 the number has never risen above 25." (In 1966–67, it went up to 28.)

## V. The Challenge

1. The quote on Broadway is by Otis L. Guernsey Jr., editor of *The Best Plays of 1965–1966,* New York: Dodd, Mead & Co., 1966, p. 41.
2. For additional statistics on Broadway theater audiences, see William J. Baumol and William G. Bowen, *Performing Arts: The Economic Dilemma,* New York, Twentieth Century Fund, 1966, pp. 64–67, 458–465.
3. The most encouraging "sign" on Broadway, as this report goes to press, is the announcement (*New York Times,* January 29, 1968) of the creation of the Theater Development Fund, Inc., "a New York nonprofit organization, armed with grants totaling $400,000, including Federal money, [which] will buy tickets . . . at box office prices for up to five weeks to plays it regards as meritorious and in need of time to find their audiences." The tickets, said the Fund's president, John E. Booth, "will be sold at discount prices to selected groups [including] students, college faculty members, and professional people who might be interested in seeing the plays but who for a variety of reasons no longer attend the theater. . . . The Fund's intention is to maintain flexible and innovative operating procedures which would enable it to provide other forms of subsidy, . . . such as helping to secure rights and translations and helping to cover marginal costs for a limited period." The Fund, it was explained, can "give worthy productions a chance to find an audience, and a new audience a chance to find the theater."
4. Samuel Selden's address on "Future Directions of Educational Theatre" was published as one of a series of lectures entitled *Futures in American Theatre* by the Department of Drama, The University of Texas, Austin, 1963.
5. The quote on university theater programs is from Joseph Golden's *The Death of Tinker Bell: The American Theatre in the 20th Century,* Syracuse, N. Y.: Syracuse University Press, 1967, pp. 155–156.
6. Hume Cronyn's remarks on the Tyrone Guthrie Theatre appear in *The Best Plays of 1965–1966, op. cit.,* pp. 58–62.
7. This quotation on regional theater, by Otis L. Guernsey Jr., is from *The Best Plays of 1965–1966, op. cit.,* p. 41.

# BIBLIOGRAPHY

## Books

Ayers, Richard G. (ed.). *Directory of American College Theatre,* second edition. Washington, D. C.: American Educational Theatre Association, 1967.

Baumol, William J., and Bowen, William G. *Performing Arts: The Economic Dilemma.* New York: Twentieth Century Fund, 1966.

Blau, Herbert. *The Impossible Theater: A Manifesto.* New York: Macmillan, 1964.

Blum, David C. (ed). *A Pictorial History of the American Theatre, 100 Years—1860–1960.* New York: Chilton Co., 1960.

————. *Theatre World* (yearbooks, 1944–1964). New York: Greenberg.

Brown, John Mason. *Dramatis Personae.* New York: Viking Press, 1963.

Brustein, Robert. *Seasons of Discontent: Dramatic Opinions, 1959–1965. New York:* Simon & Schuster, 1965.

Burris–Meyer, Harold, and Cole, Edward C. *Theatres and Auditoriums.* (Second ed.) New York: Reinhold Corp., 1964.

Citron, Samuel J. *Dramatics for Creative Teaching.* New York: United Synagogue Commission on Jewish Education, 1961.

Clurman, Harold. *The Naked Image.* New York: Macmillan, 1966.

Cullman, Marguerite. *Occupation: Angel.* New York: W. W. Norton, 1963.

Dalrymple, Jean. *September Child: The Story of Jean Dalrymple by Herself.* New York: Dodd, Mead & Co., 1965.

Davis, Jed H., and Watkins, Mary J. L. *Children's Theatre: Play Production for the Child Audience.* New York: Harper, 1960.

De Grazia, Sebastian. *Of Time, Work and Leisure.* New York: Twentieth Century Fund, 1962.

Dorian, Frederick. *Commitment to Culture: Art Patronage in Europe. Its Significance for America.* Pittsburgh: University of Pittsburgh Press, 1964.

Downer, Alan M. *Fifty Years of American Drama, 1900–1950.* Chicago: Regnery, 1951.

Ehrensperger, Harold. *Religious Drama: Ends and Means.* New York: Abingdon Press, 1962.

Esslin, Martin. *The Theatre of the Absurd.* New York: Doubleday & Co., 1961.

Fergusson, Francis. *The Human Image in Dramatic Literature.* New York: Doubleday, 1957.

Fischer, Ernst. *The Necessity of Art.* Baltimore: Penguin Books, 1965.

Flanagan, Hallie. *Arena.* New York: Duell, Sloan & Pearce, 1940.

Free, William, and Lower, Charles. *History into Drama: A Source Book on Symphonic Drama.* New York: Odyssey Press, 1963.

Freedman, Morris. *Confessions of a Conformist.* New York: W. W. Norton, 1961.

Frenz, Horst (ed.). *American Playwrights on Drama.* New York: Hill & Wang, 1965.

Gard, Robert E., and Burley, Gertrude S. *Community Theatre: Idea and Achievement.* New York: Duell, Sloan & Pearce, 1959.

Gard, Robert E. *Grassroots Theatre: A Search for Regional Arts in America.* Madison: The University of Wisconsin Press, 1955.

Gardner, R. H. *The Splintered Stage: The Decline of the American Theater.* New York: Macmillan, 1965.

Gassner, John. *Directions in Modern Theatre and Drama.* New York: Holt, Rinehart and Winston, Inc., 1966.

————. *Theatre at the Crossroads: Plays and Playwrights of the Mid-century American Stage.* New York: Henry Holt, 1960.

Gohdes, Clarence. *Literature and Theater of the States and Regions of the U. S. A.: An Historical Bibliography.* Durham, N. C.: Duke University Press, 1967.

Golden, Joseph. *The Death of Tinker Bell: The American Theatre in the 20th Century.* Syracuse, N. Y.: Syracuse University Press, 1967.

Gorelik, Mordecai. *New Theatres for Old.* New York: Samuel French, Inc., 1940.

Gottfried, Martin. *A Theater Divided: The Postwar American Stage.* Boston and New York: Little, Brown, 1968.

Gould, Jean. *Modern American Playwrights.* New York: Dodd, Mead & Co., 1966.

Green, Abel, and Laurie, Joe, Jr. *Show Biz.* New York: Doubleday & Co., 1953.

Green, Paul. *Plough and Furrow.* New York: Samuel French, 1963.

Griffith, Thomas. *The Waist-High Culture.* New York: Grosset & Dunlap. 1959.

Guerard, Albert L. *Art for Art's Sake.* New York: Schocken Books, 1965.

Guernsey, Otis L., Jr. (ed.). *The Best Plays of 1965–1966,* also *of 1966–1967.* (Annually since 1899.) New York: Dodd, Mead & Co., 1966, 1967.

Guthrie, Tyrone. *A Life in the Theatre.* New York: McGraw–Hill, 1959.

Hart, Moss. *Act One.* New York: New American Library, 1960.

Heckscher, August. *The Public Happiness.* New York: Atheneum, 1962.

Hewitt, Barnard. *Theatre U.S.A. 1668–1957.* New York: McGraw–Hill, 1959.

Hobgood, Burnet M. (ed.). *Directory of American College Theatre.* East Lansing, Mich.: American Educational Theatre Association. First ed. 1960.

Hofstadter, Richard. *Anti-intellectualism in Amercan Life.* New York: Alfred A. Knopf, 1963.

Hollander, E. P. *Leaders, Groups, and Influence.* New York: Oxford University Press, 1964.

Houghton, Norris. *Advance from Broadway: 19,000 Miles of American Theatre.* New York: Harcourt, Brace & Co., 1941.

Hughes, Glenn. *A History of the American Theatre, 1700–1950.* New York: Samuel French, 1951.

Hyams, Barry (ed.). *Theatre: The Annual of the Repertory Theater of Lincoln Center.* New York: Hill & Wang, 1964 to date.

Jones, Howard Mumford. *One Great Society: Humane Learning in the United States.* New York: Harcourt, Brace & Co., 1959.

Jones, Robert Edmond. *The Dramatic Imagination.* New York: Duell, Sloan & Pearce, 1941.

Josephson, Eric and Mary (eds.). *Man Alone.* New York: Dell Books, 1962.

Keller, Suzanne. *Beyond the Ruling Class.* New York: Random House, 1963.

Kernan, Alvin B. (ed.). *The Modern American Theater: A Collection of Critical Essays.* Englewood Cliffs, N.J.: Prentice–Hall, Inc., 1967.

Kerr, Walter. *The Theater in Spite of Itself.* New York: Simon & Schuster, 1963.

Kinne, Wisner Payne. *George Pierce Baker and the American Theatre.* Cambridge, Mass.: Harvard University Press, 1954.

Kostelanetz, Richard (ed.). *The New American Arts.* New York: Horizon Press, 1965. Chapter on "The New American Theatre," by the editor.

Langner, Lawrence. *The Play's the Thing.* New York: G. P. Putnam, 1960.

Larrabee, Eric, and Meyersohn, Rolf (eds.). *Mass Leisure.* Glencoe, Illinois: The Free Press, 1958.

Laski, Harold J. *The American Democracy.* New York: Viking Press, 1948.

Lerner, Max. *America as a Civilization.* New York: Simon & Schuster, 1957.

Lewis, Allan. *American Plays and Playwrights of the Contemporary Theatre.* New York: Crown Publishers, 1965.

Lowenthal, Leo. *Literature, Popular Culture, and Society.* Englewood Cliffs, N. J.: Prentice–Hall, 1961.

Lowry, Ritchie P. *Who's Running This Town? Community Leadership and Social Usage.* New York: Harper & Row, 1965.

Lynes, Russell. *The Tastemakers.* New York: Grosset & Dunlap, 1954.

McCalmon, George, and Moe, Christian. *Creating Historical Drama: A Guide for the Community and the Interested Individual.* Carbondale, Ill.: Southern Illinois University Press, 1965.

McCarthy, Mary. *Sights and Spectacles, 1937–1962.* New York, Farrar & Straus, 1963.

McCleery, Albert, and Glick, Carl. *Curtains Going Up.* New York: Pittman, 1939.

MacDonald, Dwight. *Against the American Grain: Essays on the Effects of Mass Culture.* New York: Random House, 1962.

Macgowan, Kenneth. *Footlights Across America: Towards a National Theatre.* New York: Harcourt, Brace & Co., 1929.

Melnitz, William W. (ed.). *Theatre Arts Publications in the United States: A Five-Year Bibliography.* American Educational Theatre Association Monograph No. 1, 1959.

Miller, Herman P. *Rich Man, Poor Man.* New York: Thomas Y. Crowell, 1964.

Miller, Jordan Y. *American Dramatic Literature: Ten Modern Plays in Historical Perspective.* New York: McGraw–Hill, 1961.

Mitchell, Loften. *Black Drama: The Story of the American Negro in the Theatre.* New York: Hawthorn Books, 1967.

Morris, Lloyd R. *Curtain Time: The Story of the American Theatre.* New York: Random House, 1953.

Myers, Bernard S. *Problems of the Younger American Artist.* New York: The City College Press, 1957.

Ogden, Jean (Carter) and Jess. *Everyman's Drama: A Study of the Noncommercial Theatre in the United States.* New York: American Association for Adult Education, 1938.

Ortega y Gasset, Jose. *The Dehumanization of Art.* Garden City, N.Y.: Anchor Books, n.d.

Overmyer, Grace. *Government and the Arts.* New York: W. W. Norton, 1939.

Packard, Vance. *The Status Seekers.* New York: David McKay, 1959.

Pieper, Josef. *Leisure the Basis of Culture.* New York: Pantheon Books, 1964.

Plummer, Gail. *The Business of Show Business.* New York: Harper & Brothers, 1961.

Price, Julia S. *The Off-Broadway Theater.* New York: The Scarecrow Press, 1962.

Rappel, William J., and Winnie, John R. *Community Theatre Handbook.* Iowa City: Institute of Public Affairs, State University of Iowa, 1961.

Read, Herbert. *To Hell with Culture.* New York: Schocken Books, 1963.

Reitlinger, Gerald. *The Economics of Taste.* London: Barrie & Rockliff, 1961.

Rice, Elmer. *The Living Theatre.* New York: Harper & Brothers, 1959.

————. *Minority Report.* New York: Simon & Schuster, 1963.

Riesman, David. *Abundance for What?* Garden City, N.Y.: Doubleday & Co., 1964.

Rigdon, Walter (ed.). *The Biographical Encyclopedia and Who's Who of the American Theatre.* New York: James H. Heineman, Inc., (1st ed.) 1966.

Rockefeller Brothers Fund. *Directory of National Organizations in the Arts and the Arts and Education.* New York: 1967.

Rockefeller Panel Report. *The Performing Arts: Problems and Prospects.* New York: McGraw–Hill, 1965.

Rosenberg, Bernard, and White, David Manning (eds.). Glencoe, Ill.: The Free Press, 1960.

Rosenberg, Harold. *The Tradition of the New.* New York: Grove Press, 1961.

Rourke, Constance. *The Roots of American Culture and Other Essays.* New York: Harcourt, Brace & Co., 1942.

Santaniello, A. E. (ed.). *Theatre Books in Print.* New York: Drama Book Shop, 1963.

Schroeder, R. J. *The New Underground Theater.* New York: Bantam Books, 1967.

Selden, Samuel (ed.). *Organizing a Community Theatre.* Cleveland: National Theatre Conference, 1945. Distributed by Theatre Arts Books, New York.

Seldes, Gilbert. *The Seven Lively Arts.* New York: The Sagamore Press, 1957.

Stevens, David H. (ed.). *Ten Talents in the American Theatre,* by Robert E. Gard and Others, Norman, Okla.: University of Oklahoma Press, 1957.

Stratman, Carl J. *Bibliography of the American Theatre Excluding New York City.* Chicago: Loyola University Press, 1965.

Taubman, Howard. *The Making of the American Theatre.* New York: Coward McCann, 1965.

Taylor, Harold. *Art and the Intellect.* New York: The Museum of Modern Art, 1960.

Toffler, Alvin. *The Culture Consumers.* New York: St. Martin's Press, 1964.

Walton, Ann D., and Lewis, Marianne D. (eds.). *The Foundation Directory.* (second ed.) New York: The Russell Sage Foundation, 1964.

Weales, Gerald. *American Drama Since World War II.* New York: Harcourt, Brace & World, 1962.

Wellwarth, George E. *The Theatre of Protest and Paradox: Developments in the Avant-Garde Drama.* New York: New York University Press, 1964.

Williams, Raymond. *Culture and Society, 1780–1950.* Garden City, N.Y.: Anchor Books, 1960.

Young, John Wray. *The Community Theatre and How It Works.* New York: Harper & Brothers, 1957.

## Reports, Documents, Special Papers, Addresses, Articles, and Unpublished Dissertations

*The American Imagination,* a critical survey of the arts from the (London) *Times Literary Supplement.* Published in the U.S. by Atheneum Publishers, 1960.

*The Arts: A Central Element of a Good Society.* Eleventh National Conference, Arts Councils of America, June 16–19, 1965, Washington, D.C.

*The Arts: Planning for Change.* Twelfth National Conference, Associated Councils of the Arts (formerly Arts Councils of America), May 19–21, 1966, New York City.

Barzun, Jacques. "The New Man in the Arts," in *Arts and Society,* January 1959. Published by the University Extension Division, The University of Wisconsin, Madison.

Birkenhead, Thomas Bruce. "The Economics of the Broadway Theaters, 1962–63." Dissertation, New School for Social Research, New York, incomplete.

Briggs, William A. "Night and Day in Richmond, Va." Report on the feasibility of a cultural center in Richmond. February 1962.

Dukore, Bernard (ed.). "Professional Companies, Professionalism, and the University Theatre Department: A Symposium," *Educational Theatre Journal,* XVI (May 1964).

Fichandler, Zelda. "A Permanent Classical Repertory Theatre in the Nation's Capital." Washington, D.C., 1959.

Ford Foundation. Annual Reports.

Foundation Library Center. Annual Reports, since 1962.

Guthrie Theatre Survey. "Analysis of the (Tyrone) Guthrie Theatre Audience," prepared by Batten, Barton, Durstine & Osborn, Inc., Minneapolis, 1963.

Heckscher, August. "The Arts and National Government." Report to the President, May 28, 1963. U.S. Senate Document No. 28, 88th Congress, First Session.

Hobgood, Burnet M. "Self-Study Report for Departments and Programs in Theatre"; also "Manual of Operation." Prepared by the Standing Committee on Standards in Educational Theatre of the American Educational Theatre Association, August 20, 1967. Mimeographed.

————. "American Educational Theatre in the Present." Prepared for delivery at the annual convention of the American Educational Theatre Association in New York City, August 21, 1967.

Hyams, Barry (ed.). *Theatre: The Annual of the Repertory Theater of Lincoln Center.* New York: Hill and Wang, 1964 to date.

Levy, Richard. "University Theatre: Embarrassing Riches," *Tulane Drama Review,* X (Fall 1965).

Lowry, W. McNeil. "The University and the Creative Arts." Address before the Association of Graduate Schools, October 24, 1961, reprinted by the Ford Foundation.

Marechal, Judith R. "Off-Broadway: A Limited Engagement," *Tulane Drama Review,* X (Fall 1965).

"Mass Culture and Mass Media," *Daedalus,* Spring 1960. A symposium.

Mitchell, Arnold, and Anderson, MaryLou. *The Arts and Business.* Long Range Planning Report No. 140, Stanford Research Institute, Menlo Park, California, 1962.

Moore, Thomas Gale. "The American Theatre: Past, Present, and Future." Dissertation, Carnegie Institute of Technology, Pittsburgh, Pennsylvania, 1965. Unpublished.

————. "Broadway Theatre Myths," *Tulane Drama Review,* X (Fall 1965).

Munson, Henry Lee. "Money for the Arts: The What, How and Why of Government Aid to the Arts in Seven Free Countries of Europe." New York, H. L. Munson & Co., 1962.

Murdock, Lawrence C., Jr. "S.R.O. and S.O.S.: The Performing Arts Paradox," *Business Review,* Federal Reserve Bank of Philadelphia, March 1962

New York State Council on the Arts. Annual Reports, New York, 1965 to date.

Playbill survey, "Who's Who in the Audience," compiled and issued annually since 1955 by Playbill, Inc., New York.

Poggi, Jack. "The Beginnings of Decline," *Tulane Drama Review,* X (Fall 1965). The financial picture of Broadway in the 1920's.

Raymond, Thomas. Charles Playhouse Survey, Boston, c. 1965.

Robbins, Lionel C. R. "Art and the State," in *Politics and Economics.* New York: St. Martin's Press, 1963.

Rockefeller, John D., 3rd. "The Arts and the Community," *Music Journal,* XXI (September 1963).

Rockefeller Panel Report: Papers prepared for the Study. (Unpublished) For full list of papers, see Report, pp. 221–222. The following papers deal especially with the theatre:

Barr, Richard. "Off-Broadway Theatre."

Bloom, Murray Teigh. "Economic Problems of the American Theatre."

Houghton, Norris. "The American Theatre—Today and Tomorrow."

————. "Characteristics and Development of the Off-Broadway Theatre Movement."

Karp, Irwin. "Problems of the Professional Playwright."

Little, Stuart W. "The Broadway Producer."

Moore, Dick, and Golodner, Jack. "The Amateur and the Professional in the American Theatre."

Schechner, Richard. "Ford, Rockefeller, and Theatre," *Tulane Drama Review,* X (Fall 1965).

————. "The TDR Theatre Conference," *Tulane Drama Review,* X (Summer 1966).

Schmidt, Sandra. "The Regional Theatre: Some Statistics," *Tulane Drama Review,* X (Fall 1965).

————. "The Regional Theatre." Series of articles published in *Christian Science Monitor,* (July and August, 1964).

Scott, Mel. "Partnership in the Arts." Public and private support of cultural activities in the San Francisco Bay Area. Report published by the Institute of Governmental Studies, University of California, Berkeley, 1963.

"The Shorter Work Week and the Constructive Use of Free Time," Proceedings of the Eighth Annual AFL–CIO National Conference on Community Service Activities, New York, 1963.

Smith, Michael. "The Good Scene," *Tulane Drama Review,* X (Summer 1966).

Stoddard, Hope. *Subsidy Makes Sense.* Newark, International Press, n.d. Published by the American Federation of Musicians.

Sumner, Mark R. (ed.). "An Investigation of Existing Outdoor Drama Techniques and a Determination of Methods to Improve Training." A Research Report by the Institute of Outdoor Drama. Chapel Hill, N.C.: University of North Carolina, 1967. Mimeographed.

"Symposium: The University and the Creative Arts," reported in *Arts and Society,* II, No. 3, 1963. Published by University Extension Division, The University of Wisconsin, Madison.

UCLA Theater Subscribers' Analysis, Winter 1964. University Theater, University of California, Los Angeles. Unpublished.

United States, Department of Labor, Bureau of Labor Statistics. "Employment Outlook in the Performing Arts," Bulletin No. 1300–65. 1965.

————, House of Representatives. *Hearings on Economic Conditions in the Performing Arts* before the Select Subcommittee on Education of the Committee on Education and Labor, 87th Congress, First and Second Sessions, November 15–17, 1961: December 7–8, 1961; February 5–6, 1962. (House Hearings, II). Government Printing Office, Washington, D.C., 1962.

————, Senate. *Government and the Arts.* Hearings before a Special Subcommittee on Labor and Public Welfare, 87th Congress, Second Session, August 29–31, 1962.

———, ———. *National Arts Legislation.* Hearings before the Special Subcommittee on the Arts of the Committee on Labor and Public Welfare, 88th Congress, First Session, October 28–November 1, 1963.

van Itallie, Jean–Claude. "Playwright at Work: Off-Off-Broadway," *Tulane Drama Review,* C (Summer 1966).

Wharton, John F. *A Fresh Look at Theatre Tickets.* Report to the Legitimate Theatre Industry Exploratory Commission. New York, 1965.

"Wingspread Conference on the Arts," papers and discussion reported in *Arts in Society, II, No. 2,* Fall–Winter, 1962–63. Published by University Extension Division, The University of Wisconsin, Madison.

## Periodicals Dealing With the Theater

*American Community Theatre Association Newsletter.* (ACTA: a Division of the American Educational Theatre Association, Inc.) Currently edited at the College of Arts and Sciences, Oklahoma State University, Stillwater, Oklahoma 74075.

*Arts in Society.* Published three times a year at The University of Wisconsin, Extension Building, 432 N. Lake Street, Madison, Wisconsin 53706.

*Children's Theatre Conference Newsletter.* (CTC: a Division of the American Educational Theatre Association, Inc.) Currently edited at the Department of Drama, The University of Texas, Austin, Texas 78712. Quarterly.

*Critical Digest.* Weekly N.Y.C. Newsletter for College, Resident, and Community Theatres, and Libraries. Edited by Ted M. Kraus, GPO Box 2403, New York, N.Y. 10001.

*Cultural Affairs.* Published by the Associated Councils of the Arts, 1564 Broadway, New York, N.Y. 10036. First issued in August 1967.

*Drama Survey.* A Review of Dramatic Literature and the Theatrical Arts. Published three times a year by the Bolingbroke Society, Inc., Box 4098, University Station, Minneapolis, Minnesota 55414.

*Dramatics.* Published monthly during school by The National Thespian Society, College Hill Station, Cincinnati, Ohio 45224.

*Dramatists Guild Quarterly.* Published by The Dramatists Guild, 234 West 44th Street, New York, N.Y. 10036.

*Educational Theatre Journal.* Published quarterly by the American Educational Theatre Association, Inc., 1701 Pennsylvania Avenue, N.W., Washington, D.C. 20006.

*Equity.* Published monthly (except for three bimonthly issues) by The Actors' Equity Association, 165 West 46th Street, New York, N.Y. 10036.

*International Theatre/Informations Internationales.* Published by the International Theatre Institute, Paris. U.S. distributor: Theatre Arts Books, Inc., 333 Sixth Avenue, New York, N.Y. 10014.

*Modern Drama.* Published quarterly at the University of Kansas, Lawrence, Kansas 66045.

*The New Yorker.* Published weekly by The New Yorker Magazine, Inc., 25 West 43rd Street, New York, N.Y. 10036. Lists current Broadway and off-Broadway stage shows.

*New York Critics' Reviews.* Published in facsimile throughout the theatre season by Critics' Theatre Reviews, Inc., 150 East 35th Street, New York, N.Y. 10016.

*New York Times,* Sunday ed., Arts & Leisure Section, Times Square, New York, N.Y. 10036.

*Playbill.* Published monthly by Playbill, Inc., 579 Fifth Avenue, New York, N.Y. 10017.

*Players Magazine,* October through May, by the National Collegiate Players, University of Northern Illinois, De Kalb, Illinois 60115.

*Quarterly Journal of Speech.* Published by The Speech Association of America, Statler Hilton Hotel, New York, N.Y. 10001.

*La Scène au Canada/The Stage in Canada.* Monthly bulletin of the Canadian Theatre Centre of the International Theatre Institute, 280 Bloor Street West, Toronto 5, Ontario.

*Theatre Crafts.* Published every other month by Rodale Press, Inc. Emmaus, Pennsylvania 18049.

*Theatre Design and Technology.* Quarterly Journal (since May 1965) of the U.S. Institute for Theatre Technology, 1125 Cathedral of Learning, University of Pittsburgh, Pittsburgh, Pennsylvania 15213.

*Theatre Survey.* Semi-annual journal of the American Society for Theatre Research, 1117 Cathedral of Learning, University of Pittsburgh, Pittsburgh, Pennsylvania 15213.

*Tulane Drama Review* (Henceforth to be *The Drama Review*). Edited by Richard Schechner at New York University. Distributed by Simon & Schuster, 630 Fifth Avenue, New York, N.Y. 10020.

*Variety.* Published weekly by Variety, Inc., 154 West 46th Street, New York, N.Y. 10036.

*Washington International Arts Letter.* Published ten times a year by Allied Business Consultants, 115 5th Street, S.E., Washington D.C. 20003.

*World Theatre/Le Theatre dans le Monde.* Bimonthly review published by the International Theatre Institute, Paris. U.S. distributor: Theatre Arts Books, Inc., 333 Sixth Avenue, New York, N.Y. 10014.

# INDEX